Main Floor

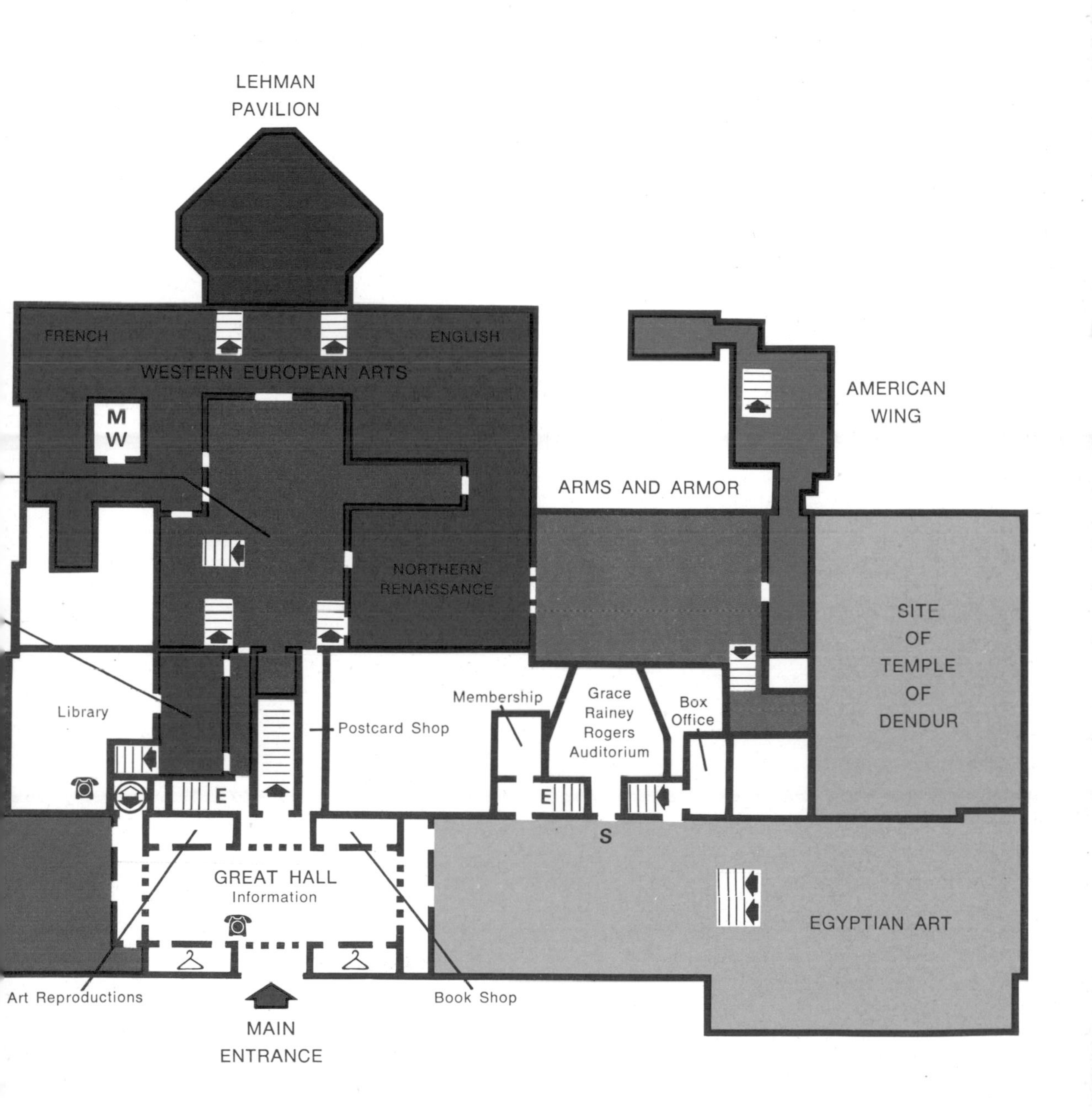
LEHMAN
PAVILION
FRENCH
ENGLISH
WESTERN EUROPEAN ARTS
M
W
AMERICAN
WING
ARMS AND ARMOR
NORTHERN
RENAISSANCE
SITE
OF
TEMPLE
OF
DENDUR
Library
Membership
Grace
Rainey
Rogers
Auditorium
Box
Office
Postcard Shop
E
E
S
GREAT HALL
Information
EGYPTIAN ART
Art Reproductions
Book Shop
MAIN
ENTRANCE

Guide to The Metropolitan Museum of Art

Published by The Metropolitan Museum of Art, New York

Acknowledgment

A grant from the Helena Rubinstein Foundation has made possible the publication of this Guide. The Foundation is dedicated to the advancement of the public good especially in those areas with which its founder was closely identified during her lifetime—the education, health, and general well-being of people. In its support of medical research, education of the young, care and assistance for the disadvantaged and elderly, and programs in the arts, the Foundation seeks to make as broad a contribution as it can to the fundamental concerns of our times.

First Edition

Published 1972 by The Metropolitan Museum of Art.

Author and General Editor: Nora B. Beeson, in cooperation with Margaretta M. Salinger for the Editorial Advisory Committee of The Metropolitan Museum of Art.
Illustrations: The Metropolitan Museum of Art Photography Studio.

Produced by Chanticleer Press, Inc., New York.
Plan: Paul Steiner and Gudrun Buettner.
Design and layout: Ellen Hsiao, assisted by Margaret Saunders, Elaine Jones.
Production: Helga Lose
Printed and bound by Amilcare Pizzi, S.p.A., Milan, Italy.

Library of Congress Catalog Card Number 72-81647.
International Standard Book Number 0-87099-118-3.

Contents

How to Use the Guide 4
Introduction 5
Services of the Museum 6
American Paintings and Sculpture 9
American Wing 25
Ancient Near Eastern Art 41
Arms and Armor 57
Costume Institute 73
Drawings 89
Egyptian Art 105
European Paintings 121
Far Eastern Art 145
Greek and Roman Art 161
Islamic Art 177
Lehman Collection 193
Medieval Art 209
Musical Instruments 225
Primitive Art 241
Prints and Photographs 257
Twentieth Century Art 273
Western European Arts 289
Credits 313
Index 316

How to Use the Guide

This Guide is easy to use. It is planned as an introduction to the collections of the Metropolitan Museum and as a practical aid to the visitor.

- Floor plans of the entire Museum are inside the front and back covers. On these plans each department has the same color as the individual fold-out of that department. This helps to locate quickly the section you want.

- The separate sections devoted to each of the departments are arranged in alphabetical order.

- At the beginning of each section is a fold-out floor plan showing the galleries of that department. (Note that some departments have galleries on more than one floor.) The small black numbers in each gallery are the ones appearing after the major works of art mentioned in the text. A map in the lower left-hand corner shows the location of each department in relation to the rest of the Museum.

- The page facing each floor plan tells you what objects, periods, and styles are represented; the numbers in red, at the left, show you in which galleries you can find the things that interest you; the numbers in black, at the right, correspond with the numbers in the text.

- The text in each section gives a short account of that department. Major works of art are discussed in chronological order, with detailed information on the most important. The heavy black number assigned to a work helps you to locate the object on the floor plan and to identify the illustration. Objects that are illustrated are distinguished in the text by heavy black type.

Introduction

When the Metropolitan Museum came into being in 1870, the founders stressed its role in giving popular instruction. Ever since then its public has expressed interest in obtaining a general guidebook to all the multiple facets of its encyclopedic collections. But a museum is a living, constantly changing institution, and the preparation of such a guide presents many problems. The scope and depth of the Museum's holdings are described with flexibility in mind, so that alterations to the building and changes in the collections can be readily accommodated in future editions of this *Guide*. The number of pages allocated to each department is restricted to multiples of eight pages; this will permit revisions in future editions.

A guidebook, however, should not be a straitjacket. It is impossible to locate accurately all works at all times because paintings and objects are constantly being cleaned, restored, loaned to other museums, or rehung within the Metropolitan.

In designing a guide that is easily portable and of interest to a large public, severe restrictions have had to be imposed. The text serves an introductory function and is not intended to give the kind of detailed information found in a catalogue or scholarly publication. Many other books published by the Museum are available to anyone wishing to follow his own special interests: a series of popular handbooks and comprehensive catalogues of various aspects of the collections are available in the Museum's bookshops; the *Bulletin of The Metropolitan Museum of Art*, a general interest magazine covering all phases of Museum activity, appears regularly throughout the year; and the *Journal of The Metropolitan Museum of Art*, a collection of scholarly monographs, is issued annually. An independent guide covers the collection at The Cloisters, our branch museum of medieval art at Fort Tryon Park.

For their excellent work in making the vast holdings of the Museum encompassable with wit and understanding, the staffs of each department in the institution deserve high praise, as do Nora Beeson, Margaretta Salinger, Paul Steiner and the staff of Chanticleer Press for their imaginative efforts in making this first *Guide* a success.

Thomas Hoving, Director

Thomas Hoving

Services of the Museum

AUDITORIUM
A distinguished series of concerts and lectures is presented in the Grace Rainey Rogers Auditorium and, occasionally, in other locations in the Museum. Lectures on art and music cover a variety of subjects, such as modern painting, antiques, great art collections, Impressionism, music in America, famous arias, and performance techniques. Concerts range from solo recitals to chamber music and orchestra performances, and from medieval music presented in a medieval setting to contemporary works. Full schedules are available in the Auditorium office.

BOOKS AND REPRODUCTIONS
Art books, catalogues, prints, postcards, slides, and precise Museum copies of ancient jewelry, sculpture, silver, pewter, porcelain, furniture, and glass are available for purchase. Inquire at the sales desks off the Great Hall (82nd Street Entrance).

CATALOGUE
The Catalogue Department is the central source of information for all Museum objects. Graduate students and scholars can consult the files and subject index for detailed descriptions, bibliography, history, and provenance of works of art in the collections. Department facilities are available on an appointment basis.

INFORMATION DESK
The Information Desk, located in the Museum's Great Hall, dispenses up-to-date information relating to current exhibitions, works of art on view, general Museum activities, and events of the day.

MEMBERSHIP
The Museum offers memberships to those who wish to enjoy a closer association with the Museum than the occasional visit can provide. Special previews, lectures, parties, and activities for children are offered only to members. Members receive free admission to the Museum, the illustrated *Bulletin,* the Calendar/News, and discounts on certain Museum publications. There are special memberships for students.

RESTAURANTS
The Fountain Restaurant and Bar are open for luncheon and also for dinner on the evenings the Museum is open. The Junior Museum Snack Bar is open during Museum hours.

Scholars doing research in the library, children searching the Egyptian wing on a treasure hunt, foreign tourists going on an introductory tour of the paintings galleries, Sunday visitors listening to a curator speak about a favorite object, high school students attending a video-tape workshop, professors looking for rare slides to illustrate their lectures, a community group seeking assistance in developing a grass-roots cultural program—all these people and thousands more are served each year by the Museum's education departments.

FOR THE GENERAL PUBLIC

Free events include introductory tours of the Museum, gallery talks, films and lectures in the Auditorium, special Sunday programs, the use of the reading room in the European paintings galleries and orientation galleries for special exhibitions. Subscription courses are offered in the Learning from the Original series, and recorded tours may be rented for certain collections.

FOR SCHOLARS AND GRADUATE STUDENTS

The Library, founded in 1881, has been named in memory of Thomas J. Watson. Privately endowed, it is the most comprehensive art and archaeology library in the Western hemisphere and has material in every field in which the Museum collects objects. It is primarily for the use of the curatorial staff but is open also to graduate students (with graduate school identification cards), researchers, and visiting scholars.

The Photograph and Slide Library maintains a collection of 290,000 slides that may be rented for lecturing, and a collection of 250,000 black and white photographs and 6,000 color prints that are available for study. These collections illustrate the history of art with a representative coverage of sculpture, painting, and the decorative arts in the Metropolitan Museum, objects from other museums and private collections, and architectural views. Photographs of objects in the Museum's collections may be purchased. The services are open to the general public who are interested in these special materials.

FOR HIGH SCHOOL STUDENTS

Free courses, events, apprenticeships, and work-study and independent-study programs are offered throughout the year, and some schools will give students credit for work done at the Museum. For information, call High School Programs.

Education

FOR CHILDREN AND THEIR PARENTS
Free talks, tours, treasure hunts, art workshops, craft demonstrations, and film showings are given. Teachers wishing to bring school groups to the Museum must make appointments in advance. The Junior Museum is open daily during Museum hours and has an exhibition area, art reference library, auditorium, studio, sales desk, and snack bar. For information, call the Junior Museum.

OUTSIDE THE MUSEUM
A variety of programs ranging from exhibitions to mobile museums to visiting lecturers or technical assistance are conducted outside the Museum. Any local organization wishing to plan joint activities with the Museum is encouraged to contact the Department of Community Programs.

Brief History

The Metropolitan Museum of Art was founded on April 13, 1870. After a nomadic existence, occupying a former dancing academy on Fifth Avenue and then the Douglas Mansion on 14th Street, the Museum moved in 1880 to its present location in Central Park, into a building designed by Calvert Vaux, one of the architects of the park itself. The Museum could now begin to apply itself to the objectives, set forth in its charter, of "encouraging and developing the study of the fine arts, and the application of arts to manufacture and practical life, of advancing the general knowledge of kindred subjects, and to that end of furnishing popular instruction."

American Paintings and Sculpture

American Paintings and Sculpture

Objects, Periods, Styles, Artists	**Numbers in Text**
ASH CAN SCHOOL or THE EIGHT: Henri, Sloan, Luks, Prendergast, Lawson, Shinn, Davies, Glackens	(55)
CHANGING EXHIBITS: water colors, drawings	
COLONIAL PORTRAITISTS	(1), (2)
COPLEY and WEST	(3-5)
EAKINS	(37), (38)
GENRE PAINTING: Mount, Bingham, Johnson	(31), (32), (36)
HISTORICAL PAINTING: West, Leutze	(22)
HOMER	(50-52)
HUDSON RIVER SCHOOL	(23-30)
IMPRESSIONISTS	(46-49)
NAÏVE PAINTERS: Hathaway, Hicks	(13), (18)
PEALE FAMILY	(10), (14), (15)
RYDER	(41)
SCULPTORS: Powers, Palmer, Rimmer, Remington, Saint-Gaudens	(33-35), (53), (54)
STUART	(7-9)
SULLY	(19), (20)
TROMPE L'OEIL: Harnett, Peto	(39), (40)
WESTERN SUBJECTS: Bingham, Blakelock, Remington	(32), (42), (53)
WHISTLER and SARGENT	(44), (45)

This page helps you to find what you especially want to see and read about.

American Paintings and Sculpture

The Metropolitan Museum's interest in American art dates from its foundation in 1870, when several prominent American artists served as founding trustees of the Museum: painters John F. Kensett, Frederic E. Church, Daniel Huntington, Eastman Johnson; the sculptor John Q. A. Ward; the architect Richard Morris Hunt; and the engraver and art dealer Samuel P. Avery. From 1870 to 1906 the growth of the collection was almost entirely dependent on gifts and bequests from such collectors as William B. Astor, Samuel P. Avery, Hamilton Fish, H. O. Havemeyer, George A. Hearn, and John S. Kennedy. The George A. Hearn and Morris K. Jesup funds have enabled the Museum to continue its program of purchasing works by American artists. Other gifts, including an outstanding selection of American naïve art given by Edgar William Garbisch and his wife, Bernice Chrysler Garbisch, have enriched the holdings.

A Department of American Paintings and Sculpture was formed in 1949; in 1967 the works of artists born after 1875 came under the administration of the newly created Department of Twentieth Century Art.

The Museum's collection of American painting and sculpture is probably the finest in this country and illustrates almost all phases of the history of American art. Miniatures, primarily dating before 1860, include works by the Peales, Edward G. Malbone, John Ramage, and Thomas S. Cummings. Drawings and water colors by John S. Copley, Arthur B. Davies, Thomas Eakins, Winslow Homer, John La Farge, Maurice Prendergast, John S. Sargent, and others, are kept in the Drawings Department and are available for study purposes by appointment. American prints and architectural drawings are preserved in the Department of Prints and Photographs and may be seen after making an appointment.

In the future, the construction of the proposed extension to the American Wing on the northwest side of the building will allow for the exhibition of a larger percentage of the Museum's holdings in American art. The plans include an orientation area; exhibitions of paintings and sculpture in period rooms and period settings; galleries devoted to paintings and sculpture; facilities for readily accessible study storage; and exhibition space for smaller, more specialized shows, including one-man retrospectives.

The earliest painting in the American colonies was closely allied to practical affairs such as making shop signs or weather vanes, painting coaches, and, in general, decorating houses. Only with increasing time and leisure were portraits commissioned from artists who gradually became able to live entirely from their skill in handling brush and paint. The Museum has in its collection portraits painted before the Revolution by about a dozen artists, some born in England or Scotland, others in the colonies along the eastern seaboard. In the towns they found the needed patronage of wealthy merchants and politically and socially prominent figures. Some painters were more successful than others in rendering accurate likenesses of their sitters and in conveying the richness of velvet, satin, and lace. More often than not, English mezzotints served as samples for the formal poses, costumes, accessories, and backgrounds of such portraits.

Though John Smibert was born in Edinburgh, he sailed to the New World in 1728 and eventually settled in Boston. Here he quickly reached the top of his profession, painting portraits of an artistic excellence unprecedented in New England, organizing the first art exhibition held in the colonies, and operating his studio as a kind of academy where younger men could learn the traditions of European painting. His portraits **(1)** in the Museum were done between 1729 and about 1735. Though Smibert's portraits were usually fashionably elegant, the likeness of Nathaniel Byfield shows well the pugnacious character of this New England judge.

A younger man than Smibert and one born in the colonial world was Robert Feke, who came under Smibert's influence in Boston. His fine portrait of *Tench Francis* **(2)** presents this prominent political figure with great conviction. Other portraitists active in the middle years of the 18th century and present in the Museum's collection were John Wollaston, a most prolific painter with approximately 300 known portraits to his name; Joseph Blackburn, whose delicate Rococo portraits were often repetitious in composition; Joseph Badger, represented here by his grandson's portrait, done in a charmingly provincial manner; Jeremiah Theüs, the most popular colonial painter in South Carolina; and John Hesselius, who was active around Annapolis.

Although the colonies provided their craftsmen with work and patronage, England continued to exert an irresistible pull. Some of the best 18th-century painters availed themselves of the opportunities that London could offer. John Singleton Copley and Benjamin West, both born in 1738 and the best artists that America had produced, eventually settled and worked in England. Copley was undoubtedly America's foremost 18th-century painter. Born in Boston, where he established himself as a professional painter when he was not yet 20, Copley was soon able to forgo stock compositions, relying on his native talent to breathe life into his portraits. In *Mrs. Sylvanus Bourne* **(3)**, painted in 1766, this artist presents a remarkable character study of the 71-year-old sitter. His understanding of paint in conveying textures was brilliantly employed in most of the portraits. Anxious to improve his work, Copley went to Europe in 1774 and became a respected figure in London, where other painters, notably Benjamin West, had already settled. One of ten Copley paintings in the Museum, **Midshipman Augustus Brine (4),**

4

6

dating from 1782, was painted seven years after Copley had moved to England. It shows his freer style and the looser brush strokes, a technique adopted from his English colleagues.

The center of London's American art colony was the house and studio of Benjamin West. Born near Philadelphia, West was drawn to Italy in his desire for improvement, and finally settled in London. A proponent of the Neoclassic style, he chose subjects from history and the Bible; these enormous canvases in "the grand manner" were eminently successful, and some of the many coming from his studio had been, following standard practice, filled in or completed by studio assistants. *The Battle of La Hogue* **(5)**, for more than a decade considered one of his most successful history paintings, depicts a final moment in a battle fought near Cherbourg, France, between French and British forces. The Museum's painting is a version done by John Trumbull, with touches by West.

Because West was one of the most advanced artists, enjoying the 40-year protection of George III, and succeeding Joshua Reynolds in 1792 as president of the British Royal Academy, American artists flocked to study with him. One of them, Matthew Pratt, a portrait painter from Philadelphia, has given us in **The American School (6)** a picture of West's studio depicting a group of American painters under the tutelage of their friend and teacher.

Among West's pupils, Gilbert Stuart was to become one of the most prominent portraitists of the late 18th century. The

7

13

Museum owns more than 20 of his paintings, of which the George Washington portraits are probably the most familiar. Stuart painted his first portrait of **George Washington (7)** from life in 1795, two years after his return to the United States, and his second in 1796. These portraits were so successful in conveying the noble character of the country's great hero that they were duplicated many times by Stuart himself. His other work represented in the Museum includes portraits of American notables, members of his family, and the recent acquisition *Louis-Marie, Vîcomte de Noailles* **(8)**. Stuart at times dispensed with all external paraphernalia, concentrating on the features of his sitters, as in his unfinished *Portrait of the Artist* **(9)**.

Also receiving some instruction from West in London was Charles Willson Peale, a versatile jack-of-all-trades who, despite his admiration for West's historical canvases, turned to painting miniatures and portraits. While on active duty during the Revolution, Peale immortalized many army officers, as well as General George Washington. The Metropolitan's *George Washington* **(10)** is a replica made by Peale of the very successful portrait commissioned in 1779 by the Supreme Executive Council of Pennsylvania. A full-length portrait of *Washington* **(11)** by John Trumbull, another pupil of West's, also depicts his subject in uniform. Ralph Earl, who also worked with West, has left a full-length painting of *Colonel Marinus Willett* **(12)**, which splendidly represents this artist's individual style; the somewhat stiff figures of Earl's canvases are often surrounded by landscape or parlor backgrounds. Rufus Hathaway, a man some 20 years younger than Earl, with little professional training, worked in a similarly primitive yet sophisticated style. His **Lady with Her Pets (13)** is his earliest

14

15

known painting, dating from 1790. This charming picture still has its original frame, painted to simulate marble. After a few years Hathaway abandoned his career in painting for one in medicine.

While American painting of the 18th century consisted almost exclusively of portraits, with standing figures forming the exception, the range of subjects was greatly enlarged after the turn of the century. Thus, the talented Peale family contributed some exceedingly fine still lifes. James Peale, the youngest brother of Charles Willson Peale, in his **Still Life: Balsam Apple and Vegetables (14)**, probably dating from the 1820s, painted a rather casual arrangement of many different shapes and forms in which the thick application of pigment admirably suits the texture of the vegetables. Charles's

18

oldest son, Raphaelle Peale, one of the finest of still-life painters, is well represented in the Museum's collection by his **Still Life with Cake (15)** from 1818; the fine drawing and subtle colors against a neutral background are reminiscent of earlier Dutch and Flemish paintings. Still another son, Rembrandt Peale, was known mainly for his portraits.

The Deluge **(16)**, a dramatic canvas strewn with corpses, became a landmark in that it presented a world of fantasy and landscape, both topics new to American painting. At first attributed to Washington Allston, it is now known to have been done by Joshua Shaw, a British-born painter who worked in America after 1817. Allston's landscapes and his moody figure paintings, such as *The Spanish Girl in Reverie* **(17)**, are romantic and tend toward sentimentality. And Edward Hicks, one of the best of the so-called naïve painters, who worked in the Pennsylvania countryside, transmitted his Quaker faith in many versions of *The Peaceable Kingdom* and conveyed the natural wonders of the North American continent in **The Falls of Niagara (18)**.

Despite the proliferation of new subject matter, portraiture was, of course, not forgotten. Thomas Sully was a most productive portraitist, with some 2,500 commissions completed before his death in 1872. He visited the studios of England's foremost portrait painters and was particularly attracted by Sir Thomas Lawrence's flowing style, which was the genesis of his own manner. The subjects of his portraits **(19)** included Philadelphia notables, such as *Major John Biddle* and *Mrs. John Biddle* (in the American Wing); members of his own family—one daughter in *The Student*, and another daughter in *Mother and Son*; and himself, such as the self-portrait of 1821 in the Museum. His most famous sitter, **Queen Victoria (20)**, posed a number of times in 1838, shortly after her accession to the throne. The Metropolitan's oil sketch, with two separate sketches of crown jewels on the lower right, shows the great beauty of the young queen and the artist's fine handling of pigment.

20

Samuel F. B. Morse, now mostly remembered as the inventor of the telegraph, was until 1837 a painter by profession, but his career in art brought him close to starvation. In the exquisite painting of his daughter Susan Walker Morse, called *The Muse* **(21)**, the artist has given the figure an elegant costume and surrounded her with an opulent, imaginary setting; the glowing tones of the fabrics and the charming characterization of the 16-year-

23

28

old girl elicited the highest praise. Unfortunately this was one of Morse's last works, and he afterward devoted himself almost exclusively to science.

As the 19th century progressed, American painters turned more and more to native subject matter. Awed by the beauties of the American countryside, they created romantic landscapes, pictured typical American pastimes, and depicted scenes from history, such as *Washington Crossing the Delaware* **(22)** by Emanuel G. Leutze. The Hudson River School of landscape painters flourished in the second and third quarters of the century; the principal founder was Thomas Cole, together with Thomas Doughty, though many other landscapists belonged to this loosely organized group. The Museum has a representative collection of these grandiloquent canvases, which, in a half-romantic and half-realistic manner, often on a large scale, reveal the artists' reverence for nature. **The Oxbow (The Connecticut River near Northampton)** by Cole **(23)**, dating from 1836, is rather typical of these paintings in its panoramic vista, detailed foreground, and expanse of sky with clouds or bursts of sunlight, done in fresh and glowing colors. Doughty's landscapes **(24)** were either painted from nature or were composed of a set of favorite landscape elements; grazing cows, plowing farmers, and young fishermen were often included in these bucolic scenes. Asher Brown Durand, another founding member of the Hudson River School, made numerous paintings of trees. His monumental landscapes, like *The Beeches* **(25)**, were painted in his studio from sketches done from nature.

Some members of the second generation of the Hudson River School continued to paint scenes around the upper Hudson River, the Catskills, and New England. *Lake George* **(26)** was superbly monumentalized by John F. Kensett; and Jasper Francis Cropsey often used shockingly brilliant colors in his Hudson autumnal scenes, though *The Valley of Wyoming* **(27)** is a more subdued Pennsylvania scene bathed in summer haze. Others went farther afield for their subjects. Frederic Edwin Church, a pupil of Thomas Cole, after two trips to South America in 1853 and 1857, completed the **Heart of the Andes (28)** in 1859; its breathtaking scope and size, the almost photographic depiction of awesome aspects of nature, and the subtle treatment of light make this canvas an important landmark in American 19th-century painting. The German-born Albert Bierstadt in 1859 joined an expedition to survey an overland wagon route to the Far West and spent that summer in Nebraska Territory. His vast panoramic studio picture of *The Rocky Mountains* **(29)**, painted in 1863 from his sketches, combines accuracy with an almost overwhelming effect of melodrama. George Inness's *Peace and Plenty* **(30)**, done after the Civil War in 1865, shows the Charles River near Medfield, Massachusetts; though the painting has traces of his earlier detailed Hudson River style, it shows the influence of contemporary French painting as well.

Many aspects of daily life and various occupations were accurately recorded. William Sidney Mount lived most of his life on Long Island, and his farm pictures are fine depictions of the rural scene he knew so well. In *Raffling for the Goose*, the lucky number is about to be drawn from

31

32

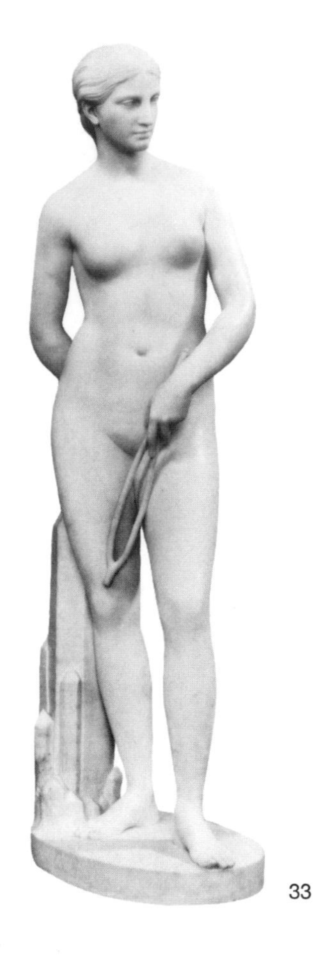

33

the hat. *Long Island Farmhouses* conveys the changeability of the weather along Long Island Sound and depicts typical farmhouses of the 1850s. **Cider Making (31)** exemplifies Mount's desire to paint pictures of popular scenes that could be understood and liked at once.

What Mount was to the East, George Caleb Bingham was to the West. Living mostly in Missouri, with trips to New York, Philadelphia, and Düsseldorf (Germany) for study, inspiration, and commissions, Bingham specialized in western genre scenes. The Metropolitan's **Fur Traders Descending the Missouri (32)** is a canvas of western river life in which the artist's classical feeling for composition and his concern for light effects are shown to masterly advantage.

American sculpture in the 18th century was the work of craftsmen and artisans. Decorative work was subordinate to the function or utility of an object; and sculpture was mainly relegated to gravestones, metal weather vanes, and woodcarving for ships, shops, buildings, and

38

gardens. By the middle of the 19th century, sculpture had come into its own as a genre. Hiram Powers, who spent most of his life in Italy, was the first American sculptor to attain international fame. The Museum's marble sculpture **California (33)**, designed in 1850, reflects an idealized classical style adapted to an allegorical representation commemorating the California gold rush of 1849. The figure holds a divining rod in her left hand; thorns hidden in the right symbolize the fickleness of fortune.

Erastus Dow Palmer in *The White Captive* **(34)** also sought for idealization, but he introduced a strong note of naturalism. He often worked from live models and probably used one of his daughters for this figure, completed in 1859. Just two years later William Rimmer executed the clay figure of *The Falling Gladiator* **(35)**, which was not cast into bronze until after the artist's death. In contrast to conventional nudes, this anatomically convincing male figure reflects the sculptor's medical training and vivid imagination.

In the second half of the 19th century America produced some of its finest artists, painters who were recognized at home and abroad. A technical skill had been achieved that could be used to express the personal vision of each individual artist, and thus styles varied enormously.

Eastman Johnson was one of the finest painters of "portrait interiors." *The Hatch Family* **(36)** is an example of the accuracy and realism with which Johnson reproduced every detail of a Victorian library. *Corn Husking* is typical of his later style.

A more unorthodox painter, Thomas Eakins, was uncompromising in his portraits of his fellow Philadelphians. In the Museum's collection *The Thinker: Portrait of Louis N. Kenton* **(37)** is a brooding study of a member of his wife's family; other portraits include one of his wife and dog in *Lady with a Setter Dog*. One of the artist's best-known works is **Max Schmitt in a Single Scull (38)**, in which

39

41

Eakins's friend, a champion oarsman, is shown on the Schuylkill River on a bright summer day; the artist has painted himself in the other scull. The careful composition and use of perspective, the excellent draftsmanship, and the fine handling of color make this one of the best genre scenes in 19th-century American art.

Exaggerated realism was the trademark of the two painters William Michael Harnett and John Frederick Peto, who deceived the eye with their *trompe l'oeil* technique of simulated textures and perspective. In Harnett's *The Artist's Card Rack*, painted in 1879, one is indeed tempted to pry away the old envelopes and calling cards tucked behind the tape. The fiddle and bow, piccolo, and sheet of music in **Music and Good Luck (39)** are hung from a slightly opened cupboard door, ready to be used at any moment; this painting dates from 1888. Peto used the subject of the *Letter Rack* **(40)** numerous times. His paintings were generally much influenced by Harnett and were even sold under the forged signature of the latter artist.

Almost completely antithetical to Harnett's and Peto's work were the canvases of Albert Pinkham Ryder. Little influenced by European art or by his American contemporaries, Ryder pursued his solitary path, painting somber, dreamlike scenes that foreshadowed the Abstract Expressionist technique used in the 20th century. Working repeatedly on one painting, Ryder applied layer after layer of pigment and glaze, forming an enamellike surface. This is evident in **Moonlight Marine (41)**, where the dark clouds, sails, and sea are reduced to expressive, almost abstract forms, creating a mysterious seascape.

Ralph Blakelock, a contemporary of Ryder's, was also haunted by his own visions. Self-taught as a painter, he traveled in the West and made hundreds of drawings. One theme, an Indian encampment under trees, formed the subject matter of many of his paintings. The one in the Museum **(42)** is typical of his dra-

44

45

matic practice of silhouetting trees against a lighter sky to create an unreal world hovering between night and day. Elihu Vedder, a painter of mystical and allegorical subjects, made the unreal plausible. *Roman Girls on the Seashore* **(43)**, completed in 1877, one year after his trip to London, reveals his affection for the English Pre-Raphaelites.

Similar to Vedder, who in the 1860s moved to Italy permanently, an entire group of American painters became expatriates in England and France. Foremost among them was James Abbott McNeill Whistler. Moving from Paris to London in 1859, he became an important and influential figure in European art circles. The portrait of Theodore Duret, entitled **Arrangement in Flesh Colour and Black (44)**, is typical of Whistler's very personal style, in which an overall formal arrangement of color and tone was just as important as the subject matter.

Also at home in London was John Singer Sargent, who enjoyed extraordinary international success as a portrait painter. Of the many portraits in the Metropolitan, one of the most famous is his painting of **Madame X—Madame Pierre Gautreau (45)**; when exhibited in 1884 the picture of this great Parisian beauty was received with derision because of the daring dress and odd skin color. Sargent himself sold it to the Museum in 1916, terming it perhaps his best picture. Later in his life he

46

47

liked to paint mostly landscapes and water colors.

Mary Cassatt, like Sargent, studied in Paris and preferred to remain in that city rather than return to her native Pennsylvania. Encouraged by Degas to join the French Impressionists, she exhibited with them in the late 1870s. **The Cup of Tea (46)**, dating from 1879, is a charming picture of her sister Lydia. But the subject for which Mary Cassatt is best known is maternity, glowingly depicted, and her many paintings of mothers attending to young children are warm and human.

Many other American artists studied with the Impressionists and adapted their ideas to individual styles. John Henry Twachtman left an evocative record of his stay in Normandy, France, in **Arques-La-Bataille (47)**, a poetic Impressionist canvas of muted greens, grays, and browns; and Monet was the chief influence in Theodore Robinson's landscapes. In the United States, city and country scenes were depicted in brilliant colors by Childe Hassam, as in *The Church at Gloucester* **(48)**; Julian Alden Weir contributed Impressionist paintings to the first exhibition, in 1898, of The Ten, a newly formed association of American Impressionists. In *The Red Bridge* **(49)**, dating from 1895, Weir made a lyrical composition out of ordinary subject matter.

Though Winslow Homer traveled abroad on various occasions, he lived and worked mostly in New York and on the coast of Maine, becoming one of America's finest realistic painters. His work is splendidly represented in the Museum. Homer at first earned his livelihood as an illustrator for *Harper's Weekly*; many of his lithographs and wood engravings of Civil War scenes and other genre topics can be seen in the Print Department of the Museum (by appointment). His early oil paintings **(50)**, such as the Metropolitan's *The Veteran in a New Field*, done in 1865 just after the Civil War, *Prisoners from the Front*, and *Snap the Whip*, are

51

52

realistic reporting, yet they show a keen eye for composition and a gift for conveying a situation quickly and often humorously.

Whether visiting the coast of England, of Massachusetts, or of the West Indies, or living for the last 25 years of his life in Prout's Neck, Maine, Homer was deeply attached to the ocean, and his paintings conjure up this great elemental force in all its many moods. The charming illustrative genre scenes of the 1860s and 70s gave way to dramatic naturalistic canvases. The seething **Northeastern (51)** and *The Gulf Stream* with its lonely shipwrecked sailor are almost totally devoid of human activity.

Homer used color for brilliant effects, often limiting his palette to a few hues ranging through many tonalities. In water color painting he was a pioneer and leader, and the Museum has an excellent selection of his landscapes and seascapes in this technique. A few sweeping brush strokes suggest a **Palm Tree, Nassau (52)**, tossed by a sudden storm in the West Indies. Successful and sought-after in his lifetime, Homer gave to the industrializing American nation a nostalgic image of the great outdoors.

Among the sculptors of the late 19th century, Frederic Remington was perhaps as "native" as Homer. Although he had become a recognized painter, he tried his hand at sculpture in the 1890s and modeled *The Bronco Buster* **(53)** after one of his drawings. With the piece an immediate success, Remington continued to make bronzes of cowboys, ranchers, and Indians in vigorous movement, often on galloping horses.

An entirely different kind of sculptor was Augustus Saint-Gaudens. Allied with the most fashionable and influential architects of the 80s and 90s, the firm of McKim, Mead, and White, Saint-Gaudens was called upon to decorate their public buildings and great mansions with murals, reliefs, and statues. The weather vane *Diana* was commissioned to stand

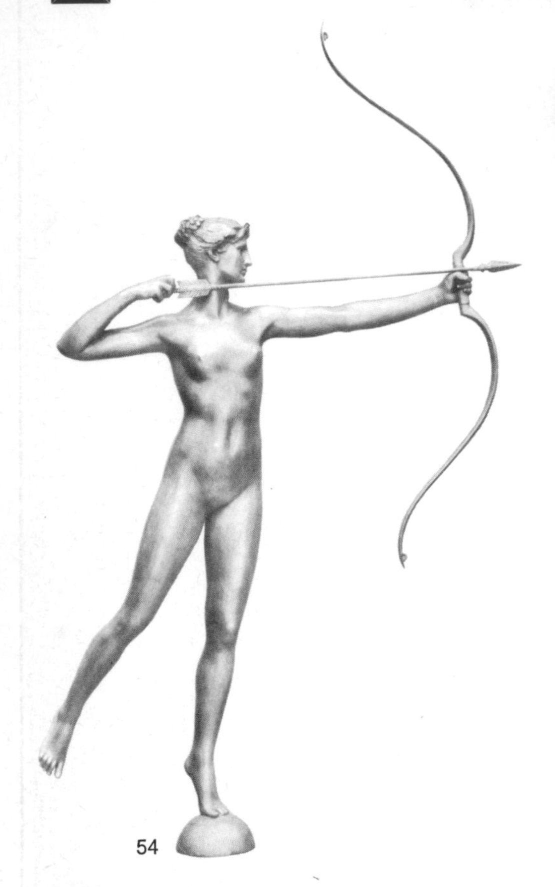

54

56

on the tower of Madison Square Garden, though the first statue proved to be too large for the building. The Museum's **Diana (54)** is a smaller version, cast in 1928 after Saint-Gaudens's death.

The early years of the 20th century were marked by two exhibitions of dissenters which may well have been indicative of the decades to follow. In 1908 eight painters exhibited together in New York. Each was an individual artist in his own right, yet all were friends who shared certain attitudes, particularly the desire to break away from existing artistic trends and from the dominance of European art. The Eight **(55)**, as they came to be called, are well represented in the Museum. Their emphasis on the ordinary human being and the commonplace scene earned them the title of Ash Can School. Indicative of The Eight's disparate interests are such canvases as Robert Henri's *Dutch Girl in White*, John Sloan's *Dust Storm, Fifth Avenue*, George Luks's *The Old Duchess*, Maurice Prendergast's *Central Park in 1903*, Ernest Lawson's *Winter*, Everett Shinn's *London Music Hall*, Arthur B. Davies's *Adventure* and *Unicorns*, and William Glackens's *Central Park in Winter*. On looking backward, this protest seems mild and their painting only a continuation, in a somewhat different direction, of the realist tradition in American art. George Bellows was also part of this "new" realism; **Up the Hudson (56)**, dating from 1908, is an evocative picture of the river's rural aspects.

In the famous Armory Show of 1913 in New York, the protest of The Eight was immersed in the international sector, in which the Fauves, Cubists, and Expressionists from Europe shocked the American public. From then on, "modern art" in America was to be considered seriously.

American Wing

American Wing

Objects, Periods, Styles	Numbers in Text
BEDROOMS	(18)
CERAMICS: earthenware and porcelain	
CHIMNEYS, FIREPLACES, MANTLEPIECES	
CHIPPENDALE STYLE	(8-10), (13)
CLOCKS	
COLONIAL PERIOD	
DINING ROOMS	(14)
DRAWING ROOMS AND PARLORS	(3), (4), (8)
EMPIRE STYLE	(16)
ENTRY HALLS	(13)
FEDERAL PERIOD: Hepplewhite and Sheraton styles	(14), (15)
FURNITURE	(1), (2), (6), (9-12), (14-17), (19), (25)
GLASS	(7)
LAMPS AND CHANDELIERS	
PENNSYLVANIA GERMAN FURNISHINGS	
PEWTER	
QUEEN ANNE STYLE	(12)
SHAKER FURNITURE	
SILVER	(5), (20-24)
TEXTILES, CREWEL WORK, NEEDLEWORK PICTURES, DRAPERIES	
WALLPAPER	(13), (18)

This page helps you to find what you especially want to see and read about.

The American Wing, housed in its own section of the Museum, was opened to the public in 1924, but the Metropolitan's involvement with American decorative arts and architecture had begun in earnest 15 years before. On the occasion of the Hudson-Fulton Celebration in 1909 the Museum held two exhibitions: one of 17th-century Dutch pictures, the other of American art to 1815. This latter undertaking—a major exhibition of American furniture, silver, glass, pottery, textiles, and paintings—was unprecedented in a public institution. Its overwhelming success and popularity led to the decision to form a permanent collection of the arts of America, to be exhibited in appropriate settings comprised of the actual interiors of early American houses.

Three men were responsible for the Americanization of the Metropolitan: Henry Watson Kent laid out the guidelines that the permanent collection was to follow; in 1920 Robert W. deForest provided the funds for constructing the building; and in 1923 R. T. Haines Halsey, a trustee and chairman of the Committee on American Decorative Art, devoted an entire year to the details of installing and furnishing more than 20 period rooms.

The wing today houses great and representative examples of all aspects of the American decorative arts. In recent years efforts have been made to acquire furniture and objects from the middle and late 19th century, and the scope of the collection has been significantly extended. The American Wing is generally strongest, of course, in 17th- and 18th-century material. In all, the American Wing collections comprise approximately 950 pieces of furniture, 850 pieces of silver, 200 pieces of pewter, 1,900 pieces of glass (of which 1,750 are 19th century), 600 examples of textile (more than half are of American manufacture), and 650 pieces of American ceramics. The pictures belong to the American Paintings and Sculpture Department and the prints to the Department of Prints and Photographs. Modern American art is now being collected by the new Department of Twentieth Century Art.

The American Wing consists of three floors with 35 rooms arranged in roughly chronological order: the top floor for the display of the 17th and early 18th centuries; the second floor for the mid-18th century; and the ground floor for the post-Revolutionary period up to 1830. In period rooms, woodwork and architectural details have been preserved from houses, many of which have long since been destroyed; the original arrangement has been kept as closely as possible. In addition, each room is provided with furniture of its period and other accessories—draperies, paintings, silver or pewter, lamps, etc. In corridors and connecting galleries, too, there are displays from the great holdings of American decorative arts: pewter, silver, porcelain, pottery, and glass.

THIRD FLOOR

The core of each floor is its large center gallery with representative pieces of furniture giving a general summary of styles. The rooms are discussed in a more or less chronological sequence, although the Museum visitor can, of course, choose his own route. On entering the central gallery on the third floor one is immedi-

1

2

ately transported into the lives of the early settlers. The heavy roof trusses, adapted from those in the Old Ship Meetinghouse at Hingham, Massachusetts (1681), recall the great English Gothic halls. In most ways the early immigrants, people of modest means largely from rural communities or small towns in the Old World, attempted to recreate the atmosphere they had left behind them. Accordingly, the work of the earliest American craftsmen tended to reflect the late Gothic style of Western Europe and not the Renaissance elegance that the more fashionable court tastes imitated. Scattered around the hall are various types of chairs, though seating accommodations were not very common in early America and tended to be straight-backed and rather uncomfortable; the average person normally sat on a stool. Wooden chairs were sometimes elaborately turned or carved, such as the Brewster chair and the wainscot chair; the earliest upholstered chairs had marsh-grass stuffing. Tables tended to be on trestles, thus easily removable, or were small to save space. A late 17th-century **folding table (1)** has heavy turned legs and a surface painted to simulate marble. The chest was used both for storage and for sitting. Many of these pieces of wooden furniture had applied moldings, bosses, turned elements, or flat carving, such as the **chest (2)** in the corridor and others in the central hall; some were gaily painted.

Two rooms on the third floor date from the 17th century; the others are from the early to mid-18th century. On either side of the oldest room, the Hart Parlor, there is a typical entry and staircase from about 1700: the tiny hallway from the John Wentworth House in Portsmouth, New Hampshire, served as the back entry; the front staircase of the same house shows more elaborate elements, such as paneling covering the bricks and spiral-turned balusters.

3

4

5

The **parlor from the Thomas Hart House (3)**, built before 1675 in Ipswich, Massachusetts, is the earliest room in the American Wing and served a multipurpose function as sitting room, bedroom, and kitchen. The structure is still clearly revealed—corner posts, horizontal supports, and the huge summer beam that spans the room from one end to the other. Though the fireplace was large and good for cooking, it was not very efficient for heating; and the small casement windows with leaded panes (some are reproductions) allowed little light to penetrate into the low-ceilinged interior. Much of the sturdy 17th-century oak and pine furniture came from Massachusetts.

A narrow passageway leads to the more spacious **room from the John Wentworth House (4)**, built in Portsmouth, New Hampshire, about 1700. One immediately senses the greater elegance and comfort. Fine wood paneling frames the fireplace and covers one entire wall; the double-hung sash windows became standard throughout the next centuries. Made of a variety of hard woods, the furniture was often veneered or, more rarely, inlaid with tiles; upholstered chairs and caning speak of greater ease. Even luxury is evident from the fine double-handled **silver cup (5)** made some years later by Jacob Hurd of Boston. Japanning, a process of painting in imitation of Oriental lacquer, was beautifully practiced on a **highboy (6)** of about 1700. Glittering quillwork on sconces was an attempt to reflect the feeble candlelight.

6

Continuing on, one enters a mid-18th-century room from Portsmouth, Rhode Island. Distinctive here are the pilastered and paneled woodwork and the tiles surrounding the fireplace. Crewel work (embroidery in wool) was much practiced on upholstery fabrics, as on the two armchairs, or on bed covers. The next room belonged to the John Hewlett House in Long Island (about 1740-50). The blue-gray of the painted woodwork was attractively matched by window and bed curtains of block-printed or resist-dyed material. China and glass are displayed in an elegantly carved cupboard, to the left of which a secret stairway was concealed. A four-poster bed would have been placed in such an upstairs bedroom.

On the opposite side of the central gallery are two more rooms from New England, both small and low-ceilinged. The room from Newington, Connecticut, has interesting fluted pilasters, arched panels, and rosette carvings, which recall the Renaissance influence that came to colo-

7

8

nial artisans from English books of design. These styles were always adapted to local tastes, needs, and materials. The next room, from Hampton, New Hampshire, is a simple rural upstairs chamber. New Hampshire was far removed from the more refined city styles, yet how cozy must have been this small farmhouse with its unpainted pine paneling, here even on the ceiling.

In the following gallery are pieces of painted furniture of a kind that brightened many colonial houses. Floral and fruit motifs, fantastic designs, biblical illustrations, and the imitation in paint of marble and rich woods can be found on chests and cupboards. A Dutch door in two sections, with oval green bull's-eye glass set in the top panels, leads into an alcove (1752) from New York state.

Returning through the central gallery and the hallway, one comes to a series of rooms starting with one devoted to 19th-century Shaker furniture. One of the utopian religious groups, the Shakers believed in hard work and the denial of worldly pleasures. The stark simplicity of their furnishings admirably mirrors their tenets. The central dining table, chairs, chests, tin cupboard, and child's desk have restrained lines with no excesses of any sort. Many of the pieces, of maple and pine, came from two main Shaker communities, in Hancock, Massachusetts, and New Lebanon, New York.

A gallery of 18th- and 19th-century country furnishings leads to the next room, which is devoted to yet another group of settlers, the Pennsylvania Germans, often wrongly referred to as Pennsylvania Dutch, who came to America from Germany at the urging of William Penn. Settling on the fertile land of Pennsylvania, these Germans maintained their religious and ethnic unity, and to this day have preserved their own special art form. The painted blanket and dower chests show their traditional ornaments of hearts, tulips, and birds and other animals; a dresser contains earthenware dishes with their special slip and sgraffito decoration.

The two cases of pewter show more than half of the Museum's holdings. Made mainly of tin, with small amounts of lead and antimony, pewter was used for many purposes until the end of the 19th century. The forms tended to be fairly standardized and remained much the same for long periods of time without following the fads of fashion. Still immensely pleasing to our eyes are the tankards, cups, plates, bowls, and candlesticks displayed here.

SECOND FLOOR

Returning to the staircase and descending to the second floor, one follows along a hallway in which are exhibited typical 18th-century objects that would have graced the interior of any well-to-do house along the Atlantic seaboard. Glass, some of it brightly colored, came from many glasshouses; in Maryland, John Frederick Amelung made the superb **presentation goblet (7)** dating from 1788. Interesting also are the needlework pictures, the objects made of whale and walrus ivory called scrimshaw, and the 248-piece dinner service of Chinese export porcelain.

Bearing to the left, on the way to a central gallery, one reaches the **Powel Room (8)**. Samuel Powel, from whose house this interior was taken, was the last colonial mayor of Philadelphia; a well-traveled man, Powel had the taste and money to secure the very best. The fine

9

wood paneling, with carved and molded decoration, is derived from the fashionable English Rococo style, interpreted here in the ornamental Chippendale manner. The Chinese wallpaper was hand-painted. Fine adaptations of the Chippendale style are evident in the furniture, most of which was made in Philadelphia. The craftsmen of that city were, in the third quarter of the 18th century, the most skilled and renowned cabinetmakers. The **tilt-top Chippendale table (9)** with claw and ball feet, the brightly covered armchairs, the fine tall clock, and the cut-glass chandelier made an elegant ensemble for the elite of Philadelphia.

On the second floor the rooms date mainly from the mid- to late 18th century. The central gallery, as on the floor above, serves as a summary: here is some of the best furniture of the period as well as paintings by two well-known portraitists of the 18th century—Gilbert Stuart (1755-1828) and John Singleton Copley (1738-1815). In 1754 Thomas Chip-

10

pendale in London published *The Gentleman and Cabinet-Maker's Director*, a pattern book that set the design for much of the good furniture in America. Adapted by Americans in a more subdued manner, the Chippendale style reached its most elaborate phase in the **highboys (10)** and lowboys made in Philadelphia; these pieces were elaborately carved and ornamented with scrolls, pierced shell motifs, leaves, and rosettes. The same Rococo motifs can be found on chairs and tables, even silver. Other parts of the seaboard colonies developed their own variations of the prevailing style, as in some of the silver displayed here. The Rhode Island **chest of drawers (11)** of mahogany, dating from 1765, was signed by John Townsend, one of a family of cabinetmakers in Newport. This refined example of a regional fashion diverged widely from its English pattern. More chairs and tables from Philadelphia and a remarkable Connecticut desk can be found in the little alcove off the central gallery, in which architectural elements from Gadsby's Tavern have been remounted; the marbleized and grained woodwork surrounding the fireplace was fashionable in the late 18th century. The English wallpaper, called " Les Oiseaux, " had painted and applied Chinese motifs, reflecting a desired Oriental exoticism.

Gadsby's Tavern was built in 1793 in Alexandria, Virginia, then an important stopping-off point on the route from the South (Williamsburg and Richmond) to the national capital, Philadelphia, in the North. Across the central hall is the Assembly Room from that tavern. As in the alcove, only the wooden overmantels reach from floor to ceiling, while the rest of the room is paneled as high as the chair rail. It is not difficult to imagine the noise and bustle during George Washington's last birthday ball, given here in 1798, with the musicians in the gallery providing music for the dance, and

11

12

warmth emanating from the marble-faced fireplaces. The continuation of older styles is visible in the fine mid-18th-century furniture; such pieces as the Queen Anne settee and related chairs were still being made in the colonies long after the style was no longer fashionable in England.

Just across from the end of the Assembly Room is an earlier interior from Marmion, the Virginia plantation of the Fitzhugh family. This parlor is one of the best surviving mid-18th-century American rooms, with the classical architectural details of the woodwork carried to the fullest extent. The walls were painted either to simulate marble or with landscapes and rich scroll and floral decorations. Once again the furniture comes from Philadelphia, that unsurpassed center of cabinetmaking; the mahogany **armchair (12)**, perhaps the stateliest of Queen Anne chairs, dates from about 1760.

One more mid-18th-century interior, off the central gallery, remains to be visited. This particular room comes from a brick house on the Maryland estate known as Almodington, and is representative of a gentleman's home. The walls were still paneled from floor to ceiling and painted; somewhat later than the room is the mantelpiece; decorations consist of fine portraits and fluted shell cupboards, their interiors painted a dull red, which would have displayed the best pieces of delftware from Holland, or English stoneware and porcelain. The handsome pieces of furniture include a mahogany card table attributed to John Goddard, another Newport cabinetmaker.

Leaving the Almodington Room, one takes a few steps through a narrow gallery to the Verplanck Room. The objects exhibited in this passageway illustrate an important phase of 18th-century furnishings—the taste for Oriental porcelain and other exotic objects from the Far East. England for a long time exported to her colonies Chinese wallpaper and sets of dinnerware, for it was not until the late

18th century that the first American ship, the *Empress of China*, traded directly with China and brought back in its hold such extravagances as the ivory pagoda seen here. Much of the China trade porcelain was decorated with well-known Chinese patterns, but other sets were made to order for certain families, often with their coats of arms. The English attempted to imitate true porcelains; the enameled, opaque, white Bristol glass shown in two cases did indeed look much like porcelain.

Many of the furnishings of the pre-Revolutionary drawing room belonging to the Verplanck family were reassembled from the original house in Wall Street, New York City, where it had been in use from 1763 to 1803. A comfortable uniformity of style marks the chairs, tables, and sofa and undoubtedly betrays the craftsmanship of a single New York cabinetmaker, freely interpreting the Chippendale style. The cosmopolitan taste of the well-to-do merchant Samuel Verplanck and his wife, Judith, would naturally have included imported pieces: the japanned secretary and the gilt-framed looking glass (both from England), and the China trade porcelain displayed in the cupboard. To add to the warmth and style of this cozy interior, three particularly fine portraits of Verplanck family members by John Singleton Copley were hung on the walls.

FIRST FLOOR

Descending another flight of stairs and turning right, one reaches in a few more steps the last interior dating from the colonial period, the splendid **Van Rensselaer Entry Hall (13)** from the great manor house that Stephen Van Rensselaer built near Albany, New York, between 1765 and 1768. One of the outstanding examples of Georgian architecture, this great house must have been known far and wide for its hall, extending from the front to the rear entrance and decorated with extraordinary scenic English wallpaper made in 1768 for this house. It is difficult to say whether the popular paintings of land and sea reproduced here are more imposing than the wonderful fantasy used in the scrolls and arabesques of the Rococo designs surrounding each "painting." More New York Chippendale furniture is assembled here; some chairs in particular came from the Van Rensselaer family, possibly even from this very hall.

The first floor of the American Wing is devoted mainly to interiors from the years immediately following the Revolution to about 1820, the Federal period. After leaving the Van Rensselaer Hall, one passes through a small gallery to a room from Providence, Rhode Island, in which the woodwork comes from a house built between 1794 and 1798. A charming settee and matching chairs painted with floral decoration are examples of the Sheraton style as practiced in New York. The two wall clocks are an original American contribution to clockmaking.

In the central gallery, also known as the **Phyfe Gallery (14)**, are exhibited various pieces of furniture in the most prominent styles of the Neoclassic period. Though the American arts were basically a reflection of international styles, mostly those of England and France, an American character is readily distinguishable in them, particularly in the local variations. Neoclassicism in art, a rebirth of interest in

13

14

15

16

classical lines and forms, was championed in England by Robert Adam (1728-92). Designing and building many splendid houses for the nobility, Adam extended his influence to every sphere of interior decoration and furnishing and, within ten years after his return from Italy in 1758, had revolutionized fashionable tastes. His ideas were applied to furniture designs in particular by two Englishmen, George Hepplewhite and Thomas Sheraton, and as such were adopted by American furniture-makers in the early Federal period. It is often difficult to differentiate between these two styles in America; together they are known as the Federal style. The late Federal style, roughly from 1815 to 1825, was influenced by the fashions of the English Regency (1811-20) and the French Empire (1804-15).

As in the earlier, colonial, period, the different cities developed their own variations of the dominating styles. Leading in fashion was New York, where Duncan Phyfe had his workshop, still visible today in the charming water color hung in the central gallery. The lyre-back **Federal chair (15)**, made by Phyfe for the family of William Livingston, governor of New Jersey, is typical in its sweep and fine decoration. The Frenchman Charles-Honoré Lannuier, also working in New York, incorporated the Empire style shapes, as in the fanciful **card table (16)** of about 1815 with its gilded, winged caryatid and animal legs; veneers of various woods and inlaid brass ornaments contribute to the table's refinement. Of the other pieces of furniture, especially noteworthy of the Empire style are the yellow upholstered dolphin sofa and the pair of yellow chairs with painted decorations—a version of the Greek klismos. Salem, Boston, Philadelphia, and Baltimore were additional cabinetmaking centers, each with its well-known designers and great roster of patrons. Salem furniture is closely linked to the name of Samuel McIntire, its most prominent designer, who was responsible for designs in the Salem alcove off the central gallery; the mantelpiece was

17

partially carved by McIntire, and a delicately carved **chair (17)** shows the same master's touch.

Whereas the central gallery serves as a repository for various kinds of furniture of the Federal period, it is surrounded by entire rooms from houses formerly in Maryland, Virginia, and New England that give the general flavor of the new classical vogue. In this time the fashionable houses were more spacious; rooms had higher ceilings and larger windows, often with elaborate window treatment in wood or with ornate curtains in fine textiles, their color blending with the rest of the overall scheme to create a harmonious space. Woodwork was usually confined to the mantelpiece, and walls were covered with expensive wallpaper or with textured silks or other cloth. The typical Adam ornamentation—delicate garlands, entwined floral patterns, and graceful figures from classical mythology—was imitated on ceilings, walls, mantelpieces, and wherever else possible. Rooms were no longer multipurpose but were adapted to their particular uses. Fantastic in their grace and glitter were the chandeliers and lighting fixtures.

The dining room taken from a house in Baltimore of about 1810 admirably conveys the feeling of classical refinement. Rectangular forms tended to be replaced by ovals and circles, and the entire interior was carefully composed to comply with the best taste of the Federal era. The furniture is mostly from Baltimore, and with its light wood inlays and painted glass inserts it demonstrates yet another regional variation of the Federal style. Particularly exuberant is the sideboard with its mahogany veneers, satinwood inlays, and silver and glass panels.

Immediately adjoining is a room from a house in Petersburg, Virginia. Here is an elaborate provincial interpretation of Adam's ideas: the proportions are light and airy, with a color effect deriving from the delicately patterned yellow satin covering the walls; the architectural trim abounds in stucco ornaments based on classical motifs; even the marble of the mantel is carved to blend with the fragile and varied decoration on the chimney piece. The furnishings in such wealthy Virginia homes of the early 19th century might have come from any of the middle eastern states; this room is now furnished with pieces by New York makers. European imports were still much coveted, and in all the rooms of the first floor there are displays of appropriate European cut glass, English pottery, French and China trade porcelain, and elaborate mantel clocks and mirrors.

18

On entering the next interior, the **Haverhill Room (18)**, one is instantly transported into the midst of a hunt, for the bright French wallpaper with hunting scenes is the most striking feature of this room from a house formerly in Haverhill, Massachusetts. The elaborately dressed and carved four-poster bed was made in Boston, and the superb **breakfront bookcase (19)** in Salem. Here, as in other rooms, much care is expended on the treatment of the chimney piece.

Whereas the furnishings of the American Wing's period rooms have been closely matched to the architectural features, stemming from identical periods and where possible from the same geographical regions, the interiors of the Benkard and Munn rooms have a more

19

mixed ensemble of objects, though they still represent the Federal period. In both cases the rooms honor private collectors, Mrs. Harry Horton Benkard and Charles Allen Munn. After Mrs. Benkard's death, the early 19th-century woodwork (from a Massachusetts house) and all the reassembled furniture and objects were presented to the Museum by her friends; particularly pleasing is the color scheme of blue and deep purple. The Munn Room serves as a summary and farewell to the early 19th-century American decorative arts. The Argand lamps on one mantelpiece represent an improvement in lighting because of a new type of wick. Other oil lamps and candlesticks, popularly made of glass in America, can be seen in the gallery leading out of the Munn Room. Here are also assembled some of the Museum's holdings in American glassware, miniatures, snuffboxes, rings, cloak pins, etc.

The superb selection of silver exhibited in the next gallery is only a small portion of the Museum's collection, yet a better survey of some of the finest pieces of the 18th and early 19th century can scarcely be found. The colonial silversmith was a much respected figure; banks were unknown until a later date, and much of the coinage that came to the colonies from foreign trade was melted and converted by him into cups and bowls, candlesticks, tea sets, etc. Thus refashioned into plate silver of certified weight and purity, such silver was easily traceable in case of theft, could serve as display pieces, or could, if necessary, be reconverted into money. Seventeenth-century silver is rare, as much has been melted down or reused; it consisted mostly of drinking cups,

20 21 22

bowls, tankards, porringers, and pieces for church use.

One of the most inventive of the early workers in silver, Cornelius Kierstede, obviously of Dutch ancestry, decorated a **pair of fluted candlesticks (20)** with flat-chased ornaments. His sturdy tea kettle shows an individual taste, and a double-handled **bowl (21)** displays fine workmanship in its embossed flower pattern. Saltcellars and dishes were set on little feet reminiscent of those used on furniture; a coiled serpent serves as a handle to the ornate **sugar box (22)** from New Hampshire (around 1710).

Mid-18th-century silver showed a very high standard of quality and repeated the Rococo spirit of design visible in the other decorative arts. Straight lines gave way to bulbous bodies, domed lids, and pear-shaped forms. Engraved, repoussé, or cast decorations were endlessly varied, repeating often the shell, leaf, and floral motifs applied to furniture.

The proliferation of tea sets corresponded roughly to the classic revival; a

23

24

particularly fine example is the **teapot (23)** and other accessories with Adam-like cut ornaments, made by Paul Revere, Jr., none other than the patriot remembered for his courageous deeds. Regional and stylistic differences are well represented in this display.

Animal shapes were a favorite motif of the Empire period; one of the most remarkable examples of Empire inventiveness is the **sauceboat (24)** by Anthony Rasch, who worked in Philadelphia from about 1808 to 1819. Mid-19th-century silver, at first overly ornate in its repoussé decoration, later mirrored the affluent patrons' tastes for Renaissance revival and other Victorian styles.

On leaving the American Wing one passes through a last gallery, which is a foreshadowing of things to come, for here are assembled some fine pieces from the 19th century, among them an original **desk (25)** with two tower-like bookcases. But the bulk of the 19th-century collections will be housed in a new addition to the American Wing. In time many of the items shown in the Centennial exhibit "19th Century America" will have a permanent exhibition place; then the fine Belter furniture, Victorian glass, Tiffany lamps and glass, Art Nouveau objects, silver, etc., will be on public display for the enjoyment of all.

25

Ancient Near Eastern Art

Ancient Near Eastern Art

Objects, Periods, Styles	Numbers in Text
BRONZES	(14), (21)
CUNEIFORM TABLETS	
FOUNDATION FIGURES	(2), (5)
GLAZED BRICKS	(19)
IVORIES	(8), (13), (17)
JEWELRY	
METALWORK: gold, silver, copper	(7), (9), (10), (12), (14), (18), (20-21), (25-27) (29)
POTTERY	
RELIEFS	(16), (23), (24)
SCULPTURE	(4), (15), (22)
SEALS	(3)
STATUETTES	(1), (4), (6)
WEAPONS, HELMET	(11), (28)
WINGED BULLS	(15)

Chronology

Early Anatolia	
Hacilar	c. 5700-5000 B.C.
Sumerian	
Ubaid	c. 4500-3500 B.C.
Uruk	c. 3500-3100 B.C.
Jamdat Nasr	c. 3100-2900 B.C.
Early Dynastic	c. 2900-2370 B.C.
Akkadian	c. 2370-2230 B.C.
Neo-Sumerian (Gudea and Third Dynasty of Ur)	c. 2230-2000 B.C.
Isin-Larsa-Old Babylonian	c. 2020-1600 B.C.
Kassite	c. 1550-1150 B.C.
Neo-Assyrian (Ashurnasirpal II to Destruction of Ninevah)	883-612 B.C.
Neo-Babylonian	626-539 B.C.
Achaemenid	539-331 B.C.
Seleucid and Parthian	312 B.C.-A.D. 224
Sasanian (Ardeshir I - Yazdgard III)	A.D. 226-651

☞ **This page helps you to find what you especially want to see and read about.**

Ancient Near Eastern Art

In 1932 a Department of Near Eastern Art was created, incorporating, among other material, the Ancient Near Eastern antiquities; these were made part of the Department of Egyptian Art in 1947. A separate Department of Ancient Near Eastern Art was formed in 1956. For four years, beginning in 1959, the pre-Islamic and Islamic sections were placed under a single curator. Then, in 1963, the two were finally separated into the present Departments of Ancient Near Eastern Art and Islamic Art.

The beginning of the collection of Near Eastern antiquities goes back to the 1890s, when a large number of cuneiform tablets and stamp and cylinder seals were purchased from General Luigi Palma di Cesnola and William Hayes Ward. Early in the 20th century major objects were acquired as gifts: Assyrian reliefs in 1917 from J. Pierpont Morgan and in the 1930s from John D. Rockefeller, Jr.; also ivories from Anatolia and Luristan bronzes from Mr. and Mrs. George D. Pratt. In the same decade the Museum began taking part in excavations in the Near East: at Ctesiphon in Iraq with the German State Museums, and independently at Qasr-i-Abu Nasr in Iran. The Museum again began excavations in the 1950s and 60s: with the British School of Archaeology at Nimrud in Iraq; with the American Schools of Oriental Research and the Oriental Institute of the University of Chicago at Nippur; with the University Museum in Philadelphia at Hasanlu, Ziwiyeh, and other sites in northwestern Iran; and with the British Institute of Persian Studies at Yarim Tepe in northeastern Iran. In the fall of 1968 the Museum, in collaboration with the Institute of Fine Arts, New York University, began excavations at the extensive mound of Al-Hiba in southeastern Iraq. This is the site of ancient Lagash, a city of considerable importance in the 3rd millennium B.C. In different areas of the mound a number of buildings have been uncovered, including a large oval temple of Enannatum I (c. 2500 B.C.), an Old Babylonian temple, and a Sumerian administrative building. It is planned that the excavations will continue for a number of years.

Until the collection can be reinstalled in its newly renovated galleries on the second floor, a small temporary exhibit shows a few works of art from each of the major areas or cultures in the ancient Near East.

The collection of Ancient Near Eastern art includes material from the countries extending from the eastern Mediterranean seacoast in the west to Afghanistan in the east, from Turkey and southern Russia in the north to the Persian Gulf and Arabia in the south. The objects range in date from the 6th millennium B.C. to the time of the Arab conquest, almost seven millennia later, in A.D. 626. The cultures that developed in these areas were, in the earliest periods, often unrelated; gradually contacts between the different geographical regions increased, and these can be traced through the material remains.

For the early periods, pottery gives the clearest evidence of indigenous artistic development and cultural contacts between different centers. Some of the most ancient is the burnished red-brown and cream-colored ware from the neolithic levels at Hacilar in southwestern Anatolia (5700-5000 B.C.). Much later in date, and

1

2

from another part of the Near East, is a large vase of around 3100 B.C. with a stylized ibex, which comes from Sialk on the central Iranian plateau. This type of pottery is found in other parts of Iran, and the cultural remains at Sialk indicate connections with Mesopotamia (present-day Iraq). Shortly before this time, in both Iran and Mesopotamia, the potter's wheel was first used, and slightly later, around 3000 B.C., the earliest written documents occur in Mesopotamia. These are tablets of clay inscribed in a pictographic script and, later, in wedge-shaped signs called cuneiform by modern scholars.

The most complete sequence of material, both literary and artistic, in the pre-Islamic Near East comes from the region of Mesopotamia. This is chiefly a result of the extensive archaeological excavation which has, for more than a century, produced evidence in the form of architecture, pottery, stone sculpture, metalwork, and thousands of tablets inscribed with economic, historical, and literary texts. The art of the Sumerians, who inhabited southern Mesopotamia in the 3rd millennium B.C., is well illustrated by the stone sculptures excavated in the Diyala region and at Nippur. These figures of worshipers, such as the **statuette from Square Temple (1)** at Tell Asmar, were placed as votive statues in a temple; they are stylized and unrealistic in form, some crude, others remarkably sophisticated in design. Almost all are carved in the poor gypsum easily available in southern Mesopotamia, where good stone is scarce. The hair was often covered with bitumen and the eyes inlaid with combinations of shell, black limestone, and lapis lazuli. A copper **foundation figure (2)** of about the same period is of unknown provenance, but surely came

3

from a city in Mesopotamia. This nude male carrying on his head a burden of bricks was probably buried for religious purposes in the foundations of a sacred or royal building. Other foundation figures are inscribed, and it is evident that these objects were dedications to a god or goddess on behalf of the king who had ordered construction of the building.

Much Sumerian jewelry in gold and lapis lazuli was found in graves in a royal cemetery at Ur, a site excavated by Sir Leonard Woolley from 1932 to 1934. The treasure he found gives an indication of the technical skills of the Sumerian craftsmen working in gold, silver, wood, and shell. Another gold necklace, made almost a millennium later, allegedly from the region of Babylon, repeats many of the techniques and forms found at Ur. The pendants on the necklace include some of the symbols of the gods. Throughout antiquity the jeweller's craft in the Near East remained a conservative one, with styles and designs repeated for centuries almost without change.

In the second half of the 3rd millennium B.C. a single Semitic state, Akkad, united the small city-states that had co-existed during the Sumerian Early Dynastic period. Of this culture (2370-2230 B.C.) there are far fewer remains, but the small **seals (3)** of cylindrical shape, the common form in Mesopotamia until the mid-1st millennium B.C., reveal in style and design a beauty and diversity that is unparalleled in the earlier and many of the later periods.

In contrast to the freedom and variety of Akkadian art, the sculpture produced in the time of the Sumerian revival during the Third Dynasty of Ur (c. 2100-2000 B.C.), particularly in the Sumerian city-state of Lagash, is almost all of a single type. The seated **figure of Gudea (4)**, the governor of Lagash, is characteristic in its massive proportions, in the linear designs used for the cap and eyebrows, and in the modeling that is visible in the limbs and parts of the face. The stone used for

4

5 6

7

the seated Gudea is diorite, which came possibly from Arabia. In spite of the fact that it is a hard and heavy stone, difficult to carve and transport, Gudea chose to have his statues made almost solely in this material.

There is little stone sculpture in the round from this time, although vast building complexes at Ur and at Nippur have been excavated. The latter site produced copper **foundation figures (5)**; these differ in design from those of the earlier Sumerian period, but still represent a figure, sometimes inscribed with a king's name, holding building material, such as a basket of mortar, on his head.

In the art of countries bordering on the eastern Mediterranean Sea in the 3rd and 2nd millennia B.C., there is clear evidence of contacts with Mesopotamia and also with Egypt, the Aegean islands, Greece, and Anatolia. A gold plate of around 1400 B.C. from Syria is not unlike Mycenaean works of art in its continuous, geometric design; and small bronze figurines made throughout the 2nd millennium in Syria and Palestine show connections with Egypt in the form of the crown and dress. One such **statuette of a god (6)** is still covered with the gold foil originally applied to the whole body. Syria and Palestine were throughout antiquity the crossroads or meeting place of persons and armies from Iran and Mesopotamia on the one hand, and Egypt and Anatolia on the other.

Anatolia itself is set apart to the north, and although there are signs in the 3rd millennium B.C. of Egyptian and Mesopotamian contacts, it is only at the end of that millennium and the beginning of the succeeding one that there is a large amount of artistic and literary evidence for these interconnections. At this period a number of wealthy independent states ruled in Anatolia and carried on extensive trade with northern Mesopotamia, exporting precious metals and importing textiles and tin. Finds from tombs, such as this **gold jug (7)** and other vessels,

weapons, and ritual instruments of copper, silver, and gold, illustrate the skill of the metalworkers. Perhaps the most striking remains from the period around 1900-1800 B.C. are a large and superb collection of ivory carvings such as the **sphinx (8)** from the site of Acem Hüyük in central Anatolia. These ivories indicate the extent of Egyptian and Syrian influence on Anatolia in this period. All were probably originally covered with gold foil; their present orange and gray coloring is due to the action of the soil and burning, respectively.

More closely tied to Mesopotamia in the 3rd and 2nd millennia was the southern region of Iran, the area called Elam. Geographically this area is an extension of the Mesopotamian plain, and in this period it was often under the actual domination of various Mesopotamian kingdoms. In the arts there is a close relationship, although Elamite works differ and are distinctive in style. It was in metalworking that the artisans of Elam excelled throughout history. A small **half-bovine, half-human figure (9)** holding an offering vessel is made from a number of pieces of silver skillfully formed and joined. Such combinations of animal and human forms, and representations of animals in human postures playing instruments, walking erect, or kneeling, occur in the art of both Mesopotamia and Iran. However, the closest parallels to this figure are small stone sculptures of around 3000 B.C. from Iran and representations on proto-Elamite cylinder seals. Consequently the piece has been dated to this period. Of less certain date, but probably from sometime

8

9

10

11

in the 2nd millennium B.C., is a solid cast copper **head of a ruler (10)**, said to have been found in northwestern Iran. The treatment of the face, the two small wrinkles on the forehead, the hollow eye sockets, once inlaid, and the design of the beard link this sculpture to Akkadian works of the second half of the 3rd millennium B.C., but there are other resemblances to male heads of the 2nd millennium, a period when, in Elam, the technique of solid casting for huge objects was known. The headdress, in particular, is of a type for which there is no exact counterpart.

12

Around 1000 B.C. in Iran there was a final flourishing of the arts in Elam, before the collapse of the ruling dynasty brought a period of disruption and chaos. Recent excavations have, however, revealed that there was at this time a rich culture in the north of Iran, in the mountainous, southern Caspian region. This center is the probable source of a number of remarkable objects in the collection—a bronze **helmet (11)** with one male and two female deities, surmounted by a hawk or a falcon, and a small, finely worked **gold cup (12)** with gazelles. Both are extremely fine works of art and both reflect in style or design earlier Elamite objects.

In the 1st millennium B.C. the movements of artisans, freely or as prisoners of war, and of objects, as tribute or booty, increased throughout the Near East. Each country or kingdom retained a distinctive culture of its own, but each favored or imitated to a large degree the works of other regions. Perhaps the clearest reflection of this "international" art of the 1st millennium B.C. are the ivories excavated by the British School of Archaeology in Iraq, at the Assyrian capital city of Nimrud in northern Mesopotamia. Because the Metropolitan was, for a period of 11 years, a partner in this excavation, the Museum's collection contains ivory plaques and this **ivory figurine (13)** from the palaces and temples unearthed at this site. Most of these ivories, which date from the 9th to the 7th century B.C., were originally covered with gold foil, and many were inlaid with colored glass paste as well. Few are purely Assyrian in style. Most are Syrian and Phoenician and must have been brought to Nimrud by a victorious Assyrian king returning from his expeditions in the west; or they may be the works of foreign craftsmen who were resettled at Nimrud. A pair of **bronze sphinxes (14)** from Syria, and another collection of ivories of the same period from the Syrian site of Arslan Tash, are not unlike objects found at Nimrud. Similar works were exported to the west and influenced the arts of such countries as Urartu and Phrygia in Anatolia, Cyprus and Greece, and Etruria in Italy. The

13

14

15

Assyrian style is best seen in the great carved limestone reliefs that decorated the walls of the royal residences, and in the giant mythical creatures, such as the winged, **human-headed bull (15)** from the gateway to the Palace of Ashurnasirpal II at Nimrud. Most of the 9th-century reliefs from the same palace at Nimrud,

16

such as the alabaster **winged genie (16)**, were excavated in the 19th century by the pioneer British archaeologist Sir Austen Henry Layard. They illustrate ritual and religious scenes. The carving is low, and the details of dress and hair style, and of the weapons and vessels, are precisely fashioned. Small designs are often carved in imitation of embroidery on the borders of the robes. An inscription carved across the slabs, which were originally partly painted, repeats over and over a descrip-

17

18

tion of the building of the northwest palace.

Assyria remained the major power in the early 1st millennium B.C., and the influence of her art was felt by all her neighbors in major centers and in outlying regions. This is apparent in some of the finds made at Hasanlu in northwest Iran, where an expedition of the University of Pennsylvania, co-sponsored for a time by the Metropolitan Museum of Art, has revealed much about the culture of this region, particularly in the 10th and 9th centuries B.C. Ivories found there, such as the **fragment of a box (17)**, are varied in style; some must be Assyrian works, others Syrian, and a few are in a quite distinctive, local Iranian style. The same variety is to be seen in other small finds such as cylinder seals. Regrettably almost no writing has been found on objects of any sort from this site, and its ancient name still remains unknown.

Not far from Hasanlu in Iran, a remarkable treasure was discovered by local inhabltants in 1947; it was divided and eventually spread throughout museums and private collections all over the world. The modern name of this site is Ziwiyeh, and a brief sondage there in 1964 by the University of Pennsylvania and the Metropolitan Museum of Art established the date for the abandonment of this hilltop citadel as about 600 B.C. The repoussé **gold plaques (18)**, the ivories, and the designs on the rim of the bronze coffin in which the treasure was allegedly found illustrate the usual mixture of styles—Syrian, Urartian, Iranian, Scythian, and

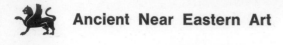

19

Assyrian. Again there is no written evidence from the site itself, and it is impossible to know for or by whom these works were made.

South of Ziwiyeh, in the Zagros Mountains, the tombs and temples of Luristan are the source of a wealth of small bronzes. Horse trappings, vessels, and weapons are covered with, or made of, decorative combinations of animal and grotesque human forms. Recent excavations in Iran suggest that some of the different types come from the 9th and 8th centuries B.C.; others are inscribed with the names of rulers of the 3rd and 2nd millennia B.C.

A combination of forces from Iran under Median leadership, supplemented by Babylonians from southern Mesopotamia and Scythians originally from the northern steppes, brought an end to the vast Assyrian empire. The short-lived Neo-Babylonian Dynasty, which succeeded the Assyrians, is a familiar one because of the fame of one of its rulers, Nebuchadnezzar II (604-562 B.C.). The city of Babylon itself was in this period greatly expanded, and the walls of its processional street, leading to the Ishtar Temple, were lined with glazed bricks in blue, black, yellow, and white, some molded to form **striding lions (19)**. In the 6th century B.C. the Iranian king Cyrus the Great, the real founder of the Achaemenid empire, captured Babylon and set himself up as ruler of Mesopotamia as well as Iran. Ruling first from Pasargadae and then from Ecbatana, the Achaemenids in the 6th and 5th centuries controlled parts of Anatolia and Egypt to the west, and Afghanistan to the east. The stone sculp-

20

tures decorating stairs, walls, and doors of the buildings at Persepolis show not only the Medes and the Persians, but peoples from all the lands tributary to Iran. The **gold rhyton (20)**, a cup or vessel terminating in an animal's head, and other bowls and weapons in silver and gold, continue the high tradition of Iranian metalwork; they also use many themes and motifs that have direct predecessors in the art of Assyria and Babylon. An over-life-size bronze **head of an ibex (21)** is an example of the skill of these Iranian craftsmen. The head is hollow cast, and the different parts are joined by fusion welding to the central piece.

The final burning and pillaging of Persepolis by Alexander the Great is one of the best-known events in the history of the ancient Near East. Under his domination a new period began, with the advent of the Greeks not only as rulers, but as craftsmen and settlers. After his death in 323 B.C., the greatest potential empire of the ancient world was divided first by Seleucid kings, then, among others, by Romans and Parthians. Little has survived from the era of Seleucid rule, but the collection contains some notable works from the succeeding Parthian period (from the 2nd century B.C. to the 2nd century A.D.). Stone sculpture, such as the **lintel from a palace (22)** at Hatra, in northern Mesopotamia, and the funerary reliefs from Palmyra in Syria still clearly reflect the traditions of Roman

21

22

23

24

art; other works, such as a stone **relief with a male figure (23)** from the south of Iran are far more "native" in style, with only a faint recollection of Western naturalism. The Parthians, who had entered Iran from the northeast, were in time weakened through wars with Rome and internal discord. Their empire fell after a relatively brief struggle to a dynasty that had risen in Fars, in southern Iran.

These Sasanians ruled Iran from A.D. 224 to 626, and at times extended their frontiers eastward into the Kushan regions, in present-day Afghanistan, northward into Armenia, and westward to the Mediterranean and briefly to Egypt. Sasanian art reflects influences from all these regions. In the 3rd and 4th centuries Western forms and styles were closely imitated, but the expansion of the kingdom to the east led to the appearance of many Indian and Central Asian elements in the last two centuries of this period. The **stucco reliefs (24)** that covered the walls of the buildings at Ctesiphon, their capital in Mesopotamia, have chiefly plant and geometric designs, although some include representations of birds, animals, and human figures. The royal vessels in silver, with mercury gilding, are the most notable remains of Sasanian art. A favorite motif was the king hunting animals, shown fleeing before him and lying dead under his horse. A king, probably Peroz or Kavadh, is hunting on the **silver-gilt dish (25)**. Less common are scenes having mythological or religious significance. The **plate with twins (26)**, whose form is derived from representations of Castor and Pollux, belongs to this category, as does a ewer with four dancing female figures. These

females are related to Western scenes connected with the cult of Dionysus, but they have been transformed by the Iranian artist and their significance remains unknown. Without parallel is the almost life-size **head of a Sasanian king (27)**, frontal and staring, made from a single piece of silver and mercury gilded. The original use of the object is uncertain; stylistically, it probably dates from the 4th century A.D. Regrettably it is torn and cut along the lower edge, and there is no way of knowing how much more of the figure once existed.

25

26

27

Almost constant war, with the Roman and Byzantine west and with the Kushan and Hephthalite forces in the east, marks the history of the Sasanian period. Conquest led as always to the exchange of artisans and craftsmen, and to the transport of peoples from their original homelands to Mesopotamia and Iran. All this is reflected in Sasanian art, in the metal-

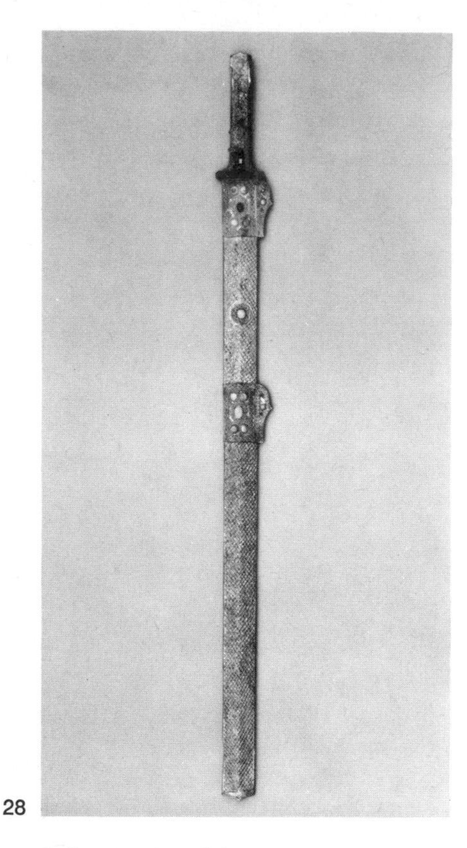

28

29

work, and in such objects as the iron **sword with gold hilt (28)**. Although the source of this piece is Iran, the closest parallels in form and decoration are among the weapons of the Avars, a tribe of Huns who came from the east and passed westward from Iran into Europe, much as the Scythians had done a millennium before. The method of suspending the gold sword from the belt, by loops on the reverse of the P-shaped attachments, is characteristic of Avar weapons and occurs in the Near East in the 6th century A.D. Indications of very early Scythian influence in Europe are apparent in the 4th-century B.C. **silver beaker (29)**, which was found in the region of the lower Danube.

The collapse of the Sasanian empire was due to a combination of forces and events: the weakness of the central authority, failure in wars against Byzantium, and the growing pressure of the armies of the Arabs. The end of the dynasty is usually marked by the defeat of the Sasanian army by the Arabs at Qadisiyah in A.D. 637 and the death of Yazdegird III, at Merv in eastern Iran, in 651. Members of the Sasanian royal family continued to rule, in name at least, for another century beyond the eastern frontiers of Iran; for a time parts of Iran itself, notably in the north by the Caspian Sea, remained outside Islamic rule. In the arts, Sasanian styles undoubtedly continued for at least a century after the Hegira (A.D. 622), the flight of Muhammad from Mecca, which traditionally marks the beginning of the Islamic period.

Arms and Armor

Arms and Armor

Objects, Periods, Styles	Numbers in Text
AMERICAN ARMS	(44)
BATTLE ARMOR	(5), (6), (13), (14)
COSTUME ARMOR	(15-17)
CROSSBOWS	(28), (29)
ENGLISH ARMOR	(26)
FIREARMS: guns, pistols, revolvers, Colts, powder horns	(39-44)
FRENCH ARMOR	(21), (27)
GERMAN ARMOR	(14), (15)
GOTHIC ARMOR	(6), (13)
HALBERDS, PARTISANS, WAR AXES, HATCHETS, MACES	(30)
HELMETS: basinet, armet à rondelle, sallet, chapel-de-fer and bevor, barbute	(1), (7-9), (22-25), (46), (47)
HISTORICAL ARMOR: French, Italian, German	(21-26)
HORSE ARMOR: spurs, stirrups, saddles	(11), (12)
ITALIAN ARMOR	(6), (13)
KNIGHTS IN ARMOR: Equestrian Court	(18)
MEDIEVAL ARMS and ARMOR before 1500	(1-10)
ORIENTAL ARMS and ARMOR	(45-64)
PARADE ARMOR	(20-27)
SHIELDS	(10)
TOURNAMENT ARMOR; LANCES	(18), (19)
SWORDS, RAPIERS, DAGGERS	(2-4), (31-38), (52), (55-58), (63), (64)

This page helps you to find what you especially want to see and read about.

Arms and Armor

The Department of Arms and Armor was officially established in 1906, though important acquisitions, gifts, and special exhibitions date from a previous period of the Museum. In 1904 the collection of the duke of Dino was acquired; two early presidents of the Metropolitan, J. Pierpont Morgan and Robert W. deForest, made notable gifts; Bashford Dean, the first curator of the department (1912), was an avid collector, and gradually most of his collection came to the Museum. By additional acquisitions and purchases from the Clarence H. Mackay and W. R. Hearst collections, from the holdings of the kings of Saxony, and from other European families, the department has been developed systematically to illustrate the technical and artistic evolution of weapons and protective equipment from the early Middle Ages.

The Museum's collection of arms and armor is the largest in this country and one of the most comprehensive in the world. It begins with material from the early medieval tribal migrations and the Vikings, and demonstrates with splendid examples man's mechanism for offense and defense, for attack and protection in war as well as in the hunt. The taste for pomp is admirably shown by armor for tournaments and parades, and by bejeweled weapons fit for the most elegant dandy at a royal court. Earlier weapons are found in the Museum's archaeological galleries—in the Egyptian, Near Eastern, and Greek and Roman departments. The Arms and Armor Department owns approximately 15,000 individual items, from as small as one arrowhead to a full suit of armor consisting of hundreds of separate elements for man and horse. It is especially strong in its European suits of armor—more than 130—many of them signed by great artist-armorers and associated with such historical personages as Emperor Charles V, Henry II of France, and Louis XIV. The richly decorated suits of parade armor are works of art that display the artistic sensibilities of their designers and makers as well as the status of their wearers. In weapons, the Museum's collection includes an impressive array of types, for example, over 1,000 swords of all countries. The making of firearms demanded a more mechanical type of skill; nevertheless, the early development of firing devices is interesting and can be studied from the many types of pistols and guns on display. Of course, beauty was no longer necessary in these weapons, and yet the ornamented firearms, usually used for hunting or dress display, can still be considered worthy of a place in an art museum.

Not only are the best examples of European arms and armor assembled in the galleries devoted to their display, but material from the high civilizations of the Far and Near East and from the colonial New World is well represented. The collection of Japanese armor and weapons is noteworthy as the largest and probably most important one outside Japan. Approximately 15 per cent of the total holdings are exhibited.

History is vividly illustrated by the Arms and Armor Galleries, and with a little imagination medieval legends, courtly etiquette, and the rigidly prescribed ways of court life are brought to life. One must not forget that before modern warfare the armorer was a respected artisan whose skill was in great demand by knights and

1

2

kings. The personal safety of a wearer of armor depended on the quality of his equipment; tournaments were won or lost by the excellence of his apparel as much as by his skill as a rider. The technical engineering of making movable parts (sometimes as many as 200) that were strong, yet light and flexible to allow freedom of movement, demanded great artistry. And ornamentation became a vital aspect of an object as much treasured as a suit of armor or a sword.

The center of the Arms and Armor Galleries is the large Equestrian Court with its colorful display of knights in armor on horseback under bright heraldic banners. Other examples from the great period of armor-making (mid-15th to end of 16th century) are grouped around the room, and an assemblage of weapons and helmets helps to create the feeling of actually being present in a medieval hall.

The earliest piece of protective equipment is the 6th-century Frankish chieftain's helmet, called a **Spangenhelm (1)**, constructed of gilded copper bands with iron lames between them; its shape derived from the headdress of the steppe nomads and was brought to the West by the Huns and other migrating tribes. The **Viking sword (2)** of the 10th century is a relic of widely ranging, warring people who covered great expanses of territory. This sword blade is forged of many layers of soft iron and hard steel to give it keen edges and toughness; the hilt is inlaid with a geometrical pattern in silver and red copper. The Viking weapons were the prototypes of the later knightly swords **(3)**, whose pommels were often richly decorated. Other typical weapons are the long-shafted halberds, partisans, war axes, and hatchets, which had many uses in medieval warfare; these are arranged on the walls and in cases throughout the

6

8

galleries. In the Middle Ages daggers **(4)** were worn by everyone, including women, for personal protection; the blades were usually short and the hilts often splendidly carved and decorated.

Armor (with helmet) and shield were the most important defense equipment. The early armor consisted of shirts of mail **(5)** constructed of thousands of hand-riveted interlinking iron rings. For greater protection separate pieces of plate armor were gradually added, as seen in the **Italian armor (6)** of about 1400 from Chalcis (Greece); little ornamentation was used in these early Gothic armors, though the red velvet covering this breast-plate is obviously a bow in the direction of elegance. To protect the head various basic shapes of helmets **(7)** were perfected: the basinet had a hinged visor shaped like a face with a nose and a stylized smiling mouth; the close-fitting armet à rondelle had five principal pieces, one of which was a circular disk (rondelle) to protect the neck; other forms were the sallet, the chapel-de-fer and bevor (the latter a special chin defense), and the barbute. A particularly fine barbute, worn only for display, is the Italian **lion-headed helmet (8)** of about 1460; the classical myth of Hercules and the Nemean lion furnished the idea for this striking piece. A very plain basinet **(9)** is said to have belonged to Joan of Arc. Painted wooden shields **(10)** completed a knight's defense.

By the 15th century the warrior and knight were encased in steel from top to toe. Many different pieces were needed to shape such a suit of armor (some are shown separately in cases, others have been composed as one armor): elbow

cops; gauntlets; arm, shoulder, thigh, and knee defense; visors and cheekpieces; tassets; toe cops, etc. Many of these pieces show one or more marks used by each armorer as his individual identifying symbol. Milan, the great center of

armor-making, was filled with workshops, some of which had specialists who worked on one kind of piece only. Some artists or families of makers became well known on the entire Continent and their services were eagerly sought by northern nobles. Owning and riding a horse was the original distinction of a knight and, thus, protecting the horse was of utmost importance. Spurs, parts of the riding equipment, became badges of chivalry. The early prick spur was changed to a less cruel form, the rowel spur **(11)**, which gradually became very elaborate and ornamented; stirrups were often gilded and decorated; elaborate curb bits and muzzles aided the rider; saddles had metal protection or, for fine occasions, were decorated with plaques or inlays of staghorn **(12)**; in many cases the horse's body was fully encased in steel.

The Milan workshops excelled in **suits of Gothic style (13)**, in which every element, often more than a hundred, was designed for maximum protection at minimum weight by an ingenious streamlining of all surfaces. The spiky decorative details and vertical elongations echo the pointed arches and turrets of Gothic

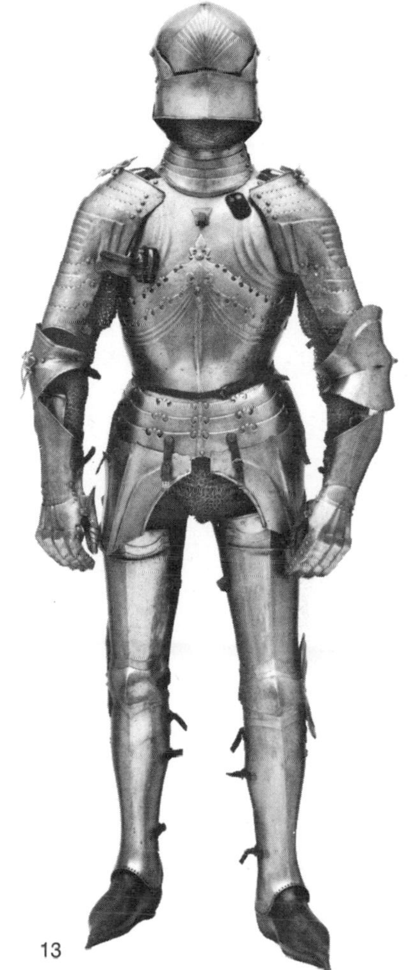

13

architecture. Contrary to popular belief, these suits of armor were light enough to enable the wearers in an emergency to vault into the saddle without using the stirrups.

The Renaissance armorers of the early 16th century somewhat changed the basic design. More compact, rounded forms gave an impression of sturdy strength and vigorous force. A special characteristic was the fluting of the larger plates; this served as a reinforcing device and re-

14

also in Germany, became known for the excellence of their armor. Since these workshops were much smaller than those in Milan, many of the artisans became well known as individual artists.

Once the functional problems were adequately solved, the imagination of the artist-armorer (and his patron) could be directed toward embellishments and fashions that had little to do with bloody warfare. The costume armor of the 16th century, probably the grandest period for armor-making, translated into articulated metal the extravagant dress of those days. Knights might imitate in metal the puffed and slashed dress of the foot soldiers, especially the German *Landsknechte*. A **German armor (15)** of about 1525 had "puffed" sleeves composed of ten steel plates for each sleeve; it was cleverly decorated by various processes of embossing, etching, and gilding to imitate the textile fashions which, in turn, by slashes in the material, had simulated wound gashes attesting to the valor of the wearer. All steel suits, including these

flected the light in a pleasing fashion. This type of armor is often called **Maximilian armor (14)** after Emperor Maximilian (1459-1519), surnamed "the Last of the Knights," who was a great connoisseur of armor, personally supervising his court workshop at Innsbruck, where he instigated numerous improvements. The illustrated suit of Maximilian armor dates from about 1535 and bears the mark of Landshut, another armor-making center. The cities of Nuremberg and Augsburg,

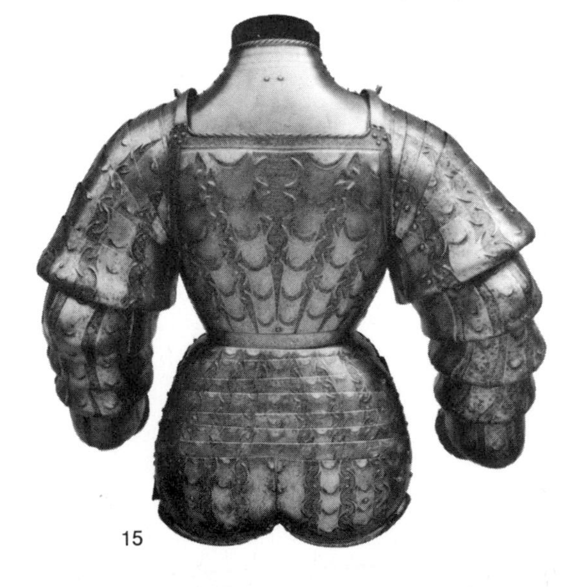
15

"fabric" suits, were worn over a special costume that served as a lining for armor; the French pourpoint and trunk hose **(16)** of about 1600 were well padded and "upholstered"—yet still elegant. Other suits of armor copied in steel the wide-skirted, fluted court coats **(17)**. How difficult it must have been to reproduce, in metal, frills and ruffles and to convey the feel of various fabric textures such as soft velvet or stiff brocade!

Already in the 15th century a trend for creating separate types of armor for battle duty and for the knightly pastime of the tournament had appeared. Armor in jousts had to fulfill a different purpose, therefore it was usually heavier and less flexible than the suit used in battle. About a dozen different types of tournament armor existed, but the variety of embellishments, plumes, costuming with fabric, banners, and so on was almost infinite and added to the sumptuous and festive quality of those grand spectacles. In jousts, the most famous form of tournament, the knights used their lances to unhorse their opponents; the blow was often directed at the head, thus making a heavy helmet an absolute necessity; the smooth surface of the armor deflected such strikes. **A mounted knight (18)** in full regalia, with the lance lowered for the charge, greets the Museum visitor in the Equestrian Court. It is interesting to note that leg armor was not needed since the rules forbade strikes below the belt. Wonderful two-dimensional representations of jousting armor can be seen in the 16th-century German Tournament Book **(19)** of 126 water colors that show all the brilliantly colored accouterments of such an event.

18

Gradually armor for sporting and festive occasions became more and more ornamented, adding to the status of the wearer and increasing the demands made on the artistry of the armor-maker. From the mid-16th century come some splendid examples of etched "garnitures" **(20)**—the complete set of armor and matching exchangeable pieces that became "a must" for the gentleman of quality. Etching with acid still kept the surface smooth, permitting an enemy's weapon to be safely deflected. But for parade purposes most functional limitations could be disregarded; as a result the most intricate work of embossing, etching, gilding, and damascening in precious metals came to be practiced in Italy, France, Germany, and England. These suits of armor and helmets became refined pieces of decorative art and the most extravagant "costume jewelry" ever designed by man. Many of the exam-

24

22

ples in this collection are known to have belonged to historical personages: the parade armor made for Henry II **(21)** was designed by Etienne Delaune (about 1550); every inch of the surface is embossed with decorations illustrating the themes of Triumph and Fame. Raised surfaces were often leaf-gilded and silvered. Other suits of embossed armor used subjects from classical history and mythology, from Christian legends, and from knightly heraldry. Aside from the French workshop of King Henry II, those in Milan, Greenwich (England), Madrid, Augsburg, and Landshut made superbly elaborate pieces. The so-called **Medici helmet (22)** is a French or Italian parade helmet from about 1550, made possibly for Henry II or for Cosimo de'Medici the Great (1519-74). Of the finest workmanship, it is embossed in low relief with the battle of the centaurs and Lapiths, with gorgons, and a Greek wave pattern on the crest. The nearby oil painting **(23)** (by a Flemish painter of the Sustermans school) depicts this very helmet held by Cosimo's grandson, Cosimo II. Of the many examples of highly decorated parade armor another **helmet (24)** from Italy, embossed in high relief, was designed by Philippo de Negroli, one of the most famous members of a Milanese clan of master armorers. The crest of this helmet is formed by a reclining mermaid who holds in her arms a Medusa head. Other Negroli armors and helmets **(25)** were made for the French and German nobility. From the most famous English armory of the 16th century, at Greenwich, came the wonderful **armor of George Clifford (26)**, third earl of Cumberland; the darkened, "blued" background provides a stunning contrast to the fancifully etched and gilded decoration. In the German centers of armor-making, the best artists of the time, such as Albrecht Dürer, were called upon to provide designs for decorating armor.

The manufacture of armor continued as late as 1700, but the later parade showpieces were used only for state occasions to proclaim the eminence of their owner. Fine late examples are the parade

26

helmet and shield of Louis XIV **(27)** made of blued silver to simulate steel, and ornamented with mountings of gilt-bronze in the shape of a fiery dragon.

Armor was, of course, designed as protection against offensive weapons. Throughout the galleries of the Arms and Armor Department are shown some of the finest specimens of swords, daggers, crossbows, and the later firearms that made the wearing of armor obsolete. More influential than any other medieval weapon was the crossbow, whose great power led directly to the development of plate armor with its glancing surfaces. It was the most important projectile weapon in Europe from the 13th through the 16th centuries. The heavy bow was drawn mechanically, making the rate of firing slow, but the bolts had tremendous penetrating power. The crossbow was used as a sporting weapon long after it was no longer efficacious in warfare; thus most of the elaborately decorated pieces on exhibition **(28)** were made for hunting. The **crossbow of Matthias I Corvinus (29)**, king of Hungary, dates from 1489. The stock is beautifully inlaid with bone figures of biblical personages, St. George and the dragon, and armorial bearings. Other Museum examples have decorations of coats of arms, animal and hunting figures, and scenes from the book of Genesis.

In hand-to-hand combat a variety of weapons was used. Of the long-shafted weapons mentioned before, the halberd **(30)** was excellently designed to hack

29

31

with an axelike blade, to stab with a spike, and to grapple down a horseman with a hook at the back of the weapon. Daggers and swords were indispensable in hand combat. The renowned Swiss mercenaries, who hired themselves out to fight battles all over the Continent, became in the late 15th century the model for infantry. The Swiss officers had a special type of dagger with a highly decorated sheath usually cast in bronze, gilded, and perforated. Favorite themes were the legend of William Tell and the Dance of Death. Designs by artists as famous as Hans Holbein still exist. The particular **dagger (31)** illustrated here, dated 1567, is decorated with a biblical scene of King Saul's death.

The development of the sword can be followed in the various galleries devoted to defensive weapons. Again the exigencies of the times and the costume with which a sword was worn determined its shape. The early knight's sword **(32)** was a large, heavy blade, counterbalanced by a massive pommel; some were two-handed swords **(33)**, difficult to handle, and the user was often awarded more pay. The hand wielding the sword was protected by a steel gauntlet. As fencing styles became more elegant, the gauntlet was regarded as a hindrance to the freer movements, and the weapon itself came to have a protective device for the hand. The swept hilt **(34)**, for example, consisted of intricately branching guards with connecting bars; these were often ornamented or covered with jewels. The later cup hilt **(35)**, often delicately chased and pierced, provided a better protection for the hand, and was much used in Spain, Italy, and France. Every gentleman of any standing wore a slim, long-bladed rapier, the design of which was undoubtedly closely matched to the occasion or to the dress of the wearer. In dueling, a left-handed dagger **(36)** was sometimes used to parry and catch the opponent's blade. Of the many examples of dress swords and rapiers in the Museum's collection, one of the finest is the **parade rapier (37)** made for Christian II, duke of Saxony and elector of the Holy Roman Empire. The hilt, signed by Israel Schuech of Dresden and dated 1606, is of cast and chiseled bronze, covered with strapwork and sculptured allegorical figures of diminutive size, and sparkling with rich gilding, multicolored jewels, and pearls. Attached to this fantastically decorated hilt, a symbol of pageantry and Baroque exuberance, was a blade made by the most renowned master of the famous Toledo swordsmiths, Juan Martinez. Though national styles in swords varied from country to country, hand weapons, particularly swords, were an international commodity.

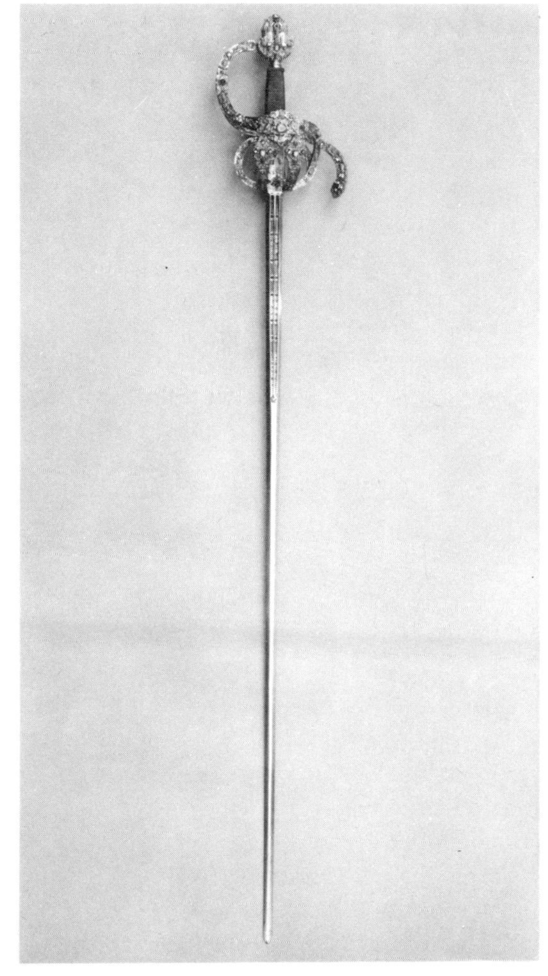
37

The famous bladesmiths of Milan, Toledo (Spain), Solingen in the Rhineland, and Passau on the Danube might receive commissions from all parts of the Continent. And the hilts might be exquisitely decorated by yet another group of artists in yet another section of the European world.

By the early 18th century precious materials were used more and more for all types of court swords, and elegance rather than strength came to be the most desired element. The rapier gradually lost its function as a weapon and was carried as an adornment to a man's attire. The former steel hilts gave way to bronze, silver, gold, even porcelain and mother-of-pearl hilts **(38)**. Blades also became more delicate while remaining deadly. Hunting swords were in keeping with the sumptuous hunting costumes of the period, and their hilts were also richly decorated.

The adaptation of gunpowder to firearms marks a decisive change in the mode of living. Knights and castles became obsolete, armies had to be reconstituted, and the pageantry of medieval courts with their knightly etiquette ceased to have any meaning. The blast of gunpowder took over what man's brute force—or skill—had previously accomplished. No precise date of invention can be set for gunpowder; it is thought that the Chinese used it in ancient times. Flaming pitch and various chemicals when ignited were known in the classical world and in the early Middle Ages. The earliest portable military firearms were developed in the first half of the 14th century, though these crude hand cannons were difficult and dangerous to utilize; they were fired by a lighted match cord that touched a chamber containing powder. Gradually a trigger was added, and this so-called matchlock gun became the standard military weapon until the 17th century. Though matchlock guns were an improvement over the earlier, clumsy portable cannons, they were still slow to fire and hazardous to prepare. Some fine examples of decorated sporting guns **(39)** form part of the extensive firearms collection.

In order to do away with the hazardous

burning match and have an instantly available ignition, the wheellock mechanism was invented, in which the igniting spark came from a revolving wheel striking a piece of pyrites. The wheellock guns were a mechanic's delight, and the most ingenious combinations of systems, such as double locks, locks with a reserve hammer, and self-winding locks, were designed to speed up the cumbersome reloading process. Since the wheellock was very expensive, extra care was taken to make it beautiful, and most wheellock arms show fine decoration; such weapons became objects of art, also important today because of their historical connotations. Many belonged to famous personages. One of the outstanding examples is the double-barreled **wheellock pistol of Emperor Charles V (40)** made by Peter Peck of Munich in about 1540, etched with the imperial double-headed eagle and the emperor's personal device. Other guns have stocks of walnut with staghorn and brass wire inlays, or the entire stock may be of ivory with various carved ornaments **(41)**. Firearms from Brescia (Italy) were much prized for their strong yet light barrels and their fine decoration. The Museum's collection includes, among other examples, some of the best Brescian pistols **(42)** made in the celebrated Cominazzo workshop.

Flintlock firearms, in which flint against steel made the spark that ignited the powder, are represented by a superb example of a **flintlock garniture (43)** made at Versailles for Napoleon Bonaparte by Nicolas Noël Boutet; the set comprises a rifle and a pair of pistols with full accessories, all with silver mounting. The rifle is spangled with gold stars, its breech decorated with flowers and foliage, the lock engraved with swans, the stock carved and engraved with miniature fishing scenes, and the trigger-guard ornamented with the figure of Diana and a Medusa mask. Other representations include a wolf caught in a trap, a Napoleonic eagle, a boar hunt, trophies of arms, serpents, and a winged caryatid. The fantastic and intricate workmanship is continued in the pistols, and the entire set is placed in a veneered mahogany case lined with light blue velvet. It is difficult to imagine a more wondrous treatment of firearms!

The collection of early American arms includes select examples from early colonial halberds and breastplates to ornamented dress swords and early Colt revolvers. One case acknowledges our former dependence on Great Britain; shown is a small collection of English firearms, with Lord Nelson's flintlock pistol representing an interesting historical piece.

40

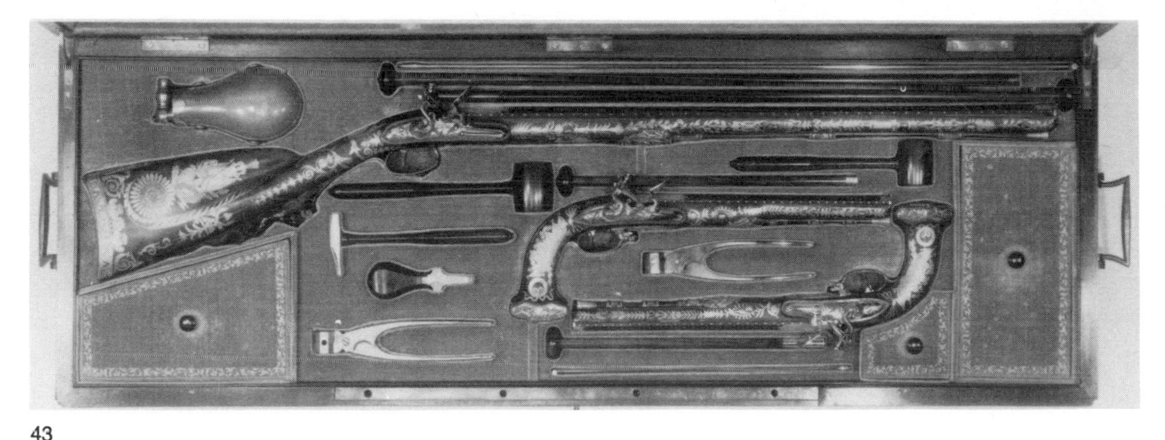

43

America's contribution to the development of weapons was the Colt revolver; patented in 1836 by Samuel Colt, this revolver solved the problem of quick reloading with an automatically revolving cylinder. Easily mass-produced, the Colt revolver became enormously popular, so much so that "Colt" is often used as a generic term for a revolver. Some representative Colts in the Museum's collection have heroic battle scenes engraved on their cylinders **(44)**. Nearby are shown powder horns used by the colonial Americans. The noteworthy collection has excellent examples of horns with finely engraved maps, forts, and scenes of specific battles and towns.

ORIENTAL ARMS AND ARMOR

The feudal societies of the Orient included a professional military caste that formed part of the nobility. A warrior had to excel not only in fighting prowess but also in the elegance of his battle gear and in his parade weapons. Highly ornamented, bejeweled arms were often presented to superiors as a token of esteem and honor. The Oriental armorer, therefore, similar to his European colleague, had to be a consummate artist as well as an excellent metalworker.

The basic features of Oriental arms and armor were already established by the 11th century and remained fairly unchanged. The emphasis in the eastern countries was not on the solidity of steel surfaces and the deflection of mighty blows that characterized European personal defense. Oriental gear was made for flexibility and speed, and consisted of many separate units that could easily be taken apart; it was also colorful, and the ornamentation often had the typical Far Eastern qualities of great sumptuousness as well as minuteness. Only a small selection of the Museum's Oriental arms and armor collection is on view, but this includes choice pieces from the great Japanese holdings, and from Indonesia, India, Persia, and Turkey.

From the earliest medieval period in Japan several primitive swords **(45)** are on display with ornamented pommels and hilts; these show signs of erosion from having been buried for a long time as treasures of the dead. (In A.D. 646 an edict was passed forbidding the burial of weapons.) A rare helmet **(46)** of the 4th century has riveted scales and bands of iron partly covered with mercury gilding. This basic helmet design changed little during the ensuing centuries. Other helmets in nearby cases have many different parts skillfully assembled to afford protection; a 16th-century helmet **(47)** has as many as 140 overlapping steel plates, secured together by more than 800 rivets.

Visually the most spectacular display is the full-standing 16th-century **Japanese suit of armor (48)**—a splendid example of the combination of elements often used in such armors; some 4,500 gold-lacquered steel scales are held together by countless rivets and interlaced with flame-colored silk braid. (The gold and flame colors indicate a general's rank.) Other parts are made of stenciled deerskin, bear pelt, and gilded wood. More suits of armor, half-armor, and pieces of armor are displayed in nearby cases. The horrifying features of the grotesque metal mask **(49)** were designed to frighten the enemy, to protect the face, and to support the helmet. Master metalworkers might fashion with such masks wonderful animal likenesses of all sizes, for which the Japanese were justly famous. A realistic life-size steel raven **(50)** was made by a member of a celebrated family of Japanese armorers; also shown are minute, delicate sword fittings, knife handles, and sword guards in shapes of exquisite animals, flowers, dragons, and floral motifs of all sorts **(51)**. Stirrups and horse trappings in fanciful shapes, sometimes lacquered or inlaid with precious metals, and a fine 17th-century saddle

48

of wood inlaid with mother-of-pearl contributed to the splendid array of a Japanese samurai, or military noble.

The classical weapons of the Japanese warrior were the huge bow and—in hand-to-hand combat—the sword. Through the centuries the Japanese developed the

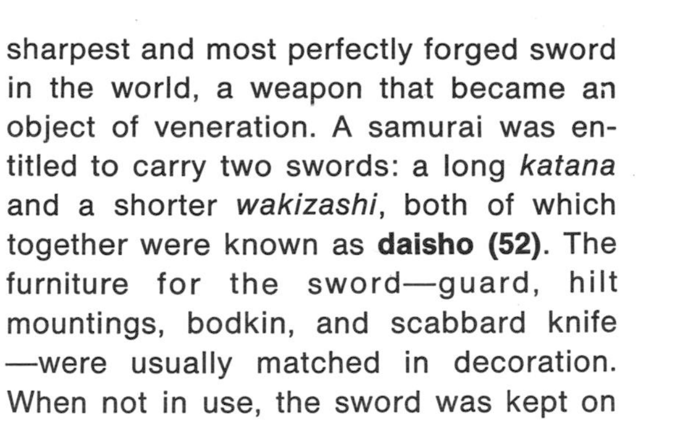

sharpest and most perfectly forged sword in the world, a weapon that became an object of veneration. A samurai was entitled to carry two swords: a long *katana* and a shorter *wakizashi*, both of which together were known as **daisho (52)**. The furniture for the sword—guard, hilt mountings, bodkin, and scabbard knife—were usually matched in decoration. When not in use, the sword was kept on a special rack **(53)**.

Many types of characteristic weapons from other parts of the Far East are on view as, for example, the *kris*, the traditional dagger used in Indonesia. Its asymmetrical blade can be straight or wavy; the small demons or other deities that usually form the grip imbue the weapon with magical qualities. The **kris stand (54)** from the Museum's collection is a fine example of a rack in which a *kris* must be deposited before its owner may enter the house; it is in the shape of a wooden male dancing figure with a grotesque face.

The Indians delighted in sumptuous decoration in precious materials. Ivory shafts and crystal grips mounted with emeralds and rubies gave to lances, daggers, and even elephant goads **(55)** a fairytale splendor. A hunting scimitar **(56)** has animal scenes carved on both sides. Typical Indian weapons are the *khattar* dagger **(57)** and the gauntlet sword **(58)**; the former was grasped by a crossbar handle for a punching stab; the latter was a steel glove that extended in one piece into a sword.

The Islamic faith forbade the representation of living beings; therefore, weapons from Islamic countries were decorated with intricate geometrical ornaments. Only

52

54

the Persians embellished their shields and helmets **(59)** with fighting or hunting scenes. The typical edged weapon of the Islamic countries was the scimitar, which had several distinctive local versions **(60)**, all well represented in our exhibits. The

62

Persian helmet **(61)**, much like its Turkish counterpart, was cone-shaped and ended in a point.

It was the Turks, of course, who posed the greatest danger to medieval Europe. These were riding warriors using bows and scimitars to hack away at the territories of the eastern Mediterranean, twice sweeping as far as Vienna. Speed and flexibility were crucial for their swift maneuvers. The best example of **Turkish armor (62)** shown here is from the 15th century; the plates of iron (for added strength) are chased with foliation and gilded; the helmet is damascened in gold

64

and silver. The Turkish daggers and swords **(63)**, many for display purposes only, are covered with the most intricate jewel-like ornamentation. The Oriental love for lavishness and pomp is amply shown in their weapons, among which one of the finest is the **state scimitar of Murad V (64)**, sultan of Turkey in 1876; the hilt is of jade with mountings of gold and silver gilt, set with diamonds and emeralds; the steel blade (dated 1688) is damascened and set with diamonds; the magnificent scabbard is of chased gold, encrusted with diamonds and emeralds.

In modern times the armorer's work has been turned into a machine-made factory product. Yet the Metropolitan Museum has in its armor workshop men who are capable of cleaning and restoring armor, and who know how to use the tools that once belonged to the armory of the dukes of Saxony. And in this workshop steel helmets and bulletproof vests were designed for soldiers in the two world wars.

Costume Institute

Costume Institute

Objects, Periods, Styles	Numbers in Text
ACCESSORIES: hats, gloves, muffs, handbags, scarves, shawls, parasols, stockings, shoes	
AMERICAN URBAN CLOTHES	(1), (5), (10), (13), (17)
CHILDREN'S COSTUMES	(17)
COATS, CLOAKS, CAPES	(5)
CONTEMPORARY FASHIONS	(4-5)
COURT GOWNS	(2), (11)
EUROPEAN URBAN CLOTHES	(2-4), (8-9), (11-12), (14-16)
EVENING DRESSES, BALL GOWNS	(1), (4-5), (14)
FASHION JOURNALS and PLATES	(6-7)
LINGERIE	
MENSWEAR	(3), (15-16), (19)
NONTEXTILE ACCESSORIES: buckles, buttons, card cases, canes, eye glasses, fans, hatboxes, snuffboxes	
PATTERN BOOKS	
PHOTOGRAPHS	
REGIONAL COSTUMES: Europe, the Americas, Africa, Asia	(18-19)
SPORT CLOTHES	
WOMEN'S CLOTHES	(1-5), (8-14), (18)

☞ **This page helps you to find what you especially want to see and read about.**

Costume Institute

The Costume Institute of the Metropolitan Museum was founded in 1937 by a small group of people involved in the arts, acting under the spirited leadership of Irene Lewisohn. Known as the Museum of Costume Art, Costume Institute, Inc., it dealt with costume and fashion at a time when no other museum in New York devoted itself exclusively to those fields. Its aim already at that time was to collect, preserve, and exhibit costumes of all countries and periods, and to serve as a research center where designers for the theater and for the clothing industry, students of design, scholars, and professionals in related fields could study original material. From 1937 to 1946 the Museum of Costume Art was located in the mid-Manhattan area and offered a program of changing exhibitions to the general public. In these early years the Museum of Costume Art developed facilities where visitors could study its collections at first hand. These included a workroom for students and designers, a storeroom designed to make the material available for immediate use, and a reference library.

In 1946 the Costume Institute moved to the Metropolitan Museum. This new association emphasized the point of view that costume design is indeed a form of art; it also enabled designers and students to draw inspiration from the many other forms of art represented in the Museum. Thus, ideas could be gained from ancient Greek sculpture, Persian miniatures, Egyptian jewelry, Oriental textiles, medieval tapestries, Renaissance paintings, and so on. And, conversely, the Museum's many other departments have been able to draw on the expertise of the Institute's staff when advice on the smallest points of apparel might aid in the identification of a print or painting, or the dating of a work of art.

From 1946 to 1960 many exhibitions were shown; "Casablanca to Calcutta" in 1948 featured costumes and objects from North Africa and the Near East, together with textiles designed by contemporary designers who were directly inspired by this material. "Adam in the Looking Class" in 1950 was a survey of men's fashion from the 14th century to the present, with projections into the future. In 1954 "The Fine Art of Costume" displayed European and American costumes and accessories spanning five centuries. And in 1957 "Children in Style" presented European and American children's costumes, portraits, and fashion prints from the 16th to the 20th century.

In 1960 the Costume Institute terminated its independent existence and became a regular department of the Museum. As such, it fulfilled the terms of the Metropolitan's original charter "to encourage and develop . . . the application of arts to manufactures and practical life." Soon the department's increased activities and significant growth necessitated the enlargement of its facilities. In 1967 the Costume Institute moved to temporary quarters so that its space could be reconstructed. The work, based on plans by Edward Durrell Stone, was completed in the spring of 1970. With the shell finished, the interior needs had to be met. In 1971 the new Costume Institute was opened for use, with the first installation set up in ten galleries. Other facilities are three storerooms to house the collection; three (convertible to five)

1

private study rooms for designers and researchers; a library; a cataloguing room; a classroom; a conservation room; a workroom for the preparation of exhibitions; offices; and three major entrances, one directly on Fifth Avenue.

In spite of the turmoil of the last few years, the Costume Institute has given some major exhibitions. In 1961 "The Age of Louis XV to the Age of Worth" presented magnificent clothes for men and women from the mid-18th to the late 19th century. In "Period Rooms Reoccupied in Style," appropriate costumes were shown in the Museum's English and French rooms from November 1963 to January 1964. And in 1967 the most ambitious project in the department's history was the major exhibition "The Fine Art of Costume," in which 185 articles of women's clothing and accessories from 1735 through 1967 dramatically demonstrated the high level of achievement attained by costume; an extensive section showed current American fashions. The French and American **day and evening dresses (1)** of the 1920s were part of this exhibition.

The Costume Institute's collection began from a nucleus of two large gifts, one presented by Irene Lewisohn and her sister Alice Lewisohn Crowley, and the other by Lee Simonson. An example of the gifts from Irene Lewisohn, in 1937, is the French embroidered tulle **court gown (2)** of about 1902 that had been worn by Queen Alexandra of England. Early gifts by Aline Bernstein, Ethel Frankau, Aline MacMahon, and Lee Simonson included the man's French **silk suit** from the end of the 18th century, the American embroidered muslin **round robe** and brocaded **silk spencer** from the early 19th century, and the Viennese **silk taffeta**

4

2

3

dress (3) of about 1820.

Many others have contributed important gifts and bequests that have enriched and immensely enlarged the collection since its beginning in 1937. One of the gifts of Mrs. Byron C. Foy was the embroidered silk **ball gown (4)** with jacket banded in sable, by Christian Dior (1954). Through the munificence of a large body of donors, the collection has grown to comprise about 17,000 articles of dress. This includes contemporary clothes produced by leaders in the European and American dressmaking in-

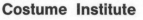

5

dustries; an example is the satin **evening dress and cape (5)**, trimmed with fox, designed by John Moore and given by him to the Museum in 1968.

A number of people have worked hard to bring the Costume Institute to realization. For over 30 years Polaire Weissman, executive director, guided the development of the organization, oversaw its activities, and supervised its growth. Under her directorship the Institute's collection became one of the largest and most comprehensive costume collections in the world. Others involved in the remarkable development were Dorothy Shaver, Eleanor Lambert, Henry Callahan, Melvin Dawley, Adam Gimbel, and Andrew Goodman, who also were among those responsible for the success of the annual Party of the Year, which raised much-needed funds for the building program.

The facilities of the Costume Institute are designed to serve the public in many different ways. The ten galleries are used to show changing installations of material from the permanent collection and also occasionally of material borrowed from outside sources. There are four different presentations every year, each lasting three months and always having a specific theme or subject matter. The exhibition that opened the newly installed department in 1971, entitled "Fashion

6

Plate," represented a succession of fashions in clothing during the past two hundred years. Two storerooms for garments and one for accessories house the material, which is arranged according to date, type, and region. This arrangement permits the staff to find costumes quickly and allows designers and scholars to study related material without difficulty. Specially designed storage cases conserve the perishable garments in humidity- and temperature-controlled rooms.

In addition, three large study rooms, two of which can be divided in half, can be used by designers and other interested people. A staff member helps the visitor select his material from study storage; this he may then study in private in the study room reserved for him. A classroom enables the staff to work with school and professional groups. Yet another strength of the department is the reference library. Some 22,000 items include books on costume design and history, or allied fields, fashion journals, pattern books, photographs, clippings, and fashion plates of the 19th and 20th centuries. The fashion plate of the two **concert gowns (6)** is from *La Mode Illustrée* of 1865; the **evening coat (7)** by Charles Frederick Worth is from the *Gazette du Bon Ton* of 1923. Other fashion drawings and costume prints are in the Department of Prints and Photographs.

The services of the Costume Institute are extended to many different types of people. Students in professional schools and colleges visit the department for the purpose of studying the design of street clothes, and with inquiries into merchandising or related fields. Many schools from different parts of the United States

7

and Canada inspect the collections, the study storage, and the total facilities. The Costume Institute has been a pioneer in its field, and its ideas have spread to many parts of the world.

Working with designers in the fashion industry is an important aspect of the department. They may be considering special clothes, such as children's clothes or lingerie, or accessories, such as hats, gloves, bags, or shoes. Others may be textile designers or artists working on advertising projects.

In the retailing trade, groups of buyers, or buyers and designers, may study period forms or special colors related to their subjects. Some want to study fashions of the past in order to get new ideas or new perspectives on the future. Representatives of fashion periodicals, writers, and researchers for the theater

8

or for television programs consult the department on costume history or usage. And, finally, museums and societies in this country and abroad come to the Costume Institute with problems about costume history, conservation, exhibition techniques, storage, and many other topics of mutual interest. After making an appointment by telephone, all specially motivated people are free to use the facilities.

The greatest strength of the Costume Institute's collection is its comprehensiveness. The 17,000 articles of dress and

9

10

accessories span the years from about 1500 to the present; they represent urban and regional costumes from Europe, Asia, Africa, and the Americas. Although the department has some fine examples of clothing from the Far and Near East, the major portion of the Museum's holdings from those areas is kept in the Departments of Far Eastern Art and Islamic Art. The Department of Arms and Armor has a few examples of dress worn under armor.

Particularly noteworthy are the American and European urban women's costumes dating from the late 17th century to the present. One of the earliest is the English striped **woolen dress (8)**, embroidered with gilt silver yarns, dating from 1690-95. From mid-18th century France comes a **gown and petticoat front (9)** made of silk, brocaded with silk and metal yarns; and a late 18th-century example is the American painted **silk taffeta gown (10)**.

13

12

11

A costume associated with a historical personage is the mid-19th century **court gown and train (11)** from the Court of Naples, worn by Princess Doria d'Angri; it is made of silk and embroidered with gilt yarns.

From 1867 comes the French **afternoon dress (12)** by Mme. Depret, made of striped piña cloth, trimmed with satin and fringe, and a matching bonnet.

The American blue velvet and faille **visiting dress (13)** with its bustle shows

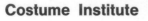

14

the fashion of the early 70s. The balloon sleeves typical of the 1890s are part of the French **formal gown (14)** designed by Worth; it is silk satin, trimmed with sequins, painted flowers, and chiffon.

Other high points of the collection are American and European wedding dresses from the 18th to the mid-20th century; coats, cloaks, capes and other outerwear; a selection of lingerie; many different types of accessories, including a varied and extensive collection of hats and bonnets, of which one of the earliest is from England—a knitted cap of the early 16th century; a representative group of gloves and mittens; handbags and purses; stockings and a fine collection of shoes, particularly high-fashion examples from the 16th to the 20th century; muffs, parasols, scarves, and shawls; and nontextile accessories such as buckles, buttons, card cases, canes, eyeglasses, fans, hatboxes, and snuffboxes.

Another kind of clothing that is well represented are the articles worn for sports. Bathing suits of wool, cotton, or

15

other materials, including sequins and plastic, date from the last 100 years. From 1900 comes an American bicycling skirt with matching knickers; a white satin exhibition-fencing costume was made in America in 1924; skating costumes and tennis and ski outfits attest to the increasing participation of women in sporting events.

Menswear is less well represented in the Metropolitan, and in general in any museum, because men's clothing is less glamorous than women's (except for the late 17th and all of the 18th century) and thus not preserved. Most of the surviving European clothing for men, dating as far back as the 16th century, was associated with royalty and famous personages and thus was treasured for reasons of historical perspective. The Costume Institute has many European and American suits, coats, capes, waistcoats, breeches, and trousers; an elegant example is the French three-piece **men's suit of patterned velvet (15)** from the second quarter of the 18th century. The small but varied collection of dressing gowns includes the late 18th-century striped satin **banyan and waistcoat (16)** from Europe. Many accessories form part of the collection: hats and all kinds of headgear, including tricorns, night caps, and house caps; collars, socks, ties, and so on.

The department's collection of children's costumes is exceptionally comprehensive, with boys' and girls' clothing from around 1800 to the present. It represents different age groups as well as various periods. During most of the 18th century, children's fine clothes closely resembled those of their parents. In the 19th and 20th century, modified forms developed. Thus a boy might wear trousers like his father's and a short version of his mother's dress. The boy's American sateen **coat dress (17)** from about 1830 shows this combination. In addition to the European and American children's costumes for all ages, there are special collections of elaborate christening robes, visiting dresses, richly trimmed party dresses for girls and dark, short-trou-

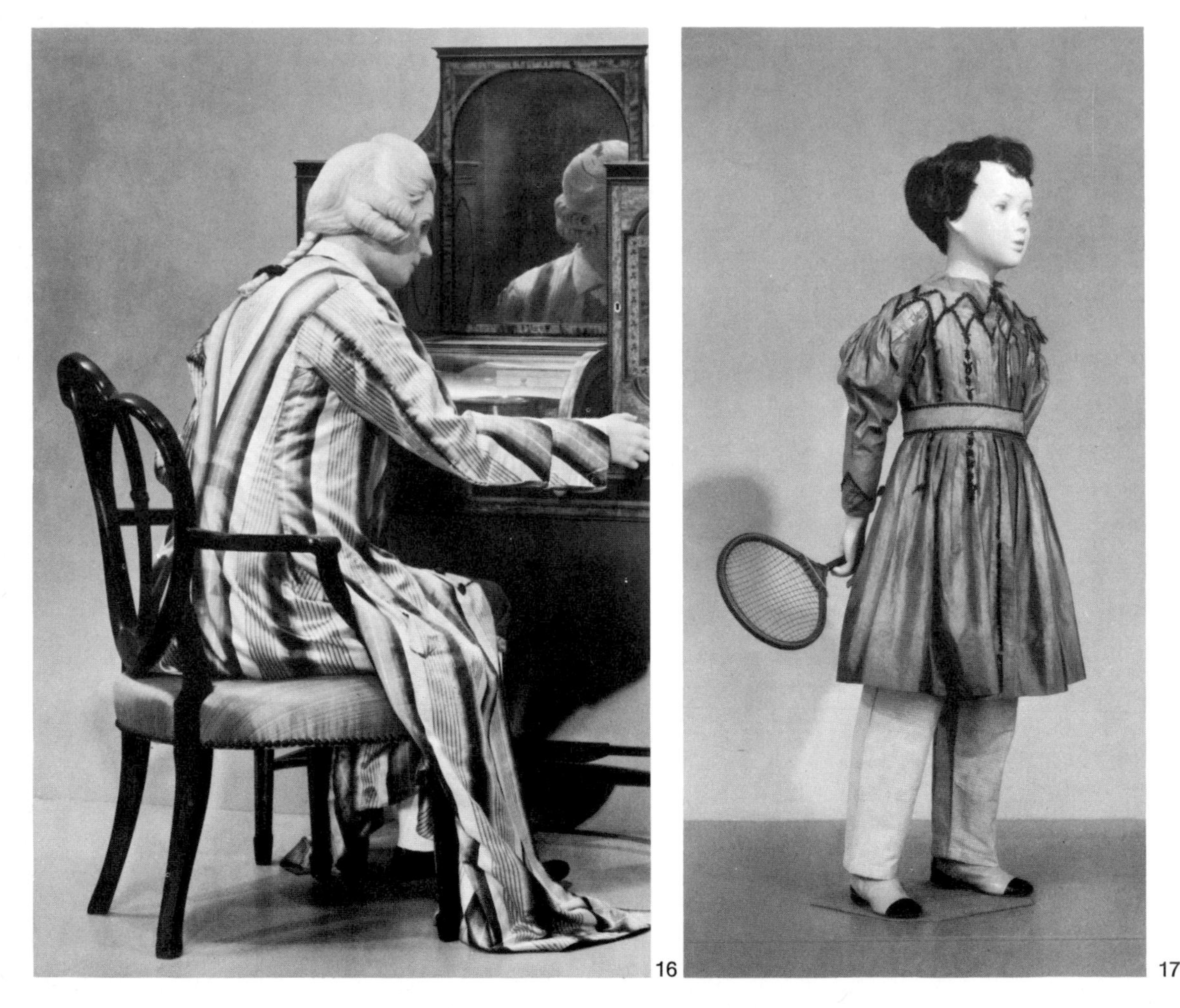

16

17

18

sered suits for boys, "costume" clothes like sailor suits and dresses, Kate Greenaway dresses, kilts, and lederhosen; and a group of children's dresses designed by European designers in the 1950s and another by American designers in 1958.

Regional clothing constitutes one of the Costume Institute's greatest treasures. Thousands of objects, including many complete costumes for men, women, and children, represent the cultures of Asia, Africa, Europe, and the Americas. In addition to their importance in terms of design, these clothes reflect the customs and manners of the people who made and wore them, often also expressing the social and marital status of the wearer, sometimes even his religion.

Only a few representative examples can be given here: from Scandinavia, a Norwegian bridegroom's costume, as well as women's and men's costumes from Sweden and Denmark; from Brittany, France, a man's and woman's festival costume and a group of Breton coifs; from Holland, costumes from Vollendam; a fisherwife's contemporary holiday costume from Newhaven, Scotland, and some children's Scottish kilts; from Central Europe —Swiss costumes from Berne and Appenzell; headdresses and costumes from Germany, Austria, and Czechoslovakia; a woman's **ceremonial coat (18)** of purple velvet, decorated with needlework in me-

19

tallic yarns, probably from Serbia; a man's **Polish holiday suit (19)** from the Tatra Mountains, in wool embroidered with woolen yarns; a Circassian man's costume from Russia; from the Mediterranean region—Spanish costumes including bullfighters' costumes and capes; a bride's costume from Sardinia, Italy; an Evzone costume from Greece; from Africa—a man's ceremonial tunic and a bride's costume from Tunis; a witch doctor's costume of the Senufo tribe from the Ivory Coast; a chieftain's ceremonial trousers from Upper Volta; from Asia Minor and Asia—a woman's trousers and sleeveless jacket of embroidered velvet from Turkey; a group of silk ikat robes for men and women from Turkistan; from the Far East—a bridal robe, and boots and shoes from Tibet; a large collection of Japanese kimonos; dancers' costumes from Bali and Java and batik sarongs from Java; from North America, a small but choice collection of costumes for men and women of the Seminole Indians, as well as other garments and mocassins, some beaded, from other Indian tribes from the West; and from the Caribbean region and Latin America—a Mexican sequined skirt for the traditional China Poblana costume, and men's traditional charro costumes, also from Mexico; costumes from Guatemala, Panama, Haiti, and the San Blas Islands; a gaucho costume from Argentina, and other garments from Peru and Bolivia.

Drawings

Drawings

Objects, Periods, Styles, Artists	Numbers in Text
AMERICAN DRAWINGS and WATER COLORS	
BAROQUE DRAFTSMEN	(8), (9)
BRITISH DRAWINGS	(17-19)
CARICATURES and SATIRES	(17), (22)
DÜRER	(7)
FLEMISH and DUTCH DRAWINGS	(10), (11)
FRENCH DRAWINGS	(6), (15), (16), (21-25)
GERMAN DRAWINGS	(7)
INGRES	(21)
ITALIAN DRAWINGS	(1-5), (8), (9), (12-14)
LANDSCAPES, GARDENS, CITY VIEWS	(13), (14), (19)
LEONARDO DA VINCI	(3)
MICHELANGELO	(4)
PORTRAITS	(6), (21), (23), (24)
RENAISSANCE DRAWINGS	(2-6)
SKETCHES and STUDIES	(1), (3-5), (7-10), (12), (15)
SPANISH DRAWINGS	(20), (26)
TECHNIQUES: conté crayon, chalk, charcoal, gouache, metal-point, pastel, pen and ink, pencil, wash	
TIEPOLO	(12)
WATER COLORS	

☞ This page helps you to find what you especially want to see and read about.

Drawings

The Department of Drawings was set up in 1960 as an independent curatorial division, whereas drawings had previously been under the aegis of the Department of European Paintings. Excellent exhibition space was provided in the arcaded loggias of the Blumenthal Patio from Vélez Blanco, Spain, and in an adjacent gallery. Drawings are extremely fragile and susceptible to fading or darkening when overexposed to light, either natural or artificial. For that reason constantly changing exhibits from the permanent collection are presented, as well as other exhibitions of special interest, often in conjunction with the Department of Prints and Photographs. A room in the Thomas J. Watson Library is available, by appointment, for the study of drawings, which are carefully preserved according to the most modern techniques.

The Museum's collection of drawings is extensive and remarkably encyclopedic. Almost every national school is represented, though the Italian and French drawings are particularly distinguished, both in quality and quantity. The first 670 drawings were given to the Metropolitan Museum in 1880 by Cornelius Vanderbilt, who had purchased them from the pioneering collector James Jackson Jarves. The public exhibition of many of these was one of the first large presentations of European drawings in an American museum, and it marked the beginning of an appreciation of a form of artistic expression that had up to then been neglected in America. In 1887 a further bequest from the painter Cephas G. Thompson enlarged the collection. However, the systematic acquisition of old master drawings became feasible only in the first decades of the 20th century, largely because of the magnificent bequest of Jacob Rogers. The English critic and painter Roger Fry made a number of wise purchases. The H. O. Havemeyer bequest of 1929 brought to the Museum some exceedingly fine 19th-century drawings and a key group of studies by Rembrandt. In 1935 the Museum was able to acquire the largest group of Goya drawings outside the Prado, and two years later it purchased the collection of the Marquis de Biron in Geneva, one of the most exceptional groups of 18th-century Venetian drawings ever assembled, particularly strong in works by Giambattista and Domenico Tiepolo and by Francesco Guardi. The Alfred Stieglitz bequest in 1949 gave the collection great strength in Postimpressionist, Fauve, and Cubist draftsmanship.

Drawings are the notations of an artist in pen and ink, chalk or pencil, pastel or water color. They are very often preparatory studies for a more definitive work of art—a painting or a sculpture—and they show us the development of a creative process. Some drawings are conceived, on the other hand, as finished works of art in their own right.

Drawings are unique, manuscript originals, so to speak. In this they differ from prints—engravings, woodcuts, etchings, lithographs—which by the very nature of their reproductive process usually exist in many examples.

The subjects of drawings are of an enormous variety. Some of the finest portraits have been drawn with pencil or pen; a nature or animal drawing can be as complete and convey as much feeling as an oil painting. It is the preferred medium for recording botanical and biological ob-

1

servations. Landscape is, of course, a favorite subject, and views seen can be recalled with elaborate precision or in a few rapid lines. Drawing is a necessary means of elaboration for the architect, sculptor, theatrical designer, and decorator. Immensely versatile, drawings mirror artistic styles and changes over the ages.

Medieval and early Renaissance draftsmen, both in the north and south of Europe, often drew with metal points—silver, gold, or lead. The use of pen and ink also extends back quite far. Black, red, and white natural chalks were used as drawing instruments until they were replaced by the modern composition lead pencil. Wood charcoal and pastel, the latter a mixture of colored chalks with a binding medium, were utilized as early as the 15th century. All these techniques could be used alone or in combination.

Draftsmanship was the fundamental artistic discipline from the Middle Ages onward, and drawings were involved in the preparation of almost all European art. In the early guilds and academies, a painting student learned his craft by copying works of the established masters or by drawing the human body; northern artists flocked to Italy to copy classical statues or Renaissance masterpieces. Indeed, for the Renaissance Italians the word "drawing" (*disegno*) embraced the intellectual concept that is the essential form of a work of art. One of the earliest Italian drawings in the Museum's collection is the **Study for the Fonte Gaia (1)**, a sketch for the left half of the fountain in

2

3

the main square in Siena, Italy. It was probably executed by the sculptor Jacopo della Quercia, who had received a commission for the project in 1408. Another transitional Tuscan draftsman who is represented in the Metropolitan is Parri Spinelli. The first flowering of the Renaissance is visible in drawings in the Museum by Filippino Lippi of Florence and Vittore Carpaccio of Venice. Raffaellino del Garbo's **Madonna and Child with Attendant Angels (2)** is a fine example of

the elegance of a late 15th-century Florentine drawing.

Leonardo da Vinci was fantastically inventive, and while drawing with his pen was always searching for the ideal solution to a problem, whether an anatomical, mechanical, or artistic one. The page called **Studies for a Nativity (3)**, executed in pen and metalpoint on slightly tinted paper, shows him investigating a composition that was much later to become the *Madonna of the Rocks*. The Metropolitan Is fortunate in possessing four drawings by this great master.

Michelangelo Buonarroti's drawings, not surprisingly, were intensely sculptural even when he was working on a figure study to be utilized in a painting. In the celebrated **Studies for the Libyan Sibyl (4)**, the artist draws with consummate authority and wonderful elaboration a nude male model, posed in the studio, who will appear, heavily draped, as the personification of the Libyan Sibyl on the frescoed ceiling of the Sistine Chapel in Rome. The model's head and torso are studied twice, and a foot, separate from the torso, appears at the lower right.

If Michelangelo as a draftsman is all sculptural force, his near contemporary, Raphael, was involved with the search for ideal grace and beauty. The red chalk drawing **Madonna and Child with the Infant St. John (5)** was probably not drawn from life but rather resulted from Raphael's concern with the overall construction and lighting of a triangular group. This study for a painting now in Vienna is one of several preparatory drawings by Raphael that have survived, and in general it is very similar to the finished picture. The reverse of this sheet bears a vigor-

4

5

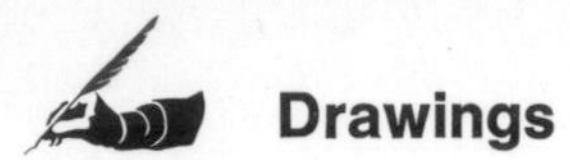

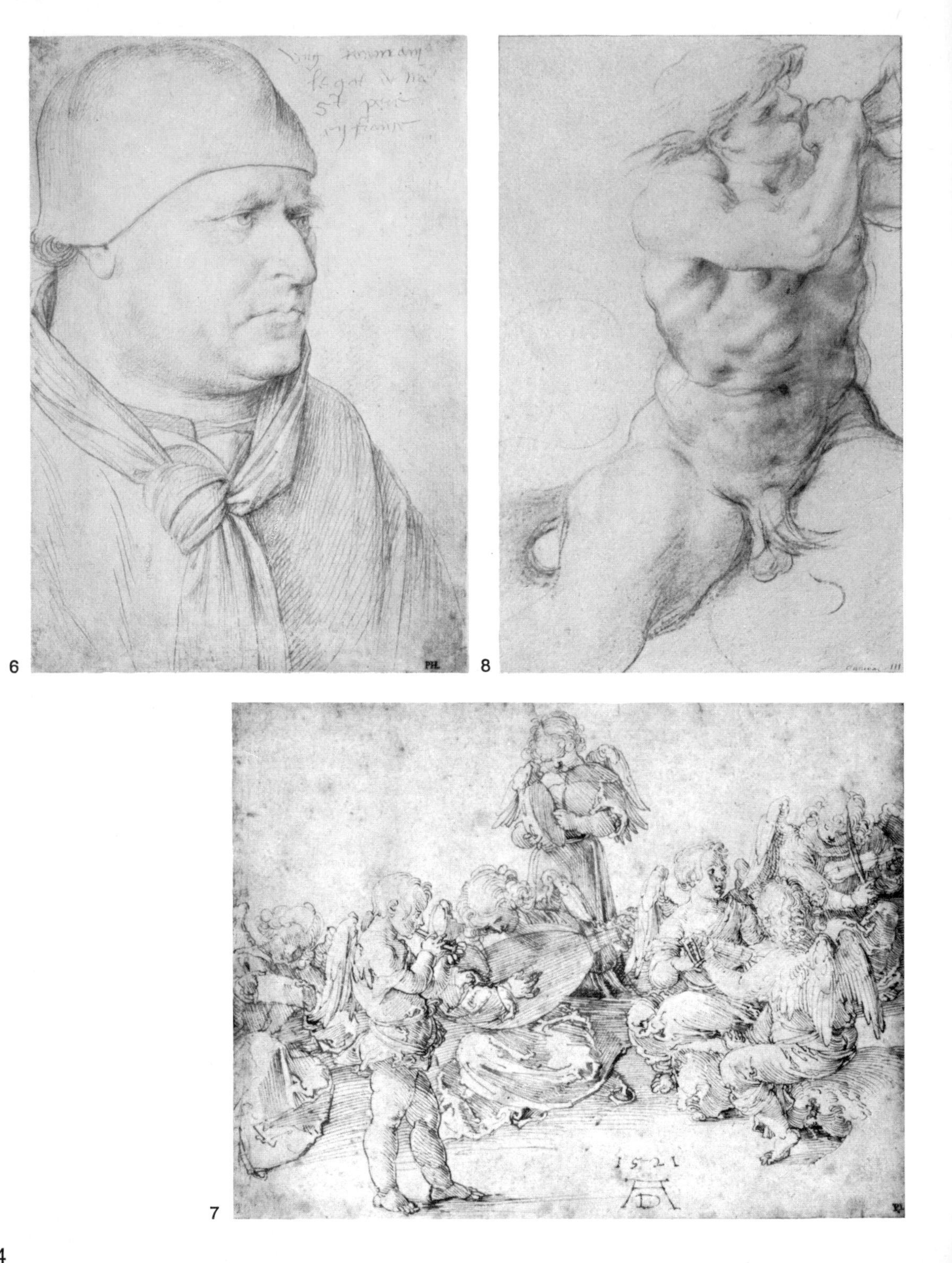

6

8

7

9

ous pen study of a nude male figure drawn from life. Important drawings in the Museum's collection by Titian and Paolo Veronese represent the Renaissance in northern Italy.

The fine metalpoint portrait by Jean Fouquet is an example of Renaissance draftsmanship in France. This **Portrait of an Ecclesiastic (6)**, one of the few surviving drawings by this great master, was identified by the artist in a manuscript annotation as a "Legate of Our Holy Father in France." Albrecht Dürer's spirited sketch of **Musical Angels (7)**, one of a group of studies for a projected altarpiece, is typical of the best Renaissance drawing in Germany. The Museum's collection contains two other excellent examples of the assured draftsmanship of this northern master.

Drawing in the 17th century was freer than in the Renaissance; wash was used for more dramatic effects, and softer chalk was preferred to the precise metalpoint favored by Renaissance artists. In the 17th century Rome was the undisputed center of Italy and, indeed, of all Europe. Great programs of building palaces and churches attracted artists from all countries. Portraiture flourished in all media, and not only official portrait painting but a new satiric style that came to be known as caricature.

The Museum's collection offers a brilliant representation of Italian Baroque draftsmanship of the 17th century. The Bolognese artist Annibale Carracci went to Rome to decorate the Gallery of the Palazzo Farnese; the vigorous **Study for a Triton (8)**, drawn from a nude model, was utilized in one of the mythological scenes executed in fresco on the ceiling of this room. Another great Baroque draftsman is Pietro da Cortona, who worked extensively in Rome and in his native Tuscany. His sensuous black chalk drawing of **A Wind God (9)** is a study for one of the frescoed ceilings he executed in the Palazzo Pitti in Florence.

The greatest Flemish master of this

period, Peter Paul Rubens, also worked in Rome. His **Study of a Standing Female Saint (10)** is a preliminary drawing in brush and wash for his early altarpiece in the Chiesa Nuova in Rome. The inscription, at the top left, of "Antonius Van Dyck" indicates that it was at one time wrongly attributed to Rubens's most talented pupil. Many phases of Rubens's prolific career are illustrated in the Metropolitan Museum, and mention should be made of the splendid studies for the woodcut version of his famous composition *The Garden of Love*.

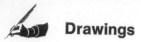

There are also in the Museum particularly brilliant examples of the draftsmanship of Rembrandt, the finest Dutch artist of the 17th century. In **Nathan Admonishing David (11)**, the biblical story of King David listening sorrowfully and repentantly to the aged prophet Nathan is masterfully conveyed; the drawing, in which pen and brown ink, brown wash, and white gouache were used, reveals the vividness of Rembrandt's hand and the intensity of his psychological penetration. In addition, he was one of the most gifted painters of landscape at a time when this subject was becoming an independent genre; this aspect is well illustrated in a fine landscape drawing depicting his favorite Dutch countryside.

In 18th-century Italy, Venice emerged once again as a major artistic center, exporting painters and paintings to the northern European countries. Venetian drawings, becoming more independent of paintings, were often produced as ends in themselves; this was likewise true in 18th-century France. Moreover, Venetian draftsmen further developed or invented new subjects, such as scenes of contemporary life, *scherzi di fantasia* (fantastic jokes), landscape capriccios, or, in contrast, realistic city views. Though Venice with Giambattista Tiepolo dominated the century, other cities—Rome, Naples, Bologna, and Genoa—also contributed original and inventive artists.

10

Giambattista Tiepolo was undoubtedly one of the greatest Italian decorators, and he was gifted with amazing productivity and virtuosity. He handled chalk, pen, and wash with marvelous ease and speed, and his vast output included highly finished compositions, notations of a fleeting idea, variations on a religious or secular theme, as well as sketches for specific paintings. His **Apollo Standing in His Chariot (12)**,

12

11

13

14

executed in 1740, is a study for the central figure in his great frescoed ceiling in the Palazzo Clerici, in Milan. The Museum possesses 20 other pen and wash drawings for this project, representing a high point in Italian draftsmanship. Tiepolo's most gifted son, Domenico, was as prolific as his father, excelling in ironical scenes, caricatures, and fantastic visions.

Venice as it exists today is almost the same as the Venice depicted in the drawings and paintings by Antonio Canaletto and Francesco Guardi, the two other important 18th-century Venetian painters. The shimmering views of the city in all its magic were eagerly bought by English gentlemen and other travelers to Italy. Architecture, water, sky with clouds, and people were accurately depicted in Canaletto's views of Venice; his inventions included a mixture of real and imaginary buildings or ruins. In the **Capriccio (13)** illustrated here, the church, farmhouse, bridge, and ruined tower may have come from elements actually seen. Guardi, 15 years younger than Canaletto, tried to capture some of Canaletto's market. He made a specialty of imaginary landscape views, but his large drawing, mostly in pen and brown ink, of the **Villa Loredan (14)** is an exact view of the demolished villa that once stood on the outskirts of Treviso.

In France, several first-rate painters also excelled as draftsmen. Antoine Watteau's **Study of a Man's Head (15)** is a preparatory drawing for the *Mezzetin*, the guitar-playing valet in the famous painting now in the Metropolitan (see page 132). Drawings by Watteau, usually executed in a combination of white, black, and red chalk, have the same delicate air as his

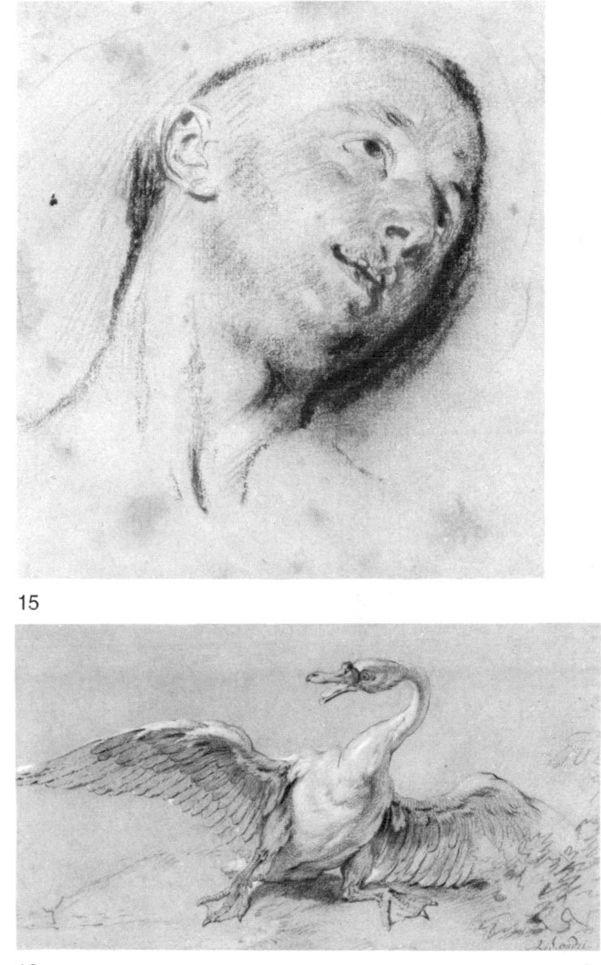

15

16

paintings and convey the Rococo ideals of grace and charm. His contemporary, Jean-Baptiste Oudry, left a series of dramatically lit garden views, which, with their receding perspective, are the predecessors of romantic stage settings. His **Angry Swan (16)**, a very recent acquisition, reveals him as a specialist in animal painting, a subject much in vogue at that time. Three other great draftsmen of the 18th century in France are present in the Department of Drawings—François

17

18

Boucher, Jean-Honoré Fragonard, and Jean-Baptiste Greuze; the first two were specialists in figure and landscape drawings, while Greuze tended toward moralizing melodrama.

In 18th-century England, Thomas Gainsborough and John Robert Cozens produced poetic water color landscapes. Gainsborough gained such a mastery of notation after nature that he could later create from memories convincing imaginary landscapes. Cozens journeyed to Italy as the official draftsman in the service of the eccentric William Beckford and recorded his travels in several series of water colors.

Social satire was excellently conveyed by many drawings, often in storytelling sequences that spelled the disasters of vice or, less entertainingly, the rewards of virtue. William Hogarth launched a satirical style that was further developed by

19

Thomas Rowlandson; with zest and humor Rowlandson caricatured life in London, ridiculing the pretensions and vulgarities of British society. **A Gaming Table at Devonshire House (17)** admirably portrays the lascivious corruptibility and greed of the gambling females and the brutish attention of the men.

No one could be more diverse from Rowlandson in spirit and technique than his exact contemporary, William Blake. A poet as well as painter, Blake filled his drawings with carefully composed, idealized figures that illustrate moral, biblical, and mystical concepts. **The Wise and Foolish Virgins (18)**, one of Blake's finest designs, was part of a series of more than 50 water colors of biblical subjects. The composition is reminiscent of the medieval sculpture that influenced Blake.

Joseph Mallord William Turner, with his highly original landscape and marine paintings and drawings, anticipated the Impressionists in his revolutionary use of light and brilliant color. He first traveled abroad in 1802 and later made annual visits to various countries on the Continent, filling many sketchbooks with drawings and water colors. **The Lake of Zug (19)** belongs to Turner's celebrated Swiss Series; the sweeping circle of the landscape surrounds the jewel-like, intensely blue lake.

The Spanish painter Francisco Goya was a virulent commentator on the late 18th- and early 19th-century scene and an exigent critic of inhumanity and brutality. He was a prolific virtuoso draftsman. **The**

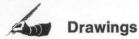

20

Swing (20) is a charming and unusually lighthearted sketch.

France, and particularly Paris, was the unquestionable artistic center of the 19th century. In the first half of the century Romanticism and classical tendencies confronted one another. Later, various artistic movements emanated from Paris, representing circles of revolt against the traditions upheld by the official French Academy. Jean-Auguste-Dominique Ingres, one of the greatest draftsmen of the century, was the principal exponent of Neoclassicism, a style based on the rediscovery of Greek and Roman ideals of art. He excelled in studies of the nude

21

figure and drew portraits of great penetration. The black chalk **Study for the Portrait of Louis-François Bertin (21)**, a painting now in the Louvre, is probably one of the most powerful of Ingres's small portraits and is one in which the sitter becomes a symbol of the solidity of the French bourgeoisie.

Of the mid-19th-century artists, Honoré Daumier stands apart as an original figure who made his living as a pictorial pamphleteer and social satirist. Few were able with the same energy, vitality, and satiric dash to capture the essence of a situation, be it the drabness of marriage, the pretensions of the middle class, or the injustices of the French legal system. In **L'Amateur (22)**, Daumier represents half-satirically and half-sympathetically a self-satisfied collector enjoying his accumulated works of art. The Museum has other fine drawings by Daumier.

Direct recourse to nature characterizes the drawings of the Impressionist painters. Hilaire-Germain-Edgar Degas, a

22

23

highly original artist associated with the Impressionists, was above all a figure draftsman, and he drew dancers, bathers, and horsemen with an authority reflecting his great interest in the movement of the human body. His portraits are alive with the psychological presence of his sitters. The **Portrait of Edouard Manet (23)**, his friend, is a preparatory study for two etchings made about 1864. This drawing and nine other masterful sketches were purchased at the sale of the contents of Degas's studio in 1918.

Georges Seurat, some years younger than most of the Impressionists, began his career painting in their manner. The monumental **Portrait of Edmond-François Aman-Jean (24)**, a painter and friend of Seurat's, was shown by the artist in the Salon des Artistes Indépendants in 1883. He perfected the individual style for which

24

25

26

he is famous; by placing small dots of pure color side by side, he created a special effect that came to be known as Pointillism. Seurat's drawings are built in a similar fashion in conté crayon, which is thickly and painstakingly applied to produce the subtlest effects ranging from light gray to velvet black. He attached great importance to his drawings, sometimes exhibiting them as independent works of art.

No two drawings can more aptly sum up the proliferation of styles after 1900 than Henri Matisse's **Nude (25)** and Pablo Picasso's **Nude Woman (26)**. These nearly contemporary works were done by two leading 20th-century artists. Whereas one consists of a few boldly drawn, sensuous curves, the other is all lines, angles, and cones, typical of Cubism. Both were first publicly exhibited in the United States before World War I by the pioneering photographer and dealer Alfred Stieglitz.

In addition to European drawings, the Museum possesses a remarkably rich and complete collection of American drawings and water colors. Winslow Homer, Thomas Eakins, John Singer Sargent, John Marin, and Charles Demuth are exceptionally well represented.

Egyptian Art

Egyptian Art

Objects, Periods, Styles	Numbers in Text
AKHENATEN and the AMARNEH PERIOD	(38), (39)
ALABASTER JARS, VASES, GOBLETS	(20)
ANIMAL FIGURES	(5), (6), (53)
CANOPIC JARS	(3), (40)
CHAPEL OF RAEMKUY	(12)
GOLD ROOM: cosmetic jars, faïence, glass, jewelry, scarabs, toys and games	(49-54)
JEWELRY	(30), (49-51)
MASTABA OF PERYNEBY (Perneb)	(11)
MIDDLE KINGDOM SCULPTURE	(23-27)
MUMMIES, MUMMY MASKS and SARCOPHAGI	(4), (55)
NEW KINGDOM SCULPTURE	(28-31), (33), (35-37), (41-45)
OLD KINGDOM GALLERIES	(9), (10), (13-20)
POTTERY	(1)
SCULPTORS' MODELS	(48)
SPHINXES	(26), (28), (30), (31)
STELAE	(7), (8), (25), (34), (47)
TOMB MODELS	(21), (22)

Chronology

Prehistoric Period	before 3100 B.C.
Early Dynastic Period, I-II Dynasty	3100-2780 B.C.
Old Kingdom, III-VI Dynasty	2780-2280 B.C.
First Intermediate Period, VII-X Dynasty	2280-2052 B.C.
Middle Kingdom, XI-XII Dynasty	2134-1786 B.C.
Second Intermediate Period, XIII-XVII Dynasty	1786-1567 B.C.
New Kingdom, XVIII-XX Dynasty	1567-1085 B.C.
Late Dynastic Period, XXI-XXX Dynasty	1085-332 B.C.
Ptolemaic Period, Conquest by Alexander the Great	332-30 B.C.
Roman Period	30 B.C.-A.D. 364

This page helps you to find what you especially want to see and read about.

Egyptian Art

The Museum's Department of Egyptian Art is one of the greatest in the world and includes objects of major importance from all periods of ancient Egyptian history. Nevertheless, the Egyptian collection was almost nonexistent until 1881, when the erection of the obelisk in Central Park, near the Museum's new home, aroused the interest of New Yorkers, and gifts of Egyptian antiquities began to stream into the Museum. In 1906, encouraged by the continued growth of the collection and the increase of public interest in the civilization of ancient Egypt, the trustees voted to establish a Department of Egyptian Art and to undertake a program of excavation in Egypt. During its nearly 30 years in the field, the Museum's Egyptian expedition excavated in areas representing all periods, from prehistoric to Roman times, concentrating, however, at the site of Lisht in the north and at Thebes, opposite the modern Luxor, in the south. The importance of the department is derived to a large extent from its excavated material—many thousands of objects with recorded histories; and notes, plans, and photographs that have contributed to the science of Egyptology everywhere. In addition, the expedition's epigraphic branch executed over 400 facsimile copies of wall paintings, thus recording many scenes which have since been destroyed.

Among the outstanding Egyptian antiquities acquired by gift, bequest, and purchase are the tombs of Peryneby (better known as Perneb) and Raemkuy, bought from the Egyptian government; the Temple of Dendur; the Carnarvon Collection, the finest ever assembled by a private individual; the Theodore M. Davis Collection, which, like the Carnarvon, includes excavated material; the collection of Albert Gallatin, particularly rich in sculpture; the Lahun Treasure; the statue of General Horemheb; and the recently acquired statue of the Chief Archivist Ptahshepses.

Owing to the rebuilding of the galleries, only a small proportion of the antiquities are on view. This comprises, however, a selection of the finest objects from every period of ancient Egyptian history, including the collection of jewelry in its entirety. After the reinstallation, the department will continue to occupy the first floor of the north wing of the Museum. The collection will then be arranged for the most part in chronological order, with certain rooms devoted to Egyptian life and civilization and other special exhibitions. The great sculptures from the temple of Queen Hatshepsut at Deir el Bahri will be displayed so as to approximate their original setting. In addition, the Temple of Dendur, an Egyptian monument of the 1st century B.C., given to the United States by the United Arab Republic, will be erected in a new wing that will suggest how it once looked on the banks of the Nile.

Egypt is a long, narrow valley hemmed in by rocky escarpments and desert plateaus. The Nile River has always been the highway and the source of water. Its banks were once edged with papyrus swamps teeming with wildlife; the desert also supported a variety of wild animals; and the rocky hills, as well as the clay banks of the river, supplied fine building material. Egypt was fortunate in having easy access to most of the materials needed for a pleasant life, but usable wood was scarce and had to be imported.

1

The greatest problem until the recent construction of the High Dam has always been lack of water: drought for nine months of the year followed by the annual flooding of the Nile for the other three. Consequently, life for the ancient Egyptian peasant was an unending struggle. Fields, once drained, had to be watered constantly, dikes repaired; and this work had to be continued in the next world, for the Egyptians believed in a life after death that would be a continuation of the existence they had known on earth. Therefore, work in the fields of a rich man's estate was a favorite subject for the scenes carved or painted on the walls of tombs, scenes which by a magic process were expected to accompany the deceased into the future.

The oldest objects in the department are prehistoric, that is, they were made before the invention of true writing and actual written records. Early pottery vessels, like the **pottery jar (1)** illustrated here, made about 3400 B.C., are decorated with a form of picture writing; precise geographical settings with animals, hills, trees, and ships with human and divine figures illustrate events of whose interpretation we cannot be sure. The religious beliefs of the later Egyptians, their respect for the forces of nature and the animals of the desert, and their faith in a life after death in which they would need the equipment they had used on earth, are already evident in this early period, when, as later, possessions were buried with the dead along with sustenance for their long journey into the next world. This is illustrated in the Museum by a predynastic burial **(2)**, in which the desiccated body is shown lying on its side in a hole scooped out of the sand (here simulated); its possessions—weapons, ornaments, and containers for food and drink—are beside it and it is covered with a linen cloth.

Since the ancient Egyptians believed that the soul of the deceased remained in contact with the body, it had to be carefully preserved, that is, mummified. The body was embalmed and wrapped in yard after yard of linen bandages, and amulets were placed among them to help and protect it. A great mask representing the dead man or woman was slipped over the head and fixed in place with the last layer of bandages, and the final decorations were fastened over the breast. Meanwhile, certain organs that had been removed in the process of mummification had also been embalmed and wrapped in bandages. These were placed in the four canopic jars **(3)** which were a necessary part of every burial and which were the particular care of one of the four deities known as the Sons of Horus. The jars were fitted into specially designed chests.

The type, number, and richness of the coffin **(4)** depended on the rank and wealth of the owner and on the period in which he lived. Heavy stone sarcophagi are particularly associated with the Old Kingdom, and rectangular wooden coffins with the Middle Kingdom. The characteristic coffins of the New Kingdom are anthropoid, that is, carved in wood in the form of the wrapped body. They are painted with scenes from the Book of the Dead, our name for a collection of magic spells that were written on papyrus rolls. Anthropoid sarcophagi of stone are found in the Late Period.

About 3100 B.C. King Narmer (Menes) united the two prehistoric kingdoms that had existed in the Nile Valley (Upper Egypt) and in the Delta (Lower Egypt), and founded the I Dynasty. For the next 3,000 years Egypt was ruled by 30 dynasties, or families of kings; the last native ruler was overthrown by the Persians shortly before the conquest by Alexander the Great in 332 B.C. During this tremendous span of time Egypt formed a background for the shorter-lived empires of the ancient world. The great peaks of her own civilization are known as the Old Kingdom, the Middle Kingdom, and the New Kingdom. The breakup of the New Kingdom was followed by the Late Dynastic and Ptolemaic periods. In 30 B.C. Egypt became a province of Rome.

The early Egyptians were particularly adept at working even the hardest stones. The **figure of a lion (5)** in quartz was probably presented by a I Dynasty king to a temple. Small animal figures of faience **(6)**, the brilliantly colored glazed ware characteristic of Egypt, are of the same period, as are ivory furniture legs from royal tombs.

The beginnings of true writing are illustrated by the small limestone stela (gravestone) of Senba **(7)** and other objects from the I Dynasty (about 3000 B.C.). The large pink granite stela **(8)** was one of a pair set up by King Reneb of the II Dynasty, 120 years later. Once the Egyptians had learned to write, they became among the world's most industrious record keepers. Rich officials were soon leaving accounts of their achievements in their tombs in beautifully carved or painted hieroglyphic characters that were to speak for them forever. The early pharaohs (the Greek form of the Egyptian word for "great house") covered the walls of their monuments with religious texts and later with accounts of their own exploits.

After the tremendous burst of activity that marked the Early Dynastic period, the Egyptians entered one of the greatest eras of their civilization, the Old Kingdom, which lasted more than 500 years. The general introduction of copper tools made stone construction possible; a panel of blue tiles **(9)** in the Museum once lined a passage of the Step Pyramid at Sakkareh, the first great stone building in the world and the first of the pyramids. It was built

5

for Djoser, the second king of the III Dynasty (about 2660 B.C.), by his architect Imhotep, whose name was still revered 2,000 years later.

The pyramids were the tombs of pharaohs, and in all 35 are known, the greatest both in size and workmanship being that of Khufu (Cheops) of the IV Dynasty (about 2580 B.C.). It was believed that the buildings connected with Khufu's monument were undecorated, until the excavations of the Museum at Lisht uncovered sculptured blocks from them that had been reused later as filling for the interior of the pyramid. These reliefs—still the only ones known from the pyramid complex of Khufu—and reliefs from other pyramids of the Old Kingdom **(10)** found at the same place are on exhibition in the Old Kingdom galleries.

Officials of the Old Kingdom were buried in so-called mastaba tombs on the flat plateau around the pyramids of the pharaohs they served. Each mastaba consisted of an underground burial chamber and a superstructure, which included a room (*serdab*) where statues of the deceased were placed and from which their souls emerged to enjoy the food left in the offering chamber. The Museum's tomb and tomb chapel, dating from the V Dynasty, were formerly near each other at Sakkareh. The mastaba of Peryneby **(11)**, the lord chamberlain of Egypt, was erected about 2440 B.C. The reliefs, once brightly painted, show servants preparing and bringing food; some unfinished scenes let us see the methods of the Old Kingdom sculptor. The mastaba in which the Crown Prince Raemkuy was buried was made for one of his father's courtiers, but Raemkuy died suddenly and it was

14

appropriated for his use. The reliefs from the chapel **(12)** are remarkable for their vivacity and show scenes of daily life: farming, harvesting, hunting, boating, preparing food, and a banquet, as well as the funeral procession.

The belief that statues and portraits in relief might serve as a home for the soul resulted in the rapid perfection of the art of sculpture. A small granite figure represents Mycerinus **(13)**, the builder of the Third Pyramid at Gizeh. It shows the fifth of the eight distinct stages in which an Old Kingdom stone statue was carved and, although unfinished, it is already a recognizable portrait of the pharaoh. The statue of **Sahure with a deity (14)**, carved in the extremely hard stone diorite, is the only known representation of the king; it was made about 2545 B.C. Figures of three officials of the V Dynasty are of the much softer and more easily worked limestone. One shows the Chief Archivist Ptahshepses **(15)** striding forward; this

18

17

was to be a favorite pose for the next 2,000 years. In another, Memy Sabu **(16)** is represented with his arm around his wife's shoulders, while her arm is around his waist. The third shows **Nykure and his family (17)**, the man seated while his wife crouches at his feet clasping his leg; their small daughter stands at his other side sucking her finger in an attitude that means childhood. All three statues were once painted, the flesh of the theoretically sports-loving men in red, that of the more sheltered women in yellow. The imposing figures of **Mitry and his wife (18)** are of imported coniferous wood. The powerful figure of an unknown provincial official of the VI Dynasty is carved in quartzite **(19)**. The series of fine alabaster jars, vases, goblets, and a headrest **(20)** is associated with kings of the VI Dynasty.

By the end of the Old Kingdom a philosophy of art had been established that was to remain in effect until the Christian era. When we talk of Egyptian art we must remember that our examples are drawn from the tombs or homes of the wealthy. A rich official is represented either full of youthful vigor or, more rarely, with the corpulence that indicates a successful career. Sculpture and writing are

allied—each of the poses allowed the sculptor or painter in a rather limited repertoire immediately tells us about the subject. The scale, particularly of relief sculpture and painting, shows the relative importance of the figures: the largest are the gods, then the royal figures, next the noble tomb owner, and last—and least—the small employees pictured working in the fields and shops of an estate.

In all two-dimensional art, the most striking or characteristic aspect of a scene or figure was the one shown: the head of a human figure was in profile; the shoulders, seen from the front, were joined so skillfully by a twisted torso to legs and feet, seen from the side, that the distortion is not disturbing. Perspective as understood by the Egyptians simply placed the objects nearest the observer at the bottom of the picture, the ones farthest away at the top.

Although Egyptian art always remained tied to religion, as time went on the figures gradually became less rigid, and the New Kingdom fashion for flowing costumes added to the more graceful effect. Increased contact with neighboring countries contributed to the store of artistic ideas until, for a brief time at the end of the XVIII Dynasty, there was a complete break with tradition in depicting the human figure. The ideas behind this revolution, which included religion and writing as well as art, are associated with the pharaoh Akhenaten and his capital city, Amarneh; the new mode of representation is known as the Amarneh style. These ideas failed to appeal to the Egyptian people and were discarded, though Egyptian art never again recaptured its old austerity.

After a period of political turbulence that followed the VI Dynasty, a second golden age, known as the Middle Kingdom, began. The well-known models from the tomb of Meketre, the chancellor and great steward of the king, date from the beginning of this period, about 2050 B.C., when the paintings and reliefs on the walls of private tombs were briefly replaced by little painted models in the round. Meketre's models, now in the Museum, are the finest known: they show their owner in the boats in which he inspected the royal estates; two barques prepared for his funeral; and various activities at his own home. Our illustration shows **Meketre's fishing and fowling skiff (21)**. From the same tomb is a larger wooden figure,

21

22

24

brightly painted, of a **girl bringing offerings (22)** of a duck, meat, and bread.

The Museum's collection excels in sculpture and relief portraits of the Middle Kingdom rulers. The pharaoh whom Meketre served, Montuhotpe II, is shown by an Osiride statue in which he appears in the guise of Osiris, god of the dead, and also by a colorful relief **(23)**; both are from his funerary temple at Deir el Bahri, Thebes. The royal portraits of the succeeding dynasty, the XIIth, are among the finest works of Egyptian art, combining the dignity and restraint associated with the office of pharaoh with a strong sense of realism that was not often applied in the ancient world to such semidivine subjects. The son of the founder of the dynasty, **Sesostris I (24)**, is represented by a wooden figure that shows him as a relatively young man wearing the Red Crown of Lower Egypt, and by a headless black basalt statue from a temple in the Fayyum. The remarkable **stela of Montuwosre (25)** was a present from Sesostris I to this official, who was his favorite steward. Its long autobiographical inscription describes Montuwosre's various duties, his generosity, and his wealth. Besides being an important historical document, this stela is an impressive work of art.

25

26

The **sphinx of Sesostris III (26)**, combining the powerful body of a lion with the head of the king, typifies the majesty of the pharaoh. The lion has always been regarded as the king of beasts; the Egyptians considered their king a lion among men. The quartzite **face of Sesostris III (27)** shows the same proud but careworn features. This is one of the finest portraits that have been preserved from ancient Egypt; although carved from this resistant material, the lined cheeks and heavy eyelids have the quality of real flesh.

The third great period of Egyptian civilization is known as the New Kingdom, the XVIII-XX dynasties (1567-1085 B.C.). The Museum's most important monuments from the early XVIII Dynasty are statues of Queen Hatshepsut that once graced the temple she built at Deir el Bahri next to that of Montuhotpe II. Of the original 200 or so, the Museum has 14 free-standing statues and the upper parts of nine Osiride figures, which were built into the columns of the temple. A special installation of these statues is planned for the future. Meanwhile, on exhibition are one of the six great granite sphinxes **(28)**

27

29

which once, in pairs, lined the approach to the temple, and the finest of the statues, a **seated figure of Hatshepsut (29)** in indurated limestone, which probably comes from the sanctuary. (Indurated limestone is a hard, marblelike material that takes a fine polish; it was much favored by the sculptors of the latter part of this dynasty.)

In the New Kingdom Egypt reached the pinnacle of its luxury and might, and the pharaohs of the XVIII and XIX dynasties brought home from their conquests booty of every description. The greatest of the Egyptian warlords and possibly the greatest of the pharaohs was Hatshepsut's stepson, Thotmose III. The Museum possesses a colossal statue of him in red granite and a small sphinx of quartzite **(30)**, as well as the jewelry of three of his minor wives, in the Gold Room. His son, Amunhotpe II, a remarkable athlete, is represented by another small sphinx, a fine kneeling statuette, and by the upper part of a diorite statue **(31)**.

Egyptians who went abroad brought back not only wealth but new ideas. One result was the so-called naturalistic movement which, though it had been gaining ground over a period of years, first became marked during the reign of Amunhotpe II's son, Thotmose IV. An arm of Thotmose's throne now in the Museum is of fine wood, though it was once overlaid with sheet gold **(32)**. The scene on the outside represents the pharaoh as a sphinx trampling on his enemies; here litheness and speed are emphasized rather than strength. Antiquities dating from the reign of Thotmose IV's son, Amunhotpe III, are remarkable for their grace and charm, exemplified by the head of the pharaoh himself **(33)**, by the two stelae of Senu **(34)**, and the small head of an unknown official **(35)**. The headless statuette of Amunhotpe III showing him in female costume **(36)** is a precursor of the style of the next reign. The famous fragmentary yellow jasper **head of Queen Teye (37)**, his wife, was actually made in the reign of their son, Amunhotpe IV Akhenaten.

The movement toward naturalism culminated toward the end of the XVIII Dynasty under Amunhotpe IV, who reigned

37

41

40

from 1379 to 1362 B.C. He moved the capital of Egypt to the site we know as Amarneh, decreed that all Egyptians should worship Aten, the disk of the sun, and changed his name to Akhenaten, "The-Aten-Is-Served." Among the finest antiquities preserved from the Amarneh period are the red quartzite head of Akhenaten **(38)** and the fragmentary indurated limestone face of the king **(39)**, in which he is represented with his facial peculiarities exaggerated in a style associated with his earlier years on the throne.

Akhenaten was succeeded by a younger half-brother, Smenkhkure, who had married the eldest of Akhenaten's six daughters, Meryetaten. Smenkhkure died soon, before his funerary equipment was ready, so a set of alabaster canopic jars prepared for his wife and bearing her name was appropriated for his use. Their stoppers were actually portraits of the **Princess Meryetaten (40)**, but the closely related husband and wife probably resembled each other. The inscriptions were erased, royal cobras (now missing) were attached over the foreheads, and the jars were then ready to receive the organs of the king. One jar is in the Museum.

Tutankhamun, another half-brother of Akhenaten and married to his third daughter, was Smenkhkure's successor. Tutankhamun's modern claim to fame rests on the magnificent treasure with which he was buried (discovered in 1922 by Lord Carnarvon and Howard Carter). His brief life ended before he was twenty, but he had lived long enough to take the court back to Thebes and restore the property of the god Amun. Our portrait is from a group showing **Tutankhamun (41)** being

42

44

blessed by the god. All that remains is the head of the young king and, behind him, the over-life-size hand of the god, gently placed on his Blue Crown. The colossal head of the **Great God Amun (42)** has the features of the reigning monarch, as was customary, and in this case Tut-

43

ankhamun is again represented.

Under these last weak kings of the XVIII Dynasty the army was controlled by General Horemheb, who eventually seized control of the throne. He became one of Egypt's most thoughtful and progressive rulers. Our portrait of **Horemheb (43)**, bent over his papyrus scroll before he became king, is considered the finest single object in our collection.

Ramesses II of the succeeding dynasty is probably the best known of all Egyptian pharaohs. A fine head in painted quartzite represents **Ramesses (44)** wearing the Blue Crown, or war helmet. The

45

46

statue of Yuny (45), Ramesses's secretary, shows him kneeling, wearing the fashionable costume of a nobleman of the time—transparent shirt, pleated kilt, curled wig, and papyrus sandals; he holds a shrine containing a figure of the god Osiris. The face was defaced in ancient times by thieves for the sake of the metal that outlined the eyebrows and eyes.

After the period of turbulence that followed the breakup of the New Kingdom, there occurred a renaissance of political power and a renewed interest in the arts. Sculptors went back to the Old Kingdom for their models, and much of their work was imitative. Their great achievement was in portrait sculpture, and their originality was expressed by an interest in the treatment of surfaces. A smooth, lustrous finish fascinated the sculptor of the XXX Dynasty who made the statue of the **Falcon God Horus (46)** with a small figure of King Nectanebos standing between his claws. Nectanebos was the last native pharaoh of Egypt, and his name also ap-

48

47

pears on the so-called **Metternich Stela (47)**. The panel in high relief on the upper face of this remarkable monument shows Horus as a child-god dominating various noxious beasts, and the inscriptions that cover every inch of the surface are for the most part spells against attacks by these animals. It is thought that such stelae were placed at the entrance to temples and that water poured over them absorbed the magic content of the spells and acquired the power to cure the ailments of the faithful.

A group of limestone plaques known as sculptors' models dates from the Greco-Roman period. The interest in surfaces has continued, but attention to delicate detail is now pre-eminent. Some plaques may have been the finest offering an artist could present to the god, others seem to have been hung in studios for pupils to study and copy. Many are obviously the work of pupils and show the master's corrections. An exceedingly fine plaque shows a **Ram-Headed Divinity (48)**.

The earliest objects in the Gold Room belong to the Middle Kingdom. The visitor should begin with the Lahun Treasure and

50

49

proceed around the gallery, ending with the Ptolemaic and Greco-Roman jewelry.

The treasure from Lahun consists of the jewelry and cosmetic equipment that belonged to Princess Sit Hathor Yunet, a daughter of Sesostris II. The most famous piece, the **Lahun pectoral (49)**, is as fine both in design and execution as any ornament surviving from antiquity. With it are shown her necklaces, girdles, bracelets, anklets, and rings, some given by her father and others by her nephew, Amunemhet III. The jewelry from Lahun should be compared with the more flamboyant treasure of three minor wives of Thotmose III. Each of these girls had similar equipment—sets of golden tableware, objects for the dressing table, and a profusion of jewelry. The most striking piece is the great **gold headdress (50)** inlaid with colored pastes and stones, one of six headdresses displayed in individual vitrines on casts of a head of Queen Nefretity now in Cairo. There is a second, smaller wig cover and, for the third girl, a circlet **(51)** decorated in front with gazelles. The gazelle, replacing the royal cobra, was a symbol of a king's concubine, and similar circlets are known only from wall paintings. The Museum's circlet with the heads of a stag and four gazelles is unique.

Among objects representing the minor arts of the New Kingdom, also in the Gold Room, is a group that belonged to the royal family **(52)** of the end of the XVIII Dynasty. Among the masterpieces of the Egyptian collection are the ivory horse

53

55

galloping at the end of a whip handle, and the little **ivory gazelle (53)** standing on a desert crag. The dog and tiny puppy were royal toys. The golden figure of the god Amun dates from the XXII Dynasty.

The Museum's collection of glass and faience is unique: some of the finest examples are in the Gold Room. Particularly noteworthy is the Carnarvon goblet **(54)**, whose delicate sides are decorated with scenes in relief illustrating plant and animal life in the marshes. Other fine examples of the minor arts include small figures of silver, bronze, and ivory.

Except when the deceased was a pharaoh, the faces of the coffins and masks of the Dynastic period bore little resemblance to their owner. Not until Egypt came under the influence of Hellenistic Greece was there an attempt at real portraiture: flat wooden panels bound over the faces of the intricately wrapped mummies of the time were painted in encaustic, a hot wax technique. In both style and material they have replaced the old conventions, yet their eyes look out on the living world, much as the eyes of mummy masks always had done. The Museum has a fine series of these masks, painted in the 2nd century A.D., such as this **portrait panel from a mummy (55)**. Most of them come from the oasis of the Fayyum.

European Paintings

European Paintings

Periods, Artists	Numbers in Text
ALTMAN COLLECTION	(6)
DUTCH PAINTINGS	(9-13)
ENGLISH PAINTINGS	(32), (33)
FLEMISH AND GERMAN PAINTINGS:	(22-28)
Van Eyck, Bouts, Van der Weyden	(22), (23)
Bruegel, Cranach, Holbein, Dürer	(24-27)
Rubens, Van Dyck	(28)
FRENCH PAINTINGS:	(14-21)
Poussin, Claude, La Tour, David	(14), (16)
Watteau, Boucher, Fragonard	(15)
Ingres, Courbet, Manet	(17), (18)
Corot, Barbizon Painters	
Impressionists and Post-Impressionists	(19-21)
ITALIAN PAINTINGS:	(1-8)
Altarpieces and High Renaissance	(1-3)
Giotto, Gaddi, Segna	(4)
Giovanni di Paolo, Sassetta, Crivelli	(5)
Pintoricchio	
Botticelli, Fra Filippo Lippi, Bellini, Carpaccio	(7)
Tiepolo, Guardi, Canaletto	(8)
Caravaggio, Carracci, Reni	
SPANISH PAINTINGS	(29-31)

☞ **This page helps you to find what you especially want to see and read about.**

European Paintings

Although a group of 174 pictures was bought in Paris and Brussels in 1871 and formed the nucleus of the collection, a Department of Paintings as such was not established until 1886. At that time, along with paintings, it included drawings and water colors, prints, photographs, and textiles. Over the years the growing institution formed new and separate departments to cope with the varied material, and most recently, after a separation of European from American paintings, the Department of European Paintings has become still more specialized; works by artists born after 1875 are cared for by the Department of Twentieth Century Art.

ITALIAN PAINTING

The monumental altarpiece, destined for a particular church or chapel from the time it was commissioned, is one of the most representative forms of painting in Italy. The great *Madonna and Child Enthroned with Saints* was painted by Raphael for the Convent of Sant'Antonio in Perugia, during the first decade of the 16th century. The influence of the Umbrian painter Perugino gave way in these years to the profound impression Raphael had received from a visit to Florence, where the most progressive art was being created, and in this large altarpiece the young artist reveals both aspects of his experience. Like most altarpieces of the Italian Renaissance, this one originally had a series of small scenes beneath the main panel, forming a *predella*. One of these scenes, the *Agony in the Garden*, after many years of separation from the altarpiece was acquired by the Museum and is now exhibited near the main panel.

1

The large canvas of *Four Saints: Peter, Martha, Mary Magdalen, and Leonard* standing against a dusky, mysterious background is by Correggio, the chief painter of Parma. The rich and deep colors are characteristic of his paintings at the beginning of his career. He was later to paint enormous frescoes, which inspired the daring illusionism of Baroque painting.

The Museum's collection of Italian paintings of the High Renaissance includes Andrea del Sarto's *Holy Family* and the impressive, somber *Entombment* by the North Italian Moretto da Brescia, dated 1554, the year of his death. There is also a pair of panels by the Florentine Francesco Granacci, with four scenes from the life of St. John the Baptist. The *Finding of Moses* by the Venetian painter

2

Tintoretto illustrates admirably the rapid brushwork characteristic of this artist. Mythological paintings from the second half of the 16th century include three sumptuous Venetian tributes to Venus, the goddess of love: Paolo Veronese's sensuous **Mars and Venus United by Love (1)**, so puzzling in its theme that it has been given other interpretations; Titian's *Venus and Adonis*; and the same artist's splendid **Venus and the Lute Player (2)**, which is endued with all the magnificence of Titian's late style. The art of the portrait in Florence is represented by Bronzino's elegant **Portrait of a Young Man (3)**.

3

This impressive group of paintings of the High Renaissance and the selection of Italian altarpieces provide a general introduction to the Museum's Italian paintings. Chronologically, the Italian section of the department begins with the *Madonna and Child* by Berlinghiero, who died in 1242 and probably painted this picture at the end of his life. He left a small group of works that show a union of Romanesque and Byzantine elements in their style.

One of the great treasures of the col-

5

4

lection is the small panel of **The Epiphany (4)**, by Giotto di Bondone (died in 1337), who has been famous for centuries as the founder of the Florentine school of painting. The Nativity, Adoration of the Magi, and Annunciation to the Shepherds, all part of this warm and sympathetic representation, are typical of Giotto's work, which combined a new concept of form and its relation to space with a human approach to subject matter.

Taddeo Gaddi, the painter of the large altarpiece *The Madonna and Child Enthroned with Saints*, followed Giotto and perhaps even collaborated with him. The way the five main panels are connected with each other today is the result of a reframing in the 15th century. Four similar and closely related panels, showing the major Old Testament prophets Abraham, Noah, Moses, and David, were painted in the first decade of the 15th century by Lorenzo Monaco, an illuminator of manuscripts.

The Sienese School stems from Duccio di Buoninsegna (died 1319) and one of his chief followers, Segna di Buonaventura. The three panels of Segna's *Madonna and Child with St. Benedict and St. Silvester Gozzolini* are the central and end sections of a five-part polyptych. The picture is one of four signed works by the artist, and the refined and elegant treatment of the slender forms is characteristic of his style. Lippo Memmi's *Madonna and Child* was intended for private devotional use, while his *St. Paul* was probably part of a large altarpiece like the Segna polyptych. *St. Catherine of Alexandria*, also a fragment of a dismembered altarpiece, is by the Sienese master Pietro Lorenzetti. The grave expression of the saint and the solid modeling of the forms testify to the influence of the Florentine Giotto and of the sculptor Giovanni Pisano.

The collection also includes a *Madonna and Child Enthroned* by the first great master of the Venetian School, Paolo Ve-

6

neziano. Paolo's style, based on the late Byzantine tradition, also shows Gothic features: the forms are treated with a new grace and refinement, but the extravagant gilding and coloring of the surface give the picture a jewel-like iconic quality. Niccolò di Pietro's *St. Ursula and Her Maidens* is a more purely decorative picture. The figures wear brocaded gowns, and the floral patterns and roundels are applied to flat fields of color without regard for the forms beneath the drapery. Extra plaster, or gesso, has been applied to the surface in the area of Ursula's crown and the buttons of her robe. This technique enjoyed considerable popularity in northern Italy, and was also employed by Michele Giambono, an artist who worked in the International Gothic style. A delicately carved and gilded arch frames the figure in his *Man of Sorrows.*

Carlo Crivelli was born in Venice but spent most of his life in the Marches, where his beautifully wrought but rather old-fashioned paintings were enthusiastically received. The **Madonna and Child (5)**, from the Bache Collection, is his masterpiece. The symbolic significance of each still-life detail would have been clear to the artist's contemporaries. At the base, on a small slip of paper pinned to the hanging, the artist has signed his work. The *Pietà*, like the other panels by Crivelli in the collection, was originally part of an altarpiece.

The later Sienese School is represented by Sassetta, Giovanni di Paolo, and Neroccio di Landi. Sassetta's *Journey of the Magi*, painted in the mid-1430s, is a fragment; the Journey of the Kings was combined with the Adoration of the Child in such a way that the star at the lower right once glowed over the spot where the Child lay. Sassetta's *Madonna and Child with Angels* is a late work in which forms of an almost geometrical clarity are combined with brilliant colors. Giovanni di Paolo, who was deeply influenced by Sassetta, painted the polyptych of the *Madonna and Child with Saints*, as well as the small picture representing the meeting of the angels and the souls of the blessed in Paradise. The refined and elegant treatment of forms is characteristic of all the masters of the Sienese School.

The collection of Benjamin Altman, bequeathed to the Metropolitan in 1913, includes a group of 15th- and 16th-century portraits, among them two important works of Titian. The Florentine School is particularly well represented, and Sandro Botticelli's **Last Communion of St. Jerome (6)** is one of the finest paintings

7

in the Museum. The saint, knowing that death is near, has risen from his bed to receive the Sacrament. Botticelli's treatment of this subject conveys something of the passionate fervor of the elderly artist's own religious convictions.

A *Madonna and Child Enthroned with Two Angels*, the central panel of a triptych painted about 1437, and the painting of a *Man and Woman at a Casement* are by Botticelli's master, Fra Filippo Lippi. The latter painting was probably executed to celebrate the engagement or marriage of the sitters. Lippi's solution of the problem of combining two profile portraits is tentative, but the restricted space is a brilliant invention, and every detail is minutely rendered. Domenico Ghirlandaio, in the presumed portrait of *Francesco Sassetti and His Son Teodoro*, painted about 1485, represented two figures with new ease and sympathy.

In only one case has the painter of an important Italian work in the Museum escaped identification. The picture, *The Birth of the Virgin*, came from the Barberini Collection, and the artist is therefore known as the Master of the Barberini Panels. Despite the religious subject, *The Birth of the Virgin* probably formed part of the decoration of a room. The figures and their costumes are exquisitely rendered, and the artist was also interested in architecture, perspective, and classical decorative motifs. A Paduan work, Andrea Mantegna's *Adoration of the Shepherds*, was painted about 1450. His contemporary, Vittore Carpaccio, worked in Venice. The Hebrew characters he painted on the stone seat provide the key to the interpretation of his *Meditation on the Passion*, with St. Jerome (left) and Job flanking the dead Christ. Giovanni Bellini's *Madonna Adoring the Sleeping Child* is one of his earliest surviving works, and the treatment of the drapery and the landscape indicates that he was still under the influence of Paduan art. By 1490, when Bellini painted the **Madonna and Child (7)**, he had been established in Venice for many years and was acknowledged as the leading master of the Venetian School.

Rome became the principal center of creative activity in the 17th century, and Baroque art flourished there. Annibale Carracci moved to Rome from Bologna in 1595, about the time he painted the Museum's *Coronation of the Virgin*. He was deeply impressed by the antique and by the work of Raphael; this comparatively small picture is characterized by nobility of form, balance, and classical restraint. Guido Reni, Carracci's pupil in Bologna, also lived for a time in Rome, and his *Immaculate Conception* may have been commissioned by the Spanish ambassador for an infanta of Spain. Carracci's contemporary, Michelangelo Merisi, called Caravaggio, was working in an entirely different style, painting from the model and experimenting with the dramatic possibilities of light and shade. The boy with the horn in Caravaggio's *Musicians* may be a portrait of the artist. A macabre portrait by a forerunner of Romantic art, Salvator Rosa, was painted toward the mid-17th century. The sitter was his friend Giovanni Battista Ricciardi, who taught philosophy at Pisa. Giovanni Pannini's two paintings *Ancient Rome* and *Modern Rome*, painted in 1757, show views of antique and contemporary monuments which were hung row upon row in a great Baroque gallery, the custom at that time. The Museum's 17th-century pictures are hung in a similar fashion today.

Throughout the 18th century painting flourished in Venice, and the Metropolitan has splendid examples of the work of this period. Among the most characteristic are the views of the city painted as souvenirs for travelers on the Grand Tour, such as Antonio Canaletto's *Venice: The Piazzetta.* The pictures of Francesco Guardi, his pupil, are admired now for their *plein-air* quality and more impressionistic brushwork. Guardi painted imaginative scenes, or *capricci*, as well as more conventional views, such as **Venice: The Grand Canal above the Rialto (8)**. Pietro Longhi was patronized by members of the Venetian aristocracy, and their manner of life is vividly recorded in such small genre scenes as *The Meeting*.

The most important Venetian of the 18th century was Giovanni Battista Tiepolo, a decorator of genius and a prolific artist. He frequently prepared a rapid oil sketch, or *modello*, to submit to his pa-

8

trons, and there are several pictures of this type on display. *St. Thecla Praying for the Plague-Stricken*, a study for his painting for the high altar in the cathedral of Este, near Padua, was commissioned in 1758. *The Triumph of Marius* and two other scenes from Roman history formed part of a cycle of decorations commissioned by the Venetian aristocrat Dionisio Dolfin.

10

DUTCH PAINTING

In the 17th century Holland was one of the most important maritime powers in Europe. The wealthy merchants, who collected paintings in the great commercial cities, set the standards of middle-class taste. No commissions came from the official Calvinist church, which frowned on art in places of worship, and very few from the Catholic church, which had been forced underground. Painters vied for portrait commissions from wealthy burghers and painted many other pictures for the open market. Artists came to specialize in certain categories of pictures, most of which reflected the everyday reality of Dutch life: landscape, seascape, scenes in domestic interiors, still life, and others.

9

An exception was Hendrick Terbrugghen, a Catholic who lived for a number of years in Italy. There he was impressed by the works of Caravaggio, whose innovations in style and content helped to set the course of Baroque painting. Terbrugghen's **The Crucifixion with the Virgin and St. John (9)** dates from the 1620s, the last decade of his life. In it he combined Italianate lighting with a north-

ern, unidealized conception of the figures: an ugly, tortured Christ and plain Dutch peasant types for Mary and John.

Whereas the largely Catholic city of Utrecht, in which Terbrugghen was born and worked, remained in close touch with Italy, the city of Haarlem nurtured a more self-sufficient school of painters. Frans Hals was the most famous painter of Haarlem. He was primarily a portraitist. In his single and group portraits he records with extraordinary verve the appearance and character of the wealthy burghers of his native country. An earthy spirit is obvious in his earlier works, such as the Museum's *Revellers at Shrovetide*; its crowded composition and bright colors typify Hals's work of the 1620s. *Young Man and Woman in an Inn (Jonker Ramp and His Sweetheart*) of 1623 is painted in a similar vein. From the 1650s comes the great **Portrait of a Man (10)**, in which the brushstrokes are broad and fluid, and the characterization is full of dignity.

It was Rembrandt Harmensz. van Rijn, of course, whose portraits were the most successful in conveying the complexities of human character. Whereas most of Hals's clients exude contentment, Rembrandt's are shown absorbed in serious and sometimes troubled thought. Rembrandt, born in Leyden in 1606, was trained in the booming commercial city of Amsterdam, worked in Leyden for a while, then returned to Amsterdam in 1632. He was an immediate success as a portraitist, as a painter of biblical and historical scenes, and as a teacher. The Museum has a distinguished collection of his works from all phases of his 40-year career. From the 1630s come the *Portrait of a Man* and *Portrait of a Woman*, a pair of energetic yet carefully executed likenesses of the sort that made Rembrandt's reputation, and the *Man in Oriental Costume (The Noble Slav)*, which shows Rembrandt's penchant for painting models in exotic trappings. **Aristotle With a Bust of Homer (11)**, dated 1653, is considered one of Rembrandt's finest paintings. It is an imaginary portrait of the great philosopher, who is paying tribute to a great poet. Remarkable is Aristotle's introspection, reinforced by the incomparable atmosphere that surrounds so many of Rembrandt's figures. The 1650s and 1660s brought increasing personal adversities and diminished patronage. Undeterred, the artist painted many of his most moving works at this time, such as the *Lady with a Carnation* and the *Man with a Magnifying Glass.*

Jan Vermeer was from Delft, where a

13

12

distinctive group of painters was occupied with interior scenes, often intimate indoor compositions with few figures. Vermeer painted little; only some 40 works are attributed to him, of which the Museum has four. The **Young Woman with a Water Jug (12)** is characteristic of Vermeer's best work. Here, as in many of Vermeer's paintings, a tranquil single figure stands in a luminous interior, with light coming from a window. Pieter de Hooch also excelled in scenes with clear perspective views into Dutch houses; like Vermeer, De Hooch's work mirrors the prosperity of Dutch life in the latter part of the 17th century.

Other notable painters not connected with Delft depicted domestic life. Gerard ter Borch's paintings are known for their easy grace as well as for their superb rendering of rich materials. In **Curiosity (13)**, the servant girl is peering over her mistress's shoulder to see what she is writing. What a complete contrast is Jan Steen's *Merry Company on a Terrace* to Ter Borch's decorous situations. Disorder, loud gaiety, and good humor resound in the painting, yet this artist, who has shown himself on the left holding a jug, composed the picture with great care and skill.

Landscape painting was another major category of Dutch painting. From the pioneer generation of landscapists, Pieter de Molyn, Jan van Goyen, and Salomon van Ruysdael are represented in the Metropolitan. More monumental are the landscapes of the next generation, such as *Wheatfields* by Jacob van Ruisdael, in which the massive cloud formations play as important a role as the detailed foreground of trees, fields, and lonely roads.

FRENCH PAINTING

Some French paintings of the 15th century are hung with the contemporary Flemish pictures. These include an important altarpiece done by an unknown French painter of the School of Avignon and a somewhat later one by Jean Bellegambe, who died in 1534. There is also an incisive portrait of the humanist Guillaume Budé, dating from about 1536, one of the very small group of extant paintings by Jean Clouet. A number of French paintings of the 16th century are displayed in the Museum's period rooms. But most of the rich collection is shown in the galleries of European paintings.

Seventeenth-century Classicism found its outstanding exponent in Nicolas Poussin. After studying in Paris, Poussin settled in Rome, where he spent almost all the rest of his life. His subjects were drawn from classical history and mythology, adapted to suit the noble character of his paintings. Even his landscapes contain small figures that supplied the subject matter for which the entire effect was created. *Midas Bathing in the River Pactolus*, one of his early works, reveals the influence of Titian in its poetic mood and mellow coloring. **The Rape of the Sabine Women (14)** is done in Poussin's mature style. It depicts the dramatic story of how Romulus, the legendary founder of Rome, populated the new city by kidnapping the women of the neighboring Sabine tribe.

Claude Lorrain, the other leading figure in French 17th-century painting, also spent most of his working life in Rome. He created a new type of landscape in which classically balanced designs are combined with subtle luminosity. *Sunrise* and *Roman Campagna* are two pictures in which his characteristically small and rather awkward figures are set against a low horizon in a receding landscape.

Georges de la Tour was a highly original 17th-century painter. A successful

14

artist in the provincial duchy of Lorraine, he was almost completely forgotten after his death and was revived only in our century. *The Fortune Teller* is one of his rare daylight scenes.

In 18th-century France many artists earned their livelihood making portraits of the aristocracy. Jean Marc Nattier was an eminently able painter who idealized his sitters to the point of foregoing their real features and personality. His double portrait, *Madame Marsollier and Her Daughter*, exemplifies his flattering manner. Sitters from the middle class posed for Joseph Siffred Duplessis, and even his aristocratic subjects had a bourgeois simplicity. *Benjamin Franklin*, when painted by Duplessis in 1778, was the rage of Paris society, yet the homespun honesty of this American ambassador is well conveyed. Jean Antoine Watteau's lyrical canvases epitomize the age of the Rococo, and it was his intimate and wistful style that set the tone for the rest of the century. The *commedia dell'arte*, a form of Italian theater, was embraced with enthusiasm by the 18th-century French, and Watteau delighted in representing characters and scenes from this form of entertainment. **Mezzetin (15)**, one of Watteau's finest paintings, shows a favorite character of the *commedia*—a confidential servant who always appeared in a striped costume.

One of the best representatives of the Rococo was François Boucher, a painter whose royal support permitted him to exert an almost dictatorial influence on French art of his day. An extremely successful artist, Boucher in his painting was always decorative, playful in mood, and elegant. *The Interrupted Sleep* and

15

The Toilet of Venus were both painted for Madame de Pompadour in 1750. In the latter, the pearly skin tone, jewels, and soft feathers of the doves combine into a delicately erotic picture.

Jean Siméon Chardin is famous for his still lifes and for his bourgeois scenes in which children often play a prominent role, such as *Boy Blowing Bubbles*. Like Chardin, Jean-Baptiste Greuze came from a modest background and worked in a style influenced by Dutch and Flemish masters of genre. His canvases, such as the Museum's *Broken Eggs*, often reflect the didactic moralizing of the period.

French society of Louis XVI's reign was elegantly portrayed by Jean-Honoré Fragonard, who, like Boucher, was a protégé of the court. His charming taste, usually joyous vein, and great technical freedom made him a brilliant interpreter of late 18th-century French society. In *The Love*

16

17

Letter there is an effect of suddenly arrested movement, as if the girl had been caught in the act of concealing a note to her lover.

Jacques-Louis David sided with the French Revolution and became the dictator of the new artistic taste. Rejecting the artificiality of the Rococo, he returned to a Classical style of painting. Classical statues and Roman bas-reliefs inspired **The Death of Socrates (16)**, a painting in which the Stoic philosopher is shown about to drink the hemlock poison that he has been condemned to take.

Jean-Auguste-Dominique Ingres became the acknowledged head of the Classical painters in the second quarter of the 19th century. Yet in his emphasis on purity and grace of line he differed markedly from his older colleagues. From 1806 Ingres lived in Rome and Florence for 18 years, and some of his fine portraits are of this period, notably those of *Joseph Antoine Moltedo*, dating about 1812, and of **Madame Leblanc (17)**, from 1823. Ingres's conception of style, which was based largely on draftsmanship, exerted a great influence on later painters. Gustave Moreau's *Oedipus and the Sphinx*, for instance, bears a general resemblance in composition to a famous painting of the same subject matter by Ingres.

Two paintings from the 1850s by two

18

very different artists show scenes of life in France: *The Horse Fair* by Rosa Bonheur is all movement and dramatic action; *Young Ladies from the Village* by Gustave Courbet is a serenely beautiful picture that the artist regarded as one of his most important works. Throughout his life, Courbet painted his native countryside in a realistic manner that shocked the critics and the public because of his completely unidealized way of presenting it. Courbet's *Woman with a Parrot* caused a scandal when it was exhibited in the Salon of 1866. Another *Woman with a Parrot* was painted by Edouard Manet in the same year and exhibited two years later. The attractive elongated figure in the pink dress was one of Manet's favorite models, who had posed as well for *Mademoiselle Victorine in the Costume of an Espada*. In 1874 Manet briefly adopted the approach to painting favored by the Impressionists; **Boating (18)** was done rapidly and retains the character of a sketch in its simplification of form. Its brilliance is partly due to the fact that, at the urging of Monet, it was painted out of doors.

The Museum has a fine collection of landscapes and figure paintings by Camille Corot, who is best known for his landscapes done in silvery-green tones with feathery trees. Corot shared his interest in nature with the Barbizon painters Jean François Millet, Théodore Rousseau, and particularly Charles François Daubigny, all of whom celebrated the beauties of the landscape near the village of Barbizon in the forest of Fontainebleau, and dignified in their works the simple tasks of peasants.

Paintings by the French Impressionists are one of the glories of the Metropolitan Museum. Claude Monet was the chief painter of the Impressionist movement, creating a system of reproducing what he saw with short brushstrokes that broke up form in an effort to achieve an effect of scintillant light and sensuous impressions. The vibrancy and intensity of his style are seen to fine advantage in his youthful **Terrace at Sainte-Adresse (19)**. Monet painted many other scenes of nature; he was a master at reproducing light and atmosphere, and in his famous series paintings he presented the same scene in different seasons and at different hours of the day.

Pierre-Auguste Renoir specialized in painting people, particularly women and children. A warm expression of intimacy and affection radiates from his imposing group portrait *Madame Charpentier and Her Children*. It was exhibited at the official Salon of 1879 and marked the beginning of Renoir's popularity. Edgar Degas's greatest talent lay in his knowledge of the human body and in his superb rendering of movement. Dancers on and off stage, musicians, figures at the race track, and milliners in their shops are

19

20

caught in exquisitely truthful moments. His **Woman with Chrysanthemums (20)** is a strangely asymmetrical composition, but the subject's unusual position in the picture intensifies the powerful effect of her personality.

Paul Cézanne was undoubtedly the most influential artist of the last half of the 19th century. At first he tried to give to Impressionism the order and discipline he felt it lacked. From the mid-80s he sought in every aspect of nature repeated forms and rhythms, and his can-

21

vases became geometrical and almost abstract, opening the way to Cubism and later abstract styles.

Although it is Cézanne who is usually associated with the southern part of France, other painters, notably Vincent van Gogh, were also inspired by the rugged landscape and color in Provence. Van Gogh lived for a brief time in Arles, reveling in the bright sunshine and expressing in brilliant paint and incisive drawing his feelings about the region and its people. His sitter for *L'Arlésienne (Madame Ginoux)* kept a café. After attacks of madness began, Van Gogh's style became increasingly violent. The Museum's *Irises* was painted in 1890, the year of his suicide.

Paul Gauguin also came under the influence of the Impressionists. Unsuccessful in Europe and pursuing a dream of the untrammeled life, he moved to Tahiti. **Ia Orana Maria (21)** (I hail thee, Mary) is a Tahitian Annunciation, with the heads of Mother and Child encircled by halos. *Two Tahitian Women* is a work in his late style.

FLEMISH AND GERMAN PAINTING

The great period of Flemish painting, the 15th century, was contemporary with the early Renaissance in Italy. The Museum has a particularly fine collection of early Flemings, a name derived from the province of Flanders that formed part of the Low Countries. Bruges, the capital of Flanders, was a port in the early 15th century and profited from the flourishing wool trade that was concentrated in that city. Other important commercial Flemish towns were Tournai, Ghent, and Antwerp. In all of these cities painters found eager patrons who commissioned portraits, altarpieces, and other religious works.

Jan van Eyck is credited with beginning the great tradition of Flemish painting. Careful observation of fine details and remarkable precision came to be distinguishing features of much of Flemish painting. The work of the Flemish artists is exhibited in a series of galleries, along with a few pictures by their French and Spanish contemporaries.

Few Flemish paintings are signed, making it often difficult to give correct attributions; thus the authorship of the **Crucifixion and Last Judgment (22)** has been much disputed, though Jan van Eyck is now believed to have painted them early in the 15th century. Originally both were wings of a triptych. The *Crucifixion* takes place in a natural world of clouds, snow-capped mountains, and towered walls and buildings; the people wear contemporary Flemish costumes

22

and the mourners display deep emotion. At a time when medieval symbolism and tradition still dominated art in Flanders, such a naturalistic scene was most unusual.

Petrus Christus was a slightly younger contemporary of Jan van Eyck. His *Annunciation* is an early work, clearly inspired by Van Eyck, to whom it was attributed for many years. The scene takes place outdoors in the midst of exquisitely painted plants, flowers, and countless other details. This was an unusual way to depict the *Annunciation*, a scene frequently shown in Flemish art with the Virgin's bedroom as its setting. A typical mature work by Christus is the *Lamentation over Christ*. The touching facial expressions and the radiant illumination of the sky and landscape reinforce the great emotional restraint and power of this tiny masterpiece.

The chief painter of the city of Brussels was Rogier van der Weyden. Trained by Robert Campin, whose Mérode Altarpiece can be seen at the The Cloisters, Van der Weyden established a trend in Flemish art very different from that of Van Eyck. In place of the serenity and naturalistic detail that Van Eyck stressed, Rogier emphasized psychological interpretation and mystical emotion conveyed by means of a tense and comparatively linear style. His **Christ Appearing to His Mother (23)** was the right wing of a triptych. Depicted here is a scene in which, according to legend, the risen Christ on Easter morning first visited His Mother. *Francesco d'Este*, of the prominent family from Ferrara, Italy, is immortalized in Rogier's distinguished portrait of him.

Dieric Bouts is represented in the

23

Metropolitan's collection by a tender *Virgin and Child*. The warmth of the relationship between Mother and Child, and their homely hands and features, are characteristic of this artist. His *Portrait of a Man*, showing a lined, introspective face, also reveals his great sensitivity.

One of the strongest artists who followed in the tradition of Rogier van der Weyden was Hugo van der Goes. His *Portrait of a Man* is a fragment cut out of a larger picture. In his last years Hugo, suffering from melancholy, entered the monastery of Roode Kloster; his brooding *Portrait of a Monk* may have depicted a member of the brotherhood.

Tommaso Portinari, the agent of the Medici banking house in Bruges, commissioned Hans Memling to paint his own and his wife's portrait, both of which are in the Museum. Memling was born in Germany but became a citizen of Bruges

24

and worked there most of his life. His colors and compositions are similar to those of Rogier van der Weyden, with whom he probably studied in Brussels. Memling's types, however, tend to be sweeter and their expressions more agreeable. Also by this artist are a *Portrait of an Old Man*, *Woman with a Pink*, and *Marriage of St. Catherine*.

The city of Bruges, in its last years of prosperity before Antwerp replaced it as the commercial and artistic center of the Low Countries, also employed Gerard David, a painter who had come from Holland. He brought with him a solid foundation of Dutch style, but in Flanders his painting soon became more opulent and richer in color. The small triptych with the *Nativity* is characteristic of his Dutch manner, and the delightful *Rest on the Flight to Egypt* shows his mature style.

Pieter Bruegel the Elder, though rooted in the Flemish tradition, developed a Renaissance attitude toward man and nature. In 1552 and 1553 he traveled in Italy and recorded his impressions in numerous drawings. Though others before him, notably Hieronymus Bosch and Joachim Patinir, had explored the possibilities of sweeping landscapes as backgrounds for human figures, it was Bruegel who perfected landscape painting as a joyous, almost pagan, setting for the trials and pleasures of man. In **The Harvesters (24)**, the artist set out to illustrate one of the labors of a particular month, probably July, when wheat is harvested. In this and four additional paintings from the same series, he observed in accurate detail the activities of peasants, set in vast landscapes that reach to the horizon, dominating mankind.

German painting, at first naïvely earnest and effective in its directness and simplicity, flourished with brilliance in the first half of the 16th century, the period of the High Renaissance in Italy. Lucas Cranach the Elder, a fine example of the German Renaissance man, was involved

25

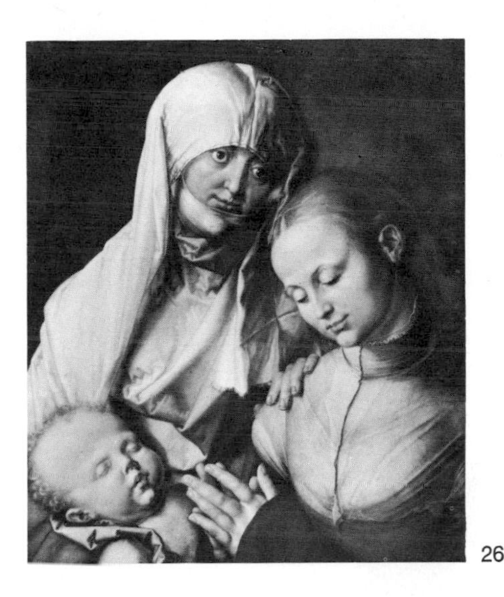

26

in many commercial and political pursuits. With the assistance of a large workshop, he also produced a huge number of paintings, engravings, and woodcuts. Cranach's works are charming, superbly finished paintings of mythological and classical subjects, such as **Judgment of Paris (25)**. The three goddesses, Juno, Minerva, and Venus, are coquettish nudes waiting for Paris, here a stolid German knight, to decide which one is the most beautiful. The portrait of *John, Duke of Saxony*, is an example of his paintings of the prominent people for whom he worked, especially the electors and dukes of Saxony.

It was Albrecht Dürer, a contemporary of Cranach, who was the most notable figure of this period and one of the first artists outside of Italy to become internationally famous. He traveled twice to Italy for the express purpose of studying Italian art and its new theories. His **Virgin and Child with St. Anne (26)** shows the three generations of the Holy Family grouped together in an expression of a traditional German theme. St. Anne, the mother of the Virgin, is thought to be an idealized likeness of the artist's wife.

Another prominent personality of the northern Renaissance and one of the world's great portrait painters was Hans Holbein the Younger. Born in Germany, he became a citizen of Basel and worked there for many years. He was persuaded to visit England and on his second trip settled permanently there, becoming the court painter of Henry VIII. He portrayed everyone of importance at the time, from the king himself to the English courtiers, as well as visiting dignitaries from foreign countries. His fine sense of composition, his use of color, and his faultless draftsmanship bestow marked distinction on **A Member of the**

Wedigh Family (27), done in 1532. The aristocratic and rather prim *Lady Lee (Margaret Wyatt)* was one of his English sitters.

By the 17th century the northern provinces of the Low Countries, zealously guarding their Protestant rights, had broken away from the south, and Dutch independence was proclaimed under the House of Orange. In the south, Flanders, under the domination of Spain, remained Catholic. Its art, robustly Baroque in style, was brought to a brilliant summit by Peter Paul Rubens. His work, as well as that of his somewhat younger contemporaries Anthony van Dyck and Jacob Jordaens, is exhibited in several adjoining galleries. The eight years that Rubens spent in Italy at the beginning of his career formed the foundations of his style. Well-educated and courtly, he was made the official painter to the Spanish governors of Flanders. So many commissions for paintings came to Rubens that he established a large workshop of pupils and assistants in Antwerp. His tremendous output included many pictures designed by him but finished by helpers; others appear to be almost entirely by the master's own hand, as in the case of the Museum's **Venus and Adonis (28)**, from the last decade of his life. This is one of his many mythological paintings that narrates a story in a remarkably vigorous style; Venus is imploring her lover, Adonis, not to leave for his last hunt for she, as goddess, knows that he will be killed. The sensuousness and vitality of the scene and the wonderfully painted flesh colors are characteristic of Rubens's pictures. Ancient Roman splendor marks *The Triumph of Henry IV*, a preparatory oil sketch for one of the paintings commissioned by Marie de' Medici.

After Rubens, Van Dyck was the most famous of the Flemish 17th-century painters. An assistant of Rubens in

27

28

Antwerp, he learned much from his master but evolved a sensitive style of his own. In London he became court painter to King Charles I. *James Stuart, Duke of Richmond and Lennox* was a cousin of the king, and in Van Dyck's portrait of him, the noble dog emphasizes the young man's commanding presence. The artist's elegant and refined manner of painting admirably suited his courtly subjects and left a lasting influence on portrait painters throughout the world.

SPANISH PAINTING

Except for a small group of early Spanish paintings from the 14th and 15th centuries, the earliest major figure of the Spanish School in the Metropolitan's collection is El Greco. He came from the island of Crete and often signed his pictures in Greek with his real name, Domenicos Theotocopoulos. After studying in Rome and Venice he moved to Spain, and sometime before 1577 settled in Toledo where he spent the rest of his life. He worked principally for the Church. His portrait of *Cardinal Don Fernando Niño de Guevara* gives a shrewd and penetrating characterization of this ecclesiastical dignitary who held the office of Grand Inquisitor. The **View of Toledo (29)** and *The Vision of St. John* are both charged with emotional intensity. The *View of Toledo*, his only true landscape, has a lowering sky and an eerily lit foreground; in it he has not hesitated to rearrange the buildings for a more dramatic composition.

Francisco de Zurbarán, Jusepe de Ribera, and Diego Rodríguez Velázquez were all born in the last decade of the 16th century and, with the somewhat younger Bartolomé Esteban Murillo, constitute a group of the greatest Spanish artists. Zurbarán's austere and personal style characterizes his large picture *The Battle with the Moors at Jerez*, in which the Virgin Mary intercedes to strengthen the Christians in a decisive battle against the Moors. *The Young Virgin*, by the same painter, shows an equally characteristic aspect of his style. Zurbarán delighted in creating intimate settings for his representations of holy people, surrounding them with still lifes of homely objects and flowers.

29

Ribera was born in Spain but did most of his work in Italy for the Spanish rulers and the Church in Naples. Italian influences and the deep impression made on him by the work of Caravaggio never obliterated the basically Spanish qualities of his art. His *Holy Family with St. Catherine*, which he painted in 1648, shows the combination of dignity and human tenderness that are typical of his late works.

Murillo worked mostly at Seville in

30

southern Spain, and he is best known for his popular religious paintings, which were multiplied in countless sentimental repetitions by less able painters. *The Virgin and Child* shows as much strength as sweetness, and exhibits the artist's fine sense of formal composition and his rich color. He also was an excellent portraitist, which is evident in the pair of standing full-length likenesses of two Spanish contemporaries.

Both of the early paintings by Velázquez are part of the Altman Collection. *The Supper at Emmaus*, with its strong chiaroscuro and its heavy textures, was painted in Seville before the artist went to work at the court of Madrid. The full-length *Philip IV* was probably made in Velázquez's workshop and strongly resembles in most details a similarly composed painting of the king in the Prado Museum. The portrait of **Juan de Pareja (30)** is a masterpiece painted in his superb mature style. It was executed in Rome in 1650, just at the time of the wonderful, but more formal, portrait of *Pope Innocent X*. Pareja, a painter himself, was Velázquez's assistant and traveling companion, whom he evidently held in affectionate regard. Ever since the portrait was first displayed to the Roman public at the Pantheon, it has astounded spectators by its vitality and lifelike appearance.

Francisco Goya in his life and career straddled the end of the courtly 18th century and the first quarter of the 19th, in which modern history and modern art had their beginnings. The Museum's paintings by him include works from both of these periods. The portrait of his friend *Don Sebastián Martínez*, lawyer and pa-

31

tron of art, is distinguished by the delicacy and urbanity of Goya's 18th-century style, as is the portrait of the *Infanta María Luisa.* In the portrait of the architect *Don Tiburcio Pérez*, Goya has shown his friend in shirt sleeves with the informal power that is prophetic of later 19th-century painting. One of the Museum's most popular pictures is Goya's painting of *Don Manuel Osorio* with his magpie and three menacing cats. In **Majas on a Balcony (31)**, the artist presents with scintillant brushwork and color two *majas*—attractive young women of Spain—accompanied by a pair of hooded escorts.

ENGLISH PAINTING

Early British pictures are shown in the Museum's period rooms. Eighteenth-century painting consisted largely of portraiture. Although the country remained somewhat apart from the artistic mainstream on the Continent, British painters traveled abroad, especially in Italy, studying Roman antiquities and the Renaissance masters. Rubens's style was much admired in England, particularly as transmitted by Van Dyck.

One of William Hogarth's earliest known works is *The Wedding of Stephen Beckingham and Mary Cox*, painted in 1729. The slim, elegantly dressed figures in the architectural setting of a famous London church have little to do with the later satiric style for which Hogarth is celebrated.

Sir Joshua Reynolds, perhaps the most influential of the British portraitists, is well represented in the Museum's collection. As the first president of the Royal Academy he held a position of importance among artists and the best of London's

32

society. He and his contemporary Thomas Gainsborough depicted a world of aristocratic leisure in bucolic settings. An individual's features were important, of course, but equally so were his social standing and rank. *Colonel George K. H. Coussmaker*, so wonderfully portrayed by Reynolds, wears the dashing uniform of his regiment and leans at ease against his highly bred horse. *The Honorable Henry Fane* shows a young and attractive aristocrat. The low horizon in so many of these portraits serves the purpose of enlarging and silhouetting the human figure.

Gainsborough's fashionable portraits, based in part on Van Dyck, are represented here by the full-length painting of the haughty and beautiful **Mrs. Grace Dalrymple Elliott (32)**. Her many admirers

33

included the Prince of Wales; he is thought to have been the father of her little daughter, Georgiana Frederica Seymour, whose portrait by Reynolds is also in the Museum. Gainsborough, himself versed in music, painted a sympathetic picture of the musician *Charles Rousseau Burney*. The artist's landscapes are poetic interpretations of the English countryside.

Sir Thomas Lawrence was one of Reynolds's most brilliant and successful pupils. His portrait of the charming actress *Elizabeth Farren* was done in 1790 when the artist was 21. It made his reputation and laid the foundations of a style that he used for over 40 years. The spirited beauty of the Queen of Comedy, caught in this alluring pose, is wonderfully conveyed. Children were also favorite subjects for English commissions. Two particularly appealing groups are *The Calmady Children* by Lawrence and *The Drummond Children* by Sir Henry Raeburn, a popular Scottish painter. Raeburn also did the Museum's portrait of these children's father, leaning on the well-curried rump of his horse.

In the first decades of the 19th century John Constable brought British landscape painting to a new level of perfection. His *Tottenham Church* and *Salisbury Cathedral* are two examples in which his luminous style and careful detail are beautifully displayed. Joseph Mallord William Turner, however, was not concerned with reproducing precisely what he saw. In **Grand Canal, Venice (33)**, painted in 1835 at the height of his career, he suggests the hazy atmosphere of the city by diffusing light, minimizing shadows, and recreating reflections of buildings.

The Pre-Raphaelite movement, initiated by a group of painters and writers in the mid-19th century, aimed at a revival in the arts of early Italian Renaissance ideals. Dante Gabriel Rossetti, one of the founders of the Brotherhood, depicted the wife of another important member of the group, *Mrs. William Morris.*

Far Eastern Art

Far Eastern Art

Objects, Periods, Styles	Numbers in Text
ALTAR SHRINES	(26)
BRONZES	(16), (17), (45), (47), (52)
CENTRAL ASIAN ART	(53)
CERAMICS	(1-15), (42)
CHINESE ART	(1-35)
INDIAN ART	(44-49)
JADES	(18), (19)
JAPANESE ART	(36-43)
JEWELRY	
LACQUER WARE	(20), (43)
NEPALESE, KASHMIRI, KOREAN, KHMER ART	(51), (52)
PAINTINGS: mural, scrolls, album leaves, tankas	(00-00)
SCULPTURE and RELIEFS	(21-25), (27-32), (41), (44-49), (52), (53)
SCREENS	(39), (40)
TEXTILES and COSTUMES	
TIBETAN ART	(50)

Chinese Chronology

Shang	1523-1028 B.C.
Chou	1027-221 B.C.
Ch'in	221-206 B.C.
Han	206-220 A.D.
Six Dynasties	220-589
Sui	581-618
T'ang	618-906
Five Dynasties	907-960
Liao	907-1125
Sung	960-1279
Chin	1115-1234
Yüan (Mongols)	1279-1368
Ming	1368-1644
Ch'ing	1644-1912
Republic of China	1912-
People's Republic of China	1949-

☞ **This page helps you to find what you especially want to see and read about.**

Far Eastern Art

The Far Eastern Art Department officially came into being in 1915, when S. C. Bosch-Reitz was appointed curator. He took over an already established collection of Chinese and Japanese ceramics, jades, paintings, sculpture, and lacquer ware. In subsequent years, substantial additions were made to the department, which now covers a time span from the 2nd millennium B.C. through the 19th century A.D. and comprises art objects from China, Japan, Korea, and a small but choice collection of Indian and Southeast Asian sculpture. Its total holdings number some 30,000 items, including prints and textiles, which are housed in the Print Department and the Textile Study Room respectively. Because of the exigencies of gallery space, only some major pieces are on exhibition. Other sections of the collection will be reinstalled as new plans for the north wing become a reality.

CHINA: Ceramics

Ceramics are one of the glories of Chinese art, and Chinese ceramic history, spanning a period of over 4,000 years, has a continuity rarely found elsewhere. The Metropolitan Museum has a splendid collection of wares from which one can trace the changes and development of this art form; unfortunately only a small percentage can be on view at any one time.

The earliest objects in the collection are the distinctive products of two Neolithic cultures that existed throughout the Yellow River area of China from around 2000 to 1523 B.C. Each of these cultures was named for the type-site where the cultural remains were first excavated and the dominant color of its distinctive ware. The Yang-shao culture is best known for its reddish bowls and jars with boldly painted designs **(1)**, examples of which can be seen in the Museum (accession numbers 27.31, 50.61.4, 60.81.1, and 50.61.3). The most typical product of the Lung-shan culture, probably slightly later in date than the Yang-shao, is a black pottery **(2)** of surprising refinement (50.61.2).

3

Although bronzes were the glory of the Shang Dynasty (1523-1028 B.C.), pottery continued to be made, and the potter often catered to the tastes of the day by making a "poor man's bronze," that is, pottery and earthenware vessels of a fine burnished gray or black ware, made in the shapes of the more expensive bronze bowls and vases. Two vases modeled after bronze prototypes, such as the **jar (3)** illustrated here, can be seen in the collection.

In the Chou Dynasty, the second re-

corded (1027-256 B.C.), shapes imitating bronze vessels continued in favor. A gray high-footed pottery bowl and cover (*tou*) **(4)** is clearly an adaptation of a bronze shape and retains some of its original polychrome pigments (50.61.9). In the years leading from the Chou Dynasty to the succeeding Han Dynasty, feldspathic glazes were developed to a point at which they can be considered the beginning of a long line of green-glazed wares. One of these is the ring-handled jar **(5)** with incised design (50.61.10), which shows remnants of its original glaze.

In 206 B.C. China was united under the Western Han Dynasty. The earlier practice of burying possessions, live animals, and even people with the dead had given way to symbolic interment. Many ceramic vessels—unglazed, painted, or with a lead silicate glaze—have been found in Han Dynasty graves. The Museum's various jars with green lead glaze have assumed a luminous irridescence due to their

6

7

many years underground, and some are almost silver today. A small unglazed earthenware **incense burner (6)** has molded scenes of men hunting among the hills, highlighted in pigments.

The Han Dynasty continued with one slight interruption until A.D. 220, when China once again splintered into many small principalities, a period usually inaccurately referred to as the Six Dynasties, after the six kingdoms that had made their capital at Nanking. A complex of kilns near Yüeh Chou (modern Shaohsing) in Chekiang Province made the famous Yüeh wares, which were now a true "green ware." The splendid **vessel (7)** in the Museum, in the shape of a crouching animal, shows sophisticated modeling.

In 581 China entered one of her great periods of unity and development, first under the Sui, then in 618 under the T'ang Dynasty. This was one of the most dynamic times in Chinese history. Ceramic forms showed a great vitality and variety, often reflecting the influence of Western countries, with which T'ang China was in constant touch. Feldspathic and lead silicate glazes were used with equal success, and a blue-glazed small jar (23.180.3) and a plate with birds and

10

14

flowers (14.66) in the Museum's collection are especially fine **(8)**. Particularly the manufacture of tomb figures **(9)** flourished, and the opulence of such figures, like the marvelous tomb guardian *lokapala* (11.83.1), was in direct proportion to the importance the deceased had enjoyed in life.

By the early 10th century China was once again divided into many small states, and the period from 906 to 960 is generally called the Five Dynasties. At this time the Yüeh kilns produced some of the finest wares of their history. Much of this production was called *pi-se-yao*, or prohibited, ware, meaning that such vases and bowls were reserved for the use of the princes of Wu-Yüeh at Hangchow. One of the most famous ceramics in the Museum's collection is an example of this 10th-century ware—the large **grayish-green bowl (10)** with three spirited dragons sporting on the inside.

The establishment of the Sung Dynasty in A.D. 960 marked the beginning of what many consider the classic period of Chinese ceramics. The country was unified, enjoying an era of prosperity, and the mood of quiet elegance that prevailed at the court was reflected in the refined Sung ware **(11)**. Shape and glaze were all important, as shown by the marblelike blue glaze of the *kuan* (imperial) dish with metal rim (24.172.1). When decoration was employed, it always complemented the total effect but never domi-

12

nated it, as in one of the great treasures of the collection—the northern celadon wine pot (26.292.73). Equally lovely, each in its own special way, are the products of the other major Sung kiln centers: the magnolia-white Ting ware bowl (26.292.98); the Chün ware cup, unusual in its crackle (18.56.44); the "bubble bowl" of northern provenance with its "oil spot" glaze (60.81.5); the fine representative of the Tz'u-chou class of stonewares, the *mei-p'ing* vase (26.292.61), and the *ch'ing-pai* (blue-white) pillow supported by the figure of a reclining woman (26.292.82). Probably the most impressive ceramics in the Museum's collection are the bigger-than-life-size pottery **statues of Lohans (12)**, glazed in shades of cream, brown, and dark green. These two disciples of Buddha are seated cross-legged on a slab of rock; the origin of these figures is obscure.

15

Sweeping down from the north, the Mongols engulfed the Chinese and established the Yüan Dynasty in 1279. Within a relatively short period of time Chinese ceramics were being manufactured to suit the rather ostentatious tastes of the new rulers. The subtle decorative effects of the Sung ceramics were replaced by bolder, more aggressive designs. Typical of this era are the bluish-white vase (23.182.1) with its fine incised scroll, and the high-shouldered Tz'u-chou ware vase with its enthusiastically painted motifs (26.292.53). New to the Yüan period was the technique of painting porcelains with cobalt oxide under the glaze to produce designs in blue and white. This manner of decoration, which was to remain preeminent in Chinese porcelains to the present, is exemplified in Yüan Dynasty wares **(13)** by the fine *mei-p'ing* vase and cover in the Museum (26.271.1).

After the fall of the Yüan Dynasty, the native Ming Dynasty was established in 1368. The difficult technique of copper red decoration on white porcelain ground under a transparent glaze is well represented in the Museum's large bowl (18.56.35). The ample blue and white **storage jar (14)** is decorated with a fierce dragon.

The Ch'ing Dynasty, from 1644 to 1912, a period of technical virtuosity in Chinese porcelains, is the one most familiar to Westerners. The Museum's large collection includes the splendid bequests of Benjamin Altman and John D. Rockefeller, Jr.; from the latter comes the fine pair of figures of the **God of Wealth (15)**, here illustrated in his civil aspect.

16

Every manner of decoration is represented; for the sake of classification the pieces decorated in polychrome are organized according to the predominating color, and are called by the French terms *famille verte*, *famille noire*, *famille jaune*, and *famille rose*. For the monochromes, *sang de boeuf* is an ox-blood red; *clair de lune* an extremely pale blue; and the highly prized "peach bloom" porcelain has a delicate rosy glaze.

CHINA: Bronze and Jade

The ritual bronze vessels of the Shang and Early Chou cultures (2nd and 1st millennia B.C.) are among the greatest treasures of China's long artistic history. Indeed it can be said that the Shang bronzes are the most refined product of any Bronze Age culture. The technical brilliance of the bronze casting, the inventive ornamentation, the refinement of their conception and form, and the importance of the inscriptions that some of them bear place these objects in a unique position in the artistic world.

The **ritual vessel (16)** in *kuang* form is an outstanding example from the late Shang Dynasty. The design motifs are raised in relief against a background of spirals; a bird, whose wings are transformed into serpents, is shown under the projecting mouth of the vessel. Fish, masks, and dragons ornament the body, and the handle is in the shape of a horned bird standing on a fish.

The 14 objects of the **Tuan Fang altar**

17

set (17) show a variety of shapes. The entire group, including an altar table, is extraordinary for its completeness as well as for the quality of the individual pieces and the wealth of the motifs. Objects from the Chou Dynasty illustrate a later phase in the long development of Chinese bronzes. One spherical vessel with intricate openwork is supported on three legs; birds and other decoration ornament it. An ovoid wine vessel is a rare example of a ritual bronze inlaid with copper ornamentation.

Jade was highly valued by the Chinese as the most precious of stones, and it was used for artistic purposes for nearly 4,000 years. Jade was treasured for the quality of the stone—its extreme hardness and rarity; for its many colors, from white to all shades of yellow, green, and brown; and also for the virtuosity required of the lapidaries who carved the stone with consummate skill, taking advantage of the texture and color shadings to create the desired object.

The Heber R. Bishop jade collection was a gift to the Museum in 1902. The approximately 1,000 pieces include archaeological objects, such as implements and weapons. Art objects, mainly from China, form by far the largest group—early jade amulets and, from a later age, snuff bottles, articles for the writing table, dress ornaments, dishes, incense burners, wine cups, and many purely decorative objects. An 18th-century disk or screen depicts in high relief **Bodhidharma Crossing the Waves on a Reed (18)**, illustrating a favorite legend about the Buddhist monk.

The Museum's holdings of jade (exclusive of the Bishop jade collection) include an outstanding pair of stags, dating from the Chou Dynasty, and a handsome carved *pi*, or symbol of heaven, from the Late Chou period. A large number of small hardstone objects, implements, amulets, archers' rings, as well as ornamental objects, form part of the collection **(19)**.

18

Also included in the department are Chinese lacquers **(20)**, in particular a rare and fine rice measure—a square box with flaring sides carved with mythological figures. The vessel is marked Chia Ching and is considered to be of that period (1522-1566).

CHINA: Sculpture

The department has an excellent collection of Chinese sculpture. Buddhism

21

came to China from its native India in about the 1st century A.D. As the religion increased in complexity, the Buddhist pantheon expanded to include a host of deities, Buddhas, and bodhisattvas—the Buddhas-to-be who one day will return and save mankind. The impact of this religion inspired and dominated Chinese artistic works for centuries. In fact, the majority of existing sculpture is Buddhist. Huge complexes of cave temples, such as the Yun-kang and Lung-men sites in China, were evidence of the religious fervor that swept China. The Museum is fortunate in having splendid examples of the sculpture from the cave temples.

The 5th-century Maitreyas from Yun-kang reflect Central Asian influences in their pose but are assimilated within the Chinese style. **Maitreya (21)** was a devoutly worshiped bodhisattva. The body forms a diamond shape, extending from the head to the arms and knees, and ending at the crossed ankles. Typical also are the long, square face, almond eyes, and archaic smile. The gesture of the deity's right hand denotes absence of fear, that of the left, fulfilling of the vow. To the devoted worshiper, these statues served as symbols of aloofness from worldly ambitions and desires.

From the Lung-men series of caves, in Honan Province, comes a near-life-size

23

25

the limestone slab are also ornamented with figures and conventionalized plant, bird, and animal forms.

The "Trübner" stele **(24)** in the Museum, bearing an inscription with the dates 533-543, is an elaborate composition with more than 50 figures. The central register depicts a scene from one of the Buddhist scriptures, the debate between the bodhisattva of wisdom, Wen Shu, and the rich sage Wei-mo-chi.

One of the largest and possibly most important Northern Wei images that has survived is a gilt bronze figure of the **Standing Buddha (25)**, on a lotus pedestal, with arms outstretched; draperies fall in swirling folds that delineate the body. An inscription around the base bears the date 477. An elaborate, shimmering **Buddhist altar shrine (26)**

limestone relief of male donors, the emperor, accompanied by his entourage wearing official hats and costumes, paying tribute to the Buddha **(22)**. It is one of China's most renowned monuments and dates from the early 6th century. This relief shows a painter's approach to sculpture, with the garments forming a decorative pattern.

A **Buddhist stele (23)** from the Northern Wei Dynasty, 5th-6th century, has three holy figures as the compelling central theme, a Buddha flanked by two bodhisattvas. The rigid, stern figures project from the background in bold relief. Other figures, dragons, and flame-shaped halos fill the stone in a beautiful and rich low-relief pattern. The back and the sides of

26

28

of gilt bronze, dated 524, can be considered a fine example of the mature Wei style. The central figure is Maitreya, the Buddha of the future. A pair of donors, bodhisattvas, and apsarases, or heavenly dancing attendants playing musical instruments, surround the figure and the flame halo in this beautifully composed, delicate shrine.

A colossal, 14-foot-tall bodhisattva **(27)** from Shansi Province towers above most of the other Chinese statues exhibited in the Museum. A fine example of the monumental Ch'i style, the columnlike figure with its crisp carving is very dignified, the face haughtily impressive, and the pose of the body rigid and ceremonious.

From the T'ang Dynasty comes a rare dry lacquer figure of a **Seated Buddha (28)**, one of the few such sculptures that have survived. The technique calls for numerous layers of lacquer-soaked cloth, which are modeled over a wooden armature into the desired thickness and form and finally painted with gesso, polychrome, and gilt. The figures were light and were often carried in religious processions. Also from the T'ang Dynasty, considered by many to be one of the great ages of Chinese art, is the beautiful **Head of a Bodhisattva (29)**. This gray sandstone head, from the temples of T'ien-lung Shan, is typical of the expressive, luxuriant style of the 8th century. A great black marble stele **(30)** with two bodhisattvas, Ta Shih Chih and Kuan Yin, is also from this time. The rigidity of the earlier Buddhist figures is replaced by a naturalistic modeling of the bodies, which have been given a posture often found in Indian sculpture, three subtle bends.

Beginning with the T'ang Dynasty, the bodhisattva Kuan Yin became the most popular and most worshiped figure in the Buddhist pantheon. He is represented in many forms, since he performed his miracles in various guises. The Museum has three seated wooden bodhisattva figures from the Sung Dynasty, two of **Kuan Yin (31)**. The faces are serene and contemplative, the bodies suggest a living being seated in a relaxed yet elegant pose. A little of the original polychrome is still visible. The same deity is depicted in a charming figure from a later date **(32)**; this sculpture is important because it bears a date in concordance with 1282, throwing light on styles in the Yüan Dynasty. Characteristic are the long oval-shaped face, the schematically arranged

29

31

hair, and the mode of drapery folds.

CHINA: Painting

A monumental Buddhist mural **(33)** is installed in the Arthur M. Sackler Gallery. A splendid example of the work of artists who painted in the Fen River area in Shansi Province, in the late 13th and early 14th centuries, this wall painting of a Buddhist assembly came from a monastery in the southwestern part of the province. A large figure of Buddha is the central image, and around him are placed in fairly symmetrical order two major bodhisattvas and many other divine, mythological, and symbolic figures. Painted by craftsmen and their apprentices, such murals were never intended to rival the masterpieces of scroll painting of the same period but were designed rather for the illiterate believer, serving as a background for the various pieces of sculpture that were the principal objects of devotion. The drawing in this great mural, though lacking in depth, is marvelously decorative. Though it is impossible to identify with certainty all the many figures, the complicated symbolism of this mural had a profound meaning.

Chinese paintings have been a part of the Far Eastern collection since 1902. Although China's painting tradition dates far back, the Museum's collection ranges from the Sung Dynasty (960-1279) through the Ch'ing Dynasty (1644-1912). Perhaps the best-known Chinese painting in the

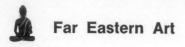

34

Museum is **The Tribute Horse (34)**, done in ink and colors on silk and dating from the Sung Dynasty, in which especially landscape painting flourished under the stimulus of enlightened patronage. Here a riderless horse heads a colorful procession of horsemen and their mounts, all richly decked with masks, helmets, and banners. Another important Chinese painting is a segment of a Buddhist holy text, the Vimalakirti sutra **(35)**; it bears a date in concordance with A.D. 1116 or 1118. The hand scroll, illuminated in gold, silver, and color on silk, depicts the meeting of Vimalakirti (Wei-mo-chi) and the god of wisdom, Manjusri (Wen Shu) who is seated on his vehicle, the lion. Landscapes, religious and mythological subjects, and figure, animal, and bird paintings are among the topics of the hanging scrolls, hand scrolls, and album leaves that comprise the Chinese painting collection.

JAPAN

Chinese culture, including the arts, exerted a profound influence on that of the Japanese, but during the Heian period (794-1185) Japan emerged with its own native art styles. Two hand scrolls in the Museum are from the Heian period and illuminate sections of the Lotus sutra with a pictorial opening scene on each scroll **(36)**. From the succeeding Kamakura period, 1185 to 1333, comes a very fine painting, a hand scroll of the *Miracles of*

38

40

Kannon **(37)**; scenes depicting the power of this god of mercy, who is the Japanese Kuan Yin, are interspersed with 33 texts describing his many miracles. A great hanging scroll from the same period shows the Buddhist deity **Aizen Myo-o (38)**, the god of lust and avarice, seated on a lotus pedestal with five of his six hands holding his attributes.

The following Muromachi period (1392-1568) saw a resurgence of Chinese influence on Japanese painting. A pair of six-fold screens by Soami shows how the Japanese artist rendered a landscape scene of the four seasons with soft brush strokes using only ink on paper.

From 1573 to 1615, in the Momoyama period, the war lords assumed supremacy. During this time of peace and prosperity a more flamboyant style prevailed—bold color on gold ground—that was especially suitable to movable screens; these decorated the lavish castles and palaces built at this time. The Museum's screen collection is especially rich. A pair of six-fold screens **(39)**, depicting the insurrection of the Hogen and Heiji eras, gives a bird's-eye view of the famous battles; sliding doors and roofs are miraculously open so that one can see the action both inside and outside the palace, with some of the figures in violent motion.

Perhaps the best-known screen in the collection is **The Wave (40)**, by Ogata Korin (1658-1716). Almost an abstraction, this dynamic and bold design, with gold and blue predominating, nevertheless embodies the Japanese kinship with nature. Also from the Rimpa, or Decorative, School, of which Korin was a leading painter, comes the superb pair of Iris Screens with brilliant blue-purple

45

46

flowers and green foliage on gold ground.

The Japanese sculpture collection **(41)** is small. Of note is a carved wooden figure of Dainichi Nyorai, one of the Buddhas of the Shingon sect; seated in a pose of meditation, the serene figure is surrounded by an elaborately carved halo, which is in marked contrast to the simplicity of the figure. There are other religious representations, particularly of Kannon. A lacquered wood portrait of a Zen priest, from the Muromachi period, is realistic in its conception.

The Japanese ceramics collection **(42)** contains an example of Yayoi pottery, a rare type of earthenware, dating from between 300 B.C. and A.D. 100. An offering jar of Sue ware from the 3rd-4th century A.D. is decorated with sculptured, incised, and cut ornamentation and has miniature libation cups around the shoulder, as well as human and animal figures. There are also later, more refined porcelains—Kutani, Nabeshima, Kakiemon ware—and some fine Raku tea bowls so prized by the Japanese.

Objects of lacquer **(43)** include writing boxes, trays, picnic containers, and a sizable collection of *inro*; these small carrying cases, usually of several compartments held together by a cord and hung over a gentleman's belt, were used to carry medicines, sweets, etc., and were often delicately decorated in gold, mother-of-pearl, and other materials.

INDIA

In India the prime influences on its sculpture were its two great religions, Buddhism and Hinduism. The historical Buddha, Prince Siddhartha, was born in the

6th century B.C., and from his preachings grew one of the world's great religions. Representations of the Buddha image did not appear until about the beginning of the Christian era, when there also emerged a Buddhist hierarchy of bodhisattvas and other deities. One such image of a bodhisattva **(44)** is a magnificent head and torso from the Gandhara region in northern India dating from the 1st-3rd century A.D.; this sculpture clearly shows the Roman influence on native Indian sculptural styles. Other Gandharan pieces in the collection illustrate scenes from the life of Buddha.

In the Gupta period a truly international style spread beyond the confines of India. The Museum's golden bronze **Standing Figure of Buddha (45)** represents the very best of what many consider to be India's high point in sculpture. The simple monastic robe clings in the typical Gupta "wet draped" fashion and reveals the outline of the body. After the Gupta period Buddhism declined and there was a resurgence of Hinduism.

Hinduism was a complex and widespread faith that dominated the huge Indian continent over various periods of time beginning more than 3,000 years ago. Its pantheon or basic trinity consisted of Shiva, the destroyer; Vishnu, the preserver; and Brahma, the creator; plus a host of lesser deities that had evolved from earlier cults. The Metropolitan's collection of Indian sculpture contains examples of the Hindu trinity. **Shiva Nataraja (46)** in his role as Lord of the Dance is shown surrounded by a flame halo, performing his cosmic dance, which symbolized the destruction of the universe and its renewal. A four-armed Vishnu of bronze **(47)** holds a flaming disk and conch shell in his upper two hands, while the lower right is in the "fear not" gesture. Brahma is present as a four-headed stone sculpture **(48)**. All these pieces from the South Indian School date from about the 10th century A.D., when the Chola Dynasty united the south of India.

49

The famous temples on the east coast of India, in the state of Orissa, were built from the 8th to the 13th century. From one of these temple complexes comes a characteristic stone fragment of a **Mithuna Couple (49)**, joyfully embracing each

52

other under a curved tree branch. Erotic themes were a facet of Hinduism found in many temple carvings. The style reached its high point in the 12th-13th century, and the Museum's couple probably comes from this period.

TIBET, NEPAL, KASHMIR, KOREA, AND CENTRAL ASIA

Buddhism, in a much modified and complex form, dominated the art of Tibet as well **(50)**. Religious paintings, or *tankas*, attest to this country's devout and unique conception of Buddhism, and the Museum has some 18th-century *tankas* that give vivid evidence of this religious zeal. Small sculptures, mostly gilt bronze, of Buddhist deities attest to the complexity of the Lamaist or Tibetan Buddhist pantheon. Beautiful necklaces, earrings, and hair ornaments were intricately made and often inlaid with precious and semiprecious stones of dazzling color.

Also forming part of the Far Eastern collection are small pieces of sculpture and jewelry from Nepal, Kashmir, and Korea **(51)**. From the last-named country come some fine pieces of ceramics and a huge and impressive painting depicting a bodhisattva with attendants, dating probably from the 14th century. In addition, there are some fine examples of the art of the Khmers, a Cambodian civilization that lasted approximately from the 9th to the 15th century and had a distinctive sculptural style. A piece that predates the construction of the famous Khmer temples at Angkor is a standing four-armed **figure of Avalokitesvara (52)** in bronze, with eyes inlaid with silver and stones; it dates probably from the 7th to the 9th century. From the Dvaravati kingdom, which preceded the Siamese kingdom, comes another Buddha figure, a standing bronze icon from about the 10th century.

Among a small group of sculptures, mostly stucco, from Central Asia, two pieces are outstanding. A wood traveling shrine with a central figure of Buddha carved in relief and set in a niche probably dates from the 6th century; it shows strong Gandharan influence in style. From the Rawak burial site in the Taklamakan desert comes a superb stucco head of Buddha **(53)**, with traces of polychrome. The serene face splendidly conveys the great power and compassion of Buddha.

Greek and Roman Art

Greek and Roman Art

Objects, Periods, Styles	Numbers in Text
ARCHAIC PERIOD (Greek)	(10-13)
BRONZES: Greek, Etruscan, Roman	(8), (12), (18), (23), (27), (28), (30)
CLASSIC PERIOD	(18-21)
CYCLADIC ART	(2), (3)
CYPRIOT ART	(4)
ETRUSCAN ART	(27), (28)
GEMS and SEALS	
GEOMETRIC PERIOD (Greek)	(7), (8)
GLASS: Greek and Roman	(34)
GRAVE MONUMENTS and RELIEFS	(11), (21), (22)
HELLENISTIC AGE	(23-26)
JEWELRY: Greek, Cypriot, Etruscan, Roman	
METALWORK: gold and silver	(26)
MINOAN and MYCENAEAN ART	(5), (6)
POTTERY and TERRA COTTAS: Attic geometric, black figure, red figure, Corinthian, Boeotian, South Italian, Etruscan, Roman	(6), (7), (9), (13-17), (28)
ROMAN ART: Portrait sculpture, sarcophagi, wall paintings, mosaic, glass, jewelry	(29-34)
ROMAN BEDROOM (Cubiculum)	(33)
SARDIS COLUMN	(1)

This page helps you to find what you especially want to see and read about.

Greek and Roman Art

The history of Greek and Roman art in the Metropolitan Museum dates from the founding of the Museum in 1870, when a Roman sarcophagus from Tarsus was the very first gift accepted. The massive collection of Cypriot antiquities gathered by General Luigi di Cesnola overshadowed other classical antiquities in the first quarter of the Museum's existence. Gifts and purchases soon widened the scope, and by the end of the 19th century classical art in the Museum included Greek vases, Etruscan art, much Roman glass, and a collection of gems. Scholarly collecting did not start until 1906, when classical antiquities were being purchased and looked after by two classical scholars. A Department of Classical Art was established in 1909, and its name was changed to the Department of Greek and Roman Art 20 years later. Its vast collection, shown in galleries on two floors of the Museum, is particularly strong in Cypriot art, painted Greek vases, Roman portrait busts, and Roman wall paintings from Campania. Its ancient glass collection is the most important anywhere, and its original Attic sculpture is the best collection outside of Athens.

The objects under the care of the department are not confined to those coming from Greece and from the Roman Empire, as the name would suggest. For classical art extends to pre-Greek and pre-Roman art and encompasses civilizations whose origins are not known. The earliest works are from the 3rd millennium B.C. The conversion of Emperor Constantine to Christianity in A.D. 313 is the date chosen to terminate the time span covered by the Department of Greek and Roman Art. This religious and political event had far-reaching consequences, but it did not mark an abrupt change in art forms and styles, many of which continued in some form in the early Christian period. Objects from this time are looked after by the Department of Medieval Art. Geographically, the scope of the department is limited to the classical lands surrounding the Mediterranean basin and beyond. In certain areas, notably Egypt and the Near East, frontiers are not so rigidly drawn, and some Greek and Roman material from those areas is shown in other departments.

Classical art in any museum is only a selected reflection of the thriving culture that contributed to the fame of Greece and Rome and that made these two civilizations, their art, architecture, philosophy, and political institutions, the very foundation on which the Western world is built. Furniture and sculpture of wood, because of the perishability of the material, have rarely survived, and the same is true for textiles. In addition, a very small percentage of sculpture has come down through the ages, and the great pieces by famous sculptors are known mostly in Roman copies, their identity established through descriptions by ancient authors. Even the sculpture that remains gave a totally different impression in ancient time; stone statues were brightly colored and bronzes were kept shiny, not discolored by patina. Few paintings have remained; and metal was often melted and reused in other forms. Greek and Roman temples, market squares, and theaters exist today because they had been covered by earth or sometimes had been used for other purposes. An important architectural re-

2

3

main now in the Museum is the Ionic capital and parts of a column from the temple of Artemis in Sardis, the capital of ancient Lydia **(1)**. The precision of detail, graceful scrolls, and deep fluting are characteristically Greek. Regardless of the ravages of time, Greek art and its Roman continuation are still the basis of Western art, having been "rediscovered" in the Renaissance and providing fresh inspiration to artists ever since.

The earliest objects in the department come from a civilization that flourished on the Cycladic Islands in the Aegean Sea during the 3rd millennium B.C. Hundreds of simple marble figures have been found on these islands, and similar statues from as far as northern Greece and Asia Minor suggest exchange of ideas in this prehistoric period. The Metropolitan has a number of these Cycladic idols, such as the **Statuette of a Woman (2)**. Most were similar in form, with arms across the chest forming part of the body and only the nose carved on the face. In comparison, the **Harp Player (3)** from the same region is very different in composition; the face, body, and arms are more detailed, and the whole figure conveys a mood.

One of the large islands situated in the most eastern basin of the Mediterranean Sea is Cyprus, and Cypriot art is exceptionally well represented by more than 5,000 objects from the Cesnola Collection. The stone sculpture, vases, terra cottas, bronzes, gold jewelry, silver objects, and other small pieces of diverse material all came from excavations conducted by General Cesnola while he was American consul in Cyprus. Most of the stone sculpture shown here was

6

7

found in a sanctuary near the town of Athieno (ancient Golgoi). These limestone figures, many of them life-size, were votive statues, showing representations of the worshipers with arms at their sides; holding offerings, such as a bird or a branch; or raising their hands in adoration or prayer. Portraiture was seldom attempted, and the statues were most likely prepared in advance, following a model, and then sold. Since Cyprus occupied a strategic position between East and West, its sculpture reflects a mixture of styles—Egyptian, Oriental, Greek, and its own native contributions **(4)**.

Another flourishing early culture existed on the island of Crete, and its art spread far beyond the confines of this small territory. The site of Knossos, first excavated by Sir Arthur Evans, revealed a remarkably intricate palace with wall paintings and many objects. The whole civilization was called Minoan, after the legendary king Minos. Cretan chronology is divided into three Minoan periods—early, middle, and late. The Museum has objects from every phase, including pottery, stone vases, bronze statuettes, metal tools, jewelry, and sealstones **(5)**.

The contemporary culture on the Greek mainland is called Mycenaean, after the famous site of Mycenae on the northeast Peloponnese. A deciphering of one of the two scripts, called Linear B, proves that the language was Greek. Mycenaean art excelled in luxurious objects of great beauty, most of which had been buried with their owners in graves. In the Museum can be seen a number of Mycenaean vases of various shapes and decoration. Quite characteristic is the **spouted jar (6)** with fish and octopus ornamentation, dated about 1200-1125 B.C.

At the end of the 2nd millennium B.C. invaders from the north introduced a change from the exuberant Mycenaean to more severe art forms, called geometric. In the early Greek, or Geometric, period, designs such as meanders, zigzags, and checkerboard patterns were mostly used on vases. When human figures were introduced in the 8th century B.C., they were presented geometrically; definite scenes, often having to do with burial and battles, can nevertheless be detected. Some of the most impressive remains from this period are the huge **kraters (7)** that served as tomb monuments. They are from Attica, the province of Greece that made some of the finest ware.

Besides pottery, the Greek Geometric period produced small bronzes, terracotta statues, and engraved seals. The bronze group in the Museum of a centaur with a man has an openwork base. Further reduced to its essentials is the **statuette of a horse (8)**, also in bronze, with a similarly perforated base. The mane, legs, and tail are the dominant features, rendered in dramatically simple lines.

Greece in its earliest historical periods was not a single country but rather a number of city states, which vied with each other for political domination, in artistic output, in athletic events, and in commerce. Of great importance were the colonies that were founded. In the 8th and 7th centuries contact with the Near East, through colonies and active trading, increased to the extent that Oriental influences brought in new forms of orna-

8

mentation. It is in this period that monumental sculpture and architecture made their first appearance. This Orientalizing phase, lasting about 100 years, forms the first stage of archaic Greek art. Painted pottery was decorated with such exotic animals as panthers and lions taken from the East, fantastic monsters, and such Oriental plants as the lotus and the palmette. The city of Corinth became the center of pottery-making, and its ware had a wide distribution. Some good examples of Corinthian pottery can be seen in the Museum **(9)**.

The archaic kouros, or nude male figure, stands at the beginning of a long line of human figures in marble and other stone. With patient determination, artistic genius, and a great appreciation of beauty, the Greeks brought the representation of the body, whether in rest or in motion, to the highest perfection. These early statues already conveyed an understanding of anatomy; muscles and even bones

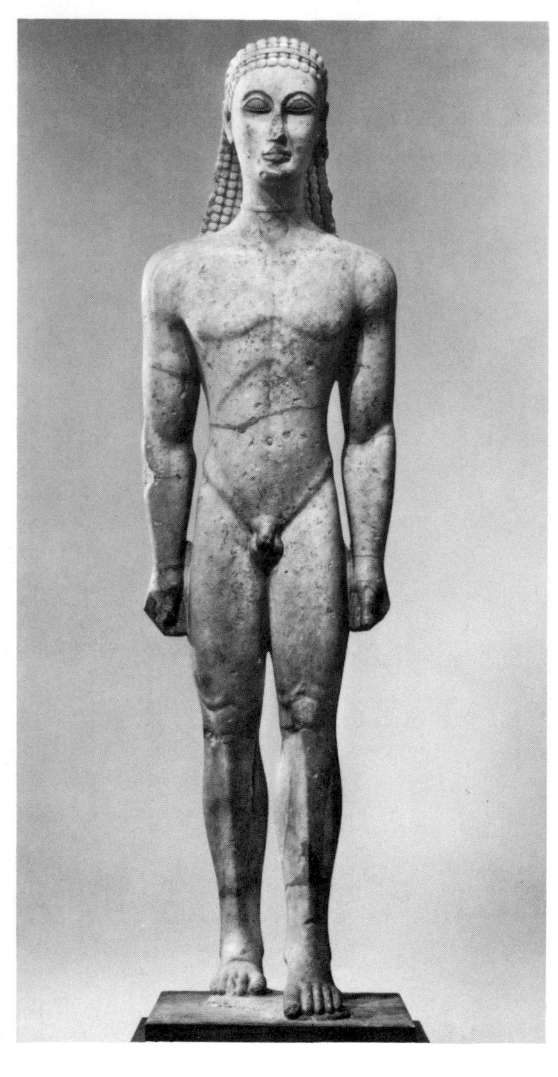

10

11

are well indicated, yet in the stiff stance and rigid frontality these statues remind one of Egyptian figures. This **kouros (10)** may have served as a tomb figure or as a votive statue dedicated to a god.

The Museum has other first-rate pieces of archaic sculpture. From the third quarter of the 6th century B.C. comes a **grave monument (11)** of a young boy and girl in relief, surmounted by a sphinx acting as guardian of the tomb. As was the custom, the figure was carved in profile, while the eye was shown as if from the front. Here some of the original paint can still be seen, different colors marking the hair, drapery, and face. A dedicatory inscription on the base indicates that the monument was erected by the parents. Other grave stelai, or slabs, some marble heads with the so-called archaic smile, and a draped female figure are from the same time.

Bronzes from the archaic period comprise utensils such as this **mirror (12)** from the 6th century, which has a handle of two cast animals and a figure attached to it. Statuettes and small terra-cotta animals are particularly charming; most are from Boeotia in central Greece. Larger and more sophisticated in style is the beautiful **Head of a Sphinx or Woman (13)**, with carefully parted hair. It was made by a Corinthian artist in about 500 B.C.

Because of the nature of the material, Greek art of all periods is best preserved in painted vases. From the 7th century many flourishing ceramic centers existed in Greece and her colonies. The whole world of Greek myths, legends, heroes, and ordinary mortals engaged in daily pursuits comes to life on painted vases. It is a fascinating world and one that tells much about the habits of the ancient Greeks. The gods were an ever-present reality and served many functions as protectors, avengers, guardians, and friends. One can meet Zeus, Athena, Apollo, Dionysos, and many more, as well as the legendary heroes of Greek mythology—Theseus fighting the Minotaur, Herakles overcoming the Nemean lion, Achilles and other heroes of the Trojan War, and the Amazons.

13

12

By the middle of the 6th century vases made in Attica came to dominate the market because of the perfection of their technique. The standard shapes became greatly refined in outline and proportions; usually a certain shape designated the vessel for its particular use—for drinking wine, carrying water, storage, general household use, or as a prize in an athletic contest. Samples of each can be studied in the Museum. In the black-figure technique of vase painting, the silhouette was enhanced by the use of accessory color—white and dark red—and articulated by incised lines. More than a hundred artists' signatures on Attic vases are known today; in addition, thousands of unsigned vases can be attributed either to artists already known from their signature or to anonymous artists who now bear made-up names, such as the Berlin Painter. This **neck-amphora (14)**, attributed to Exekias, depicts a chariot scene; exceptionally this vase has its original lid preserved.

Toward the last quarter of the 6th century a change occurred in Attic vase painting. The color scheme of the black-figure technique was reversed, with the background now painted in glossy black and the figures reserved. The red-figure technique of vase painting represents a great technical advance; the light figures are highlighted against the dark background, and the details of anatomy, garments, and accessories are drawn in lines that vary in intensity and thickness. A large number of excellent red-figured vases can be seen in the Museum; they demonstrate a progression of styles, as well as the work of individual artists. Always retaining a superb decorative sense, the 5th-century vase painter had a fine knowledge of the human body, of perspective, of rendering drapery, and of showing movement and action. An example is the Attic **amphora (15)**, or large jar, signed by Andokides as potter and attributed to the Andokides Painter; the scene retells the struggle between Herakles and Apollo for the tripod at Delphi.

The amphora signed by Andokides is

14

15

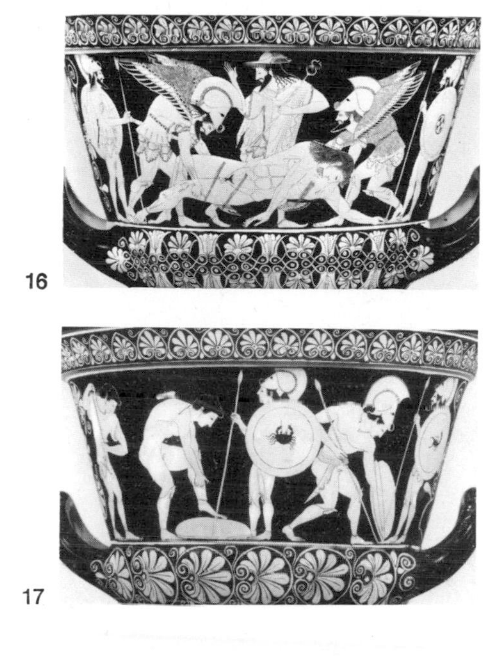

16

17

one of the earliest vases painted in the new technique. Fifteen years later Euphronios and his fellow pioneers perfected red-figure through the use of dilute glaze and washes. A **calyx-krater** is signed by the potter Euxitheos and the painter Euphronios. On the obverse **(16)** the body of prince Sarpedon is carried by the twin brothers Sleep and Death; the reverse **(17)** shows warriors arming.

Between 490 and 479 B.C. the small Greek armies and navies held their own against the warriors of the Persian invaders, insuring the freedom of Greece. The sack of the Acropolis by Persian troops called for a burial of the archaic statues and buildings that had been defiled, and a commissioning of replacements. Thus the year 480 becomes a dividing line between archaic and early classic art.

In the classic age, the severity of the archaic style was gradually replaced by a greater freedom, without losing the sense of majesty and nobility. A small bronze statuette of Athena flying her owl **(18)** is perhaps a likeness of one of the statues of Athena on the Acropolis at Athens. The goddess's helmet is pushed toward the back of her head. The Museum's figure of a **Wounded Warrior (19)**

19

20

21

is a Roman copy of the famous piece by Kresilas, a sculptor from Crete. The figure is leaning on a spear, with the weight of the body thrown backward; the face has a calm, pensive expression, without much emotion. Also attributed to Kresilas is the statue of an **Amazon (20)**, which the Museum has in a Roman copy. She is wounded in her right breast where blood flows from a gash, yet all indication of pain is concealed by her serene expression and pose.

Two reliefs of the classic period show the new treatment of the female figure. The **grave relief: Girl with Doves (21)** probably comes from the island of Paros where it was found in the 18th century. The artist has rendered a child in the demanding manner of a formal representation. The face is an artistic projection or idealization, yet the arms and feet are very much those of a child. The Relief of a Dancing Maenad, seen in the Museum in a Roman copy of a Greek original from the late 5th century, in a truly classical manner shows a serene face on a dancing body, framed by agitated, moving folds of clinging drapery.

After Pericles's great building program on the Acropolis came to an end, the many sculptors who had been employed there turned their talents to making sumptuous grave reliefs for private individuals and families. The Museum has many fine examples **(22)**.

Toward the end of the 4th century B.C. the eastern conquests of Alexander the Great increased the horizon of the Greeks, and we now speak of Hellenistic culture. New subjects were accepted, along with new means of expressing them. Greater individuality and realism marked marble and terra-cotta statuettes, The bronze statue of a **Sleeping Eros (23)**, from the 3rd century, shows early age with all its charm and the marvelous relaxation visible in a sleeping child. The statue of an old **Peasant Woman** hurrying to market with her basket **(24)**, from the 2nd century, is a frank, unrelenting depiction of old age.

24

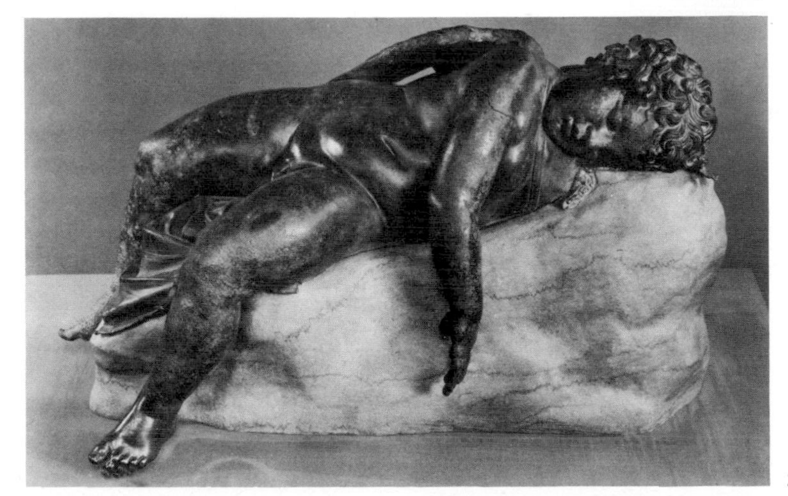

23

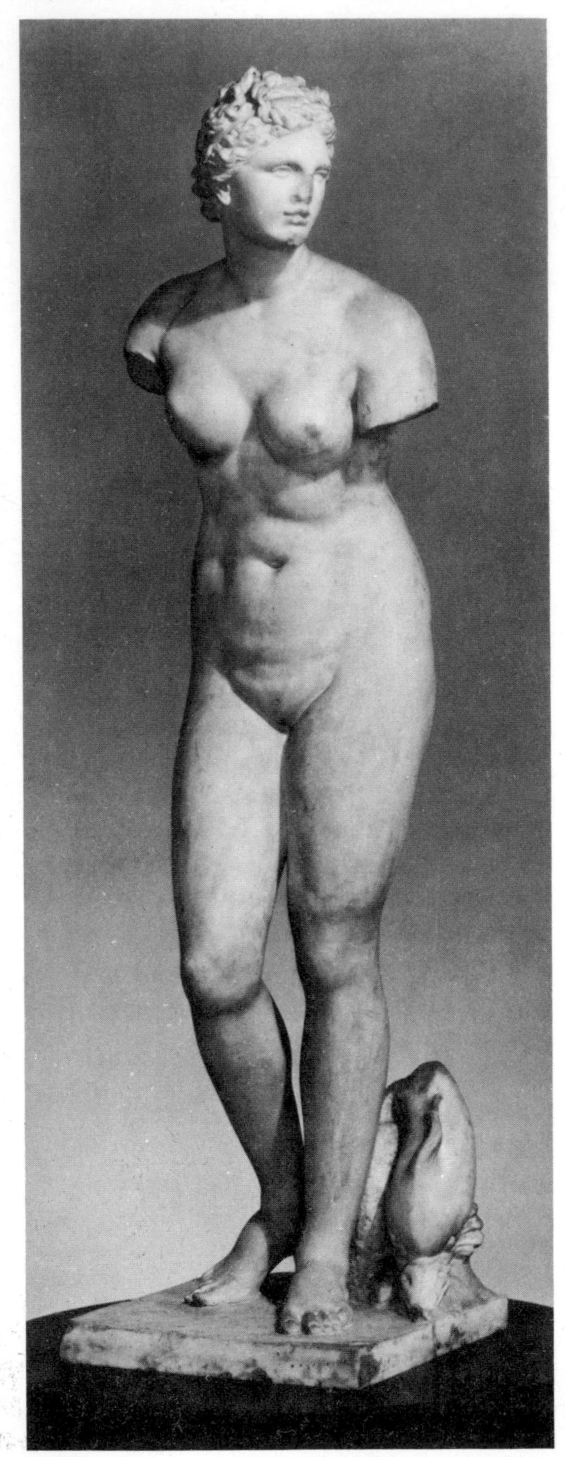

25

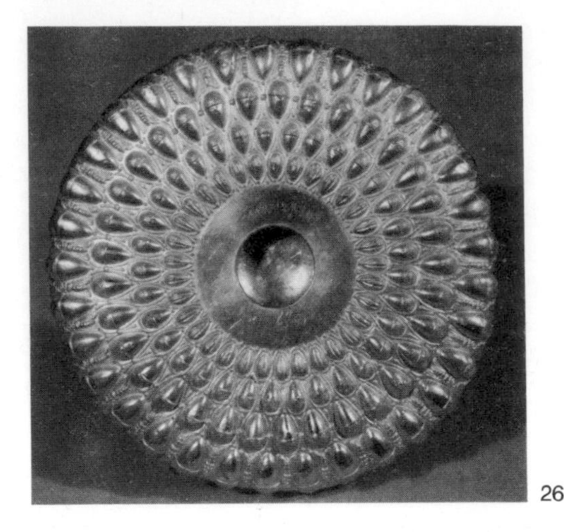

26

The sculptor Praxiteles had been the first to present the goddess Aphrodite nude, and the subject became a favorite with many successive sculptors. The Museum's **Aphrodite (25)** is a fine Roman copy of an original that was made about 300 B.C., perhaps 50 years after Praxiteles's work. Her arms, now missing, once covered parts of her body in a protective gesture.

With the advent of the Hellenistic age gold became plentiful, and some of the finest jewelry, as well as splendid gold and silver vases, were made in this period. The mode of living became more luxurious, and bronze, silver, and gold cups and dishes were used among the wealthy. Some examples now in the Museum have engraved patterns. The **gold phiale (26)**, or libation bowl, from the 3rd century, is decorated with nuts, acorns, and bees.

ETRUSCAN ART

In the beginning of the 1st millennium B.C. Italy was inhabited by many different tribes. From these humble beginnings emerged in central Italy the power of the

Etruscans. In the 6th century B.C. the Etruscans extended their influence to northern and southern Italy, and traded with the Greeks and the East. Their art took many impulses from the Greeks, yet developed in its own manner, giving an expressive vision of Greek myths. The Etruscans excelled in the working of bronze. The bronze reliefs in repoussé on this **ceremonial chariot (27)**, found in a tomb, show Etruscan art at its height in the archaic period. The subject matter is taken from Greek mythology, but native workmanship is evident.

27

The Etruscans achieved a high degree of craftsmanship also in jewelry, raising the already known techniques of filigree and granulation to a level of great virtuosity. The painted pottery was inspired by Greek models and was at times even made by potters and painters who had emigrated from Greece **(28)**.

The Etruscans continued to influence the arts of Italy even after their political decline. Their art is, in fact, the principal ancestor of Roman art, other contributors to this new power being Greek art as practiced in the Hellenistic age, and to a lesser extent the art of Ptolemaic Egypt. For it must be remembered that the Roman Empire extended from the Atlantic Ocean to the Euphrates River and included most of the countries that now form southern and western Europe.

ROMAN ART

In the Metropolitan Museum Roman art is well represented by portrait sculpture, sarcophagi, wall paintings, and glass. Roman portrait sculpture can be seen in many examples that fused two different traditions—the Etruscan and the Greek—achieving results of a high artistic nature. Its origin is connected with the cult of ancestors. The earliest portraits during the Republican period strove for true likeness, without flattery. The sitter was often shown as an old man or woman. During the period of the empire the subjects, particularly emperors and their families, were idealized; some busts attempted to convey the power with which the emperors liked to be identified. Augustus, the first emperor, and other prominent Romans are represented in the Museum.

30

29

Portrait sculptors of the late Roman Empire often attempted to suggest the mood and character of the sitter, as in the Museum's **Portrait Bust of a Young Woman (29)**, her head covered with a draped mantle.

Some of the best work is in bronze, as the **Portrait of a Boy (30)**, from the 1st

31

32

century A.D. Other portraits are full size, as the statue of a Roman prince; the quality of workmanship and the imperial nature of the subject make this one of the most important bronzes in the collection.

The Romans also excelled in the sculpture of marble reliefs, particularly those found on sarcophagi, the receptacles used in antiquity for burial. The **Badminton Sarcophagus (31)**, named after Badminton House in England to which the sarcophagus was brought from Italy in 1728, is a masterpiece from the end of classical antiquity, dating from A.D. 220-230; the young god Dionysos is seated on a panther or tiger, surrounded by satyrs, maenads, the horned god Pan, and the Four Seasons. The relief still uses classical tradition in many details but otherwise is simply a display of form without reflecting reality.

The Museum is fortunate in having two large assemblies of Roman wall paintings. Perhaps the most interesting group comes from a villa at Boscoreale, built in the mid-1st century B.C. Like the buildings at Pompeii, this house also was buried by ashes from the eruption of Mt. Vesuvius in A.D. 79. Three sections of a wall painting were cut out of a larger wall; our illustration shows a **Woman Playing a Kithara (32)**. Also from the same

33

villa is a complete **bedroom (33)** decorated with architectural vistas that may derive from stage settings. In another set of wall paintings, from Boscotrecase in the same vicinity on the slopes of Mt. Vesuvius, small scenes taken from Greek mythology are framed by architectural elements.

The Museum's collection of Roman glass is superb, reflecting all known styles and techniques from a wide geographical area and from early Mycenaean to late Roman times **(34)**. At first glass had to be modeled by hand over a core, but with the invention of glassblowing in the 1st century B.C., many new shapes evolved and centers of production flourished all over the Roman Empire. The tradition of fine craftsmanship persisted into the Middle Ages, and the continuity between the pagan and the Christian world becomes evident when the museum-goer leaves the Greek and Roman galleries and enters the galleries of medieval art.

Islamic Art

Islamic Art

Periods		Numbers in Text
THE ORTHODOX CALIPHS	A.D. 632-661	
UMAYYAD CALIPHATE	661-750	
THE UMAYYAD CALIPHS IN SPAIN	756-1031	
ABBASID CALIPHATE	750-1258	**(1-3)**
FATIMID PERIOD (Egypt)	969-1171	**(4)**
SELJUK PERIOD (Iran, Iraq, Turkey)	1037-1300	**(5-9)**
MONGOL PERIOD (Iran)	1256-1393	**(10-13)**
TIMURID PERIOD (Transoxania, Iran)	1380-1502	**(14-16)**
AYYUBID PERIOD (Egypt, Syria)	1171-1250	
MAMLUK PERIOD (Egypt, Syria)	1250-1517	**(17-19)**
SAFAVID PERIOD (Iran)	1502-1736	**(20-23)**
OTTOMAN PERIOD (Turkey)	1299-1893	**(24-25)**
MUGHAL PERIOD (India)	1525-1857	**(26)**

This page helps you to find what you especially want to see and read about.

Islamic Art

The Museum's first Islamic objects were acquired in 1874, but it was not until the 1920s that the Islamic collection was officially recognized and a subdepartment created for it, followed by the formation of an independent Near Eastern Art Department in 1932. The Department of Islamic Art came into existence in 1963 when the Near Eastern Art Department was divided into two departments—Ancient Near Eastern Art and Islamic Art.

By means of highly important gifts, bequests, purchases, and material from four successful excavation seasons in Nishapur, Iran, the Metropolitan has built up the largest comprehensive collection of Islamic art in the world. The first major private collection, given by Edward C. Moore in 1891, contained outstanding examples of Egyptian, Syrian, and Mesopotamian metalwork and glass, as well as Iranian and Spanish pottery. The next major donation was given in 1913 by Alexander Smith Cochran—a choice collection of 24 illustrated manuscripts, mostly Persian. In the same year the Benjamin Altman Bequest added a small but important group of Islamic objects, in particular Mughal Indian rugs. In 1917 a fine group of Rayy pottery and Persian carpets was added through the bequest of Isaac D. Fletcher. Other donors over the years include Henry G. Marquand, George C. Pratt, Rodman Wanamaker, Henry Walters, Edward C. Moore, Jr., J. Pierpont Morgan, Mr. and Mrs. Henry O. Havemeyer, and Horace Havemeyer. James F. Ballard in 1922 presented to the Museum the finest part of his collection of carpets. Finally, Joseph V. McMullan has donated a number of very important carpets that are representative of all the classical centers of production in the Near and Middle East.

1

Islam is an Arabic word meaning submission (to the will of God) and is the name of the religion founded by the prophet Muhammad in 622 A.D. Facing opposition to his religious teaching, he left in that year his native town of Mecca for Medina, also in Arabia. There his re-

ligion took root and spread, eventually reaching from Spain in the west to India in the east. The belief in the oneness of God and the necessity of obedience to His will form the basis of Islam. The will of Allah was revealed to Muhammad in the words that he wrote in the book called the Koran. Arabic, the language used in the Koran, became an all-important, unifying factor among the diverse national, ethnic, and cultural groups that became Muslims. Arabic script in turn became a universal basis for Islamic art.

The religion of Islam, affecting every aspect of a Muslim's life, produced a distinct Islamic culture. While the art of this culture, in the complexity, inventiveness, and variety of its designs, reflects the diversity and range of Islamic peoples, its unity and continuity show the oneness and indivisibility of God.

Following Muhammad's death in 632, the task of ruling the Muslims fell, successively, to four orthodox caliphs. During this 30-year period Egypt, Arabia, Syria, Iraq, Transcaucasia, and Iran were conquered and colonized in the name of Allah and Islam. In 661, the Umayyad Dynasty, with its capital at Damascus, came to power and there was further expansion into Spain, North Africa, and eastward into greater Iran. The Arabs came in direct contact with the tradition of Greco-Roman art, including such naturalistic motifs as the acanthus leaf and the grapevine, as well as with the art of Sasanian Iran with its more abstract motifs such as the palmette. The fusion and reinterpretation of disparate elements, and a marvelously inventive mastery of surface decoration, were to become characteristic features of Islamic art.

2

In 750 a rival dynasty, the Abbasid, seized power and moved the capital to Baghdad. In the Museum's collection a pair of **teakwood doors (1)**, probably from Samarra, which was the temporary capital of this dynasty from 836 to 892, are carved in a beveled style probably of Central Asian origin. A very unusual 9th-century pale green glass cup from Persia has alternating horizontal and vertical lozenge forms in relief, the background having been cut away.

The technique of lustre painting on pottery was invented and brought to perfection under the Abbasids. The pottery, covered with a thick white glaze, was fired, then painted with a solution containing metal oxides, and refired in a way that precipitated the metals on the surface in shades of gold, red, or brown. Another type of ceramics popular under the early Abbasids was influenced by imported Chinese T'ang ware. Also from this early period is slip-painted earthenware, as seen in the 10th-century **bowl (2)** from Nishapur. Its decoration is an outstanding

3

example of the use of calligraphy as decoration. The Arabic inscription is in the Kufic script.

Relatively little painting has survived from the Abbasid period, except for illustrations in books. Baghdad was a flourishing cultural center, and in the Museum's collection is a leaf from an Arabic manuscript made in that city and dated 1224, with an illustration of the **Preparation of Medicine from Honey (3)**; the sheet comes from *De Materia Medica*, written by the Greek Dioscorides in the 1st century A.D. The treatise was the leading text on pharmacology for many centuries.

In 969 Egypt came under the control of the independent Fatimid Dynasty ruling from Cairo, their newly founded capital. The decorative arts flourished in this cosmopolitan focal point of many influences, with Fatimid craftsmen excelling in lustreware, and wood, bone, and ivory carving. The **ivory casket (4)** of the 11th-12th century is probably from southern Italy or Sicily, earlier ruled by the Fatimids

4

5

6

7

and still then artistically dependent.

In the 11th century greater Iran, Mesopotamia, and Anatolia came under the political control of the Seljuks, a Turkic tribe from Central Asia. The Seljuk period was one of the most creative of Islamic art. The inlaid **bronze ewer (5)** from Khorasan in eastern Iran, containing zodiacal figures in lobed medallions, epitomizes the fine metal workmanship so characteristic of this time. The greatest innovation in pottery was the use of a composite body containing quartz, which permitted greater elegance of shape and variety of colors. The pottery of the Seljuk period was seldom surpassed in the excellence of its quality. The 12th-century **taboret (6)** belongs to a relatively rare group of monumental ceramic objects and was probably used as a low table for food and drink during receptions or courtly audiences; its shape resembles a secular pleasure pavilion.

Kashan and Rayy in Iran were the two main pottery-producing centers of the Seljuk period. The **lustre bowl (7)** illustrated here was produced in Kashan. The design on the garments is the typically dense Kashan pattern and includes arabesques both in lustre and reserved on the lustre ground and the background. The use of several different scripts again attests to the important place of calligraphy in Islamic art. The **jug (8)** with a

8

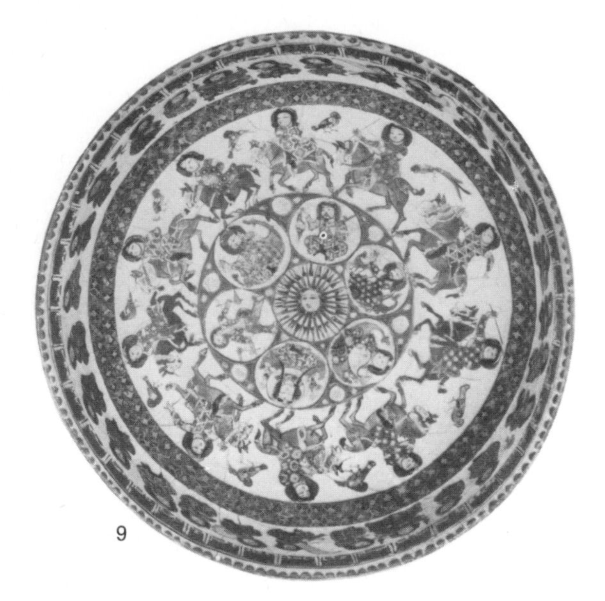
9

10

reticulated outer wall, dated 1215-16, comes from the same city, which excelled not only in lustreware but in the production of underglaze painted pottery; black under a turquoise glaze is characteristic.

Another type of painted pottery known as *minai*, that is, enameled ware, used several colors, many of which were over the glaze, and even made use of gilding. Much of this ware was probably made in Rayy. A superb **bowl (9)** of this kind is decorated in the center with the sun surrounded by the seven planets; a frieze of horsemen is next; and, finally, a group of courtiers at the sides of two enthroned personages. These motifs express good luck in astrological language and evoke a picture of the active life at the medieval Iranian court. The style of such ware often reflected Seljuk miniature painting, of which almost nothing has survived.

Early in the 13th century the Mongol hordes from the Asian steppes swept into the Islamic world destroying important cities and principalities; in 1259 Baghdad

11

fell and the Abbasid caliphate was destroyed. The relationship between the Mongols in China and those in Iran led to Chinese influences in Islamic art. In the wooden **Koran stand (10)** from Western Turkestan, dated 1360, naturalistic plant decoration of Chinese derivation mingles with the Islamic arabesques and calligraphic motifs. The engraved **brass basin (11)** from the early 14th century is inlaid with silver and gold; it is one of the most ambitious and complex figural pieces of Islamic metalwork ever produced, containing representations of 106 human figures and an equal number of fantastic creatures. The design radiates from a central eighteen-pointed star, the arms of which are extended in an interlace pattern to form a series of medallions and roundels. A faïence mosaic

12

mihrab (12) from the Madraseh Imami in Isfahan, dated 1354, continues a technique that was begun under the Seljuks and was developed to its greatest effect by the Mongols. The mihrab, or prayer niche, indicated the direction of prayer, toward Mecca, and was the most richly decorated part of a mosque or madraseh

13

(theological school). The mosaic was created by fitting together small pieces of glazed faïence that had been fired separately to produce the brightest colors.

In the Mongol capital of Tabriz, a style of painting developed in the 14th century in which the new Chinese influences gradually became amalgamated with the native traditions. An outstanding manuscript from this period is a monumental and wonderfully illustrated *Shah-nameh*, the Persian national epic written by the poet Firdowsi some three centuries earlier; shown here is the **Funeral of Isfandiyar (13)**. The intensity of the mourners' grief and the variety of expression and detail in the faces are comparatively rare in Persian art.

By the early 15th century, under the Timurid Dynasty, Persian miniature painting had achieved a style that was to remain basically unchanged for several centuries. This dynasty was founded by the savage conqueror from Central Asia, Timur, known as Tamerlane in the West. In the following generations, however, princes of the Timurid House became great patrons of the arts, and among the

14

Museum's collection of Persian miniatures is part of a manuscript probably made for Prince Baysunghur in the capital, Herat, in the 1420s. Called the *Haft Paikar*, or *Seven Portraits*, it is one of the five poems of the great poet Nizami, and relates romantic episodes of the Sasanian prince Bahram Gur. In this miniature of **Bathing Nymphs (14)**, the delicate and decorative quality of Persian painting can be clearly seen. The picture plane has been tilted up, so that the distant horizon appears at the top of the picture. Every component part is shown in its most char-

15

16

acteristic aspect—the pool from a bird's-eye view and the buildings in profile. Blooming plants and trees show the Persians' love of gardens and flowers.

18

During the latter part of the 15th century the last Timurid ruler in Iran also had his capital at Herat. Though his kingdom was much diminished, he was unsurpassed in his patronage of art. One of the greatest Persian painters of all time, Bihzad, was his protégé. While adhering to the principles established earlier, Bihzad and his school developed a new interest in humanity and the activities of the real world, as can be seen in the illustration of the **Dancing Dervishes (15)** from the manuscript of the *Divan*, or collection of poems, of the famous poet Hafiz. Delicacy of drawing, purity of color, and harmony of composition were perfected by this new vision.

Pottery and metalwork continued to thrive in this period. The Timurid **gold ring (16)** with a jade signet and dragon motif is a rare surviving object of precious metal.

The Mamluk Dynasty, originally slaves, came to power in 1250 and ruled in Egypt and part of Syria until 1517. The Mamluks brought intricate abstract ivory and wood carving to new heights of perfection. A **pair of doors (17)** from Egypt, of the late 13th or early 14th century, illustrates the Muslim predilection for infinite designs.

Magnificent metalwork was made in Cairo, and the art of glassmaking thrived. Some of the decorative motifs on Mamluk glass reflected Mongol influence, though the Mamluks successfully resisted Mongol domination. An example of this is the polychrome enameled and gilded **glass bottle (18)** from about 1320, with a frieze of horsemen and a Chinese phoenix on its neck.

Rugs are probably the form of Islamic art that is most familiar to the general public, and the department has a comprehensive collection of them. Kaleidoscopic geometric designs are dominant in Mamluk rugs. The early 16th-century

17

19

20

carpet (19) from Egypt shown here is one of the finest and largest—more than 29 feet long—of this type. Not only Egypt, but Iran, Turkey, and India became famous for their rug production. This **compartment rug (20)** from early 16th-century Iran is composed of interconnected cartouches containing dragons, phoenixes, cloud bands, and arabesques.

The rug described above was the product of a new dynasty in Iran, the Safavid, which established its rule in 1502. In the court workshops at Tabriz, the art of painting thrived under the patronage of Shah Ismail and then under his son Shah Tahmasp. A remarkable gift in 1970 from Arthur A. Houghton, Jr., of 78 miniatures from one of the greatest Iranian manuscripts constitutes a splendid collection of paintings from the early Safavid Dynasty. Most of the major Safavid artists contributed to this *Shah-nameh*, or *Book of Kings*, in which the poet tells the epic history of the Iranian people up to the Arab conquest. The manuscript, with a total of 258 miniatures, was created in Tabriz for Shah Tahmasp; one of the miniatures gives a date equivalent to 1527-28. Its illustrations show the whole range of the development of Safavid painting—from that practiced in Tabriz by the Turkmans, to the Bihzadian Herat style, and a final fusion and modification of the two. **The Feast of Sàdeh (21)** celebrates the discovery of fire by the grand-

21

22

son of the legendary first king. Here Sultan Muhammad, the court painter who taught the Shah himself, has conveyed an atmosphere of mystery and energy appropriate to the beginnings of civilization.

Characteristic of much of Safavid painting are the fantastic animals of Chinese derivation in the margins of **A Princely Hawking Party in the Mountains (22)**, a painting now in the Museum. The left half of a double-page composition, it was painted in the latter part of the 16th century in Qazvin, at that time the Safavid capital, in the elegant and poetic manner then in vogue.

Another Persian manuscript of excep-

24

tional quality was also recently acquired by the Museum. The mystical poem *The Language of the Birds*, written by the 12th-century poet Farid al-din Attar, is illustrated with eight miniatures—four that are contemporary with the copying of the text, which is dated 1483, and four that are additions from about 1600. **The Concourse of the Birds (23)** comes from the later group, painted in the city of Isfahan; it is signed by Habib Allah, one of the court painters. The artist of this exquisitely composed picture, with its fine detail in luminous colors and gold, deliberately followed the style of earlier Herat paintings in the same manuscript.

The Ottoman Dynasty ruled from Istanbul from 1517 to 1928. Among the types of rugs produced are those known today as "Holbeins," because such carpets appear in paintings by Hans Holbein the Younger, attesting to their popularity

23

in Europe. Others were made to order for European patrons and bore the coats of arms of European families. Unlike the more painterly Persian carpets, those of Anatolia bear geometrical designs.

Ottoman painting produced its own style after an initial period of Persian influence. One miniature comes from the *Fal-nameh*, or *Treatise on Divinations, Forecasts, and Fortune Telling*; **the Seven Sleepers of Ephesus (24)** is a subject that has always appealed to Muslim his-

25

26

torians and was a popular theme for illustrators as well. This one belongs to a group of Ottoman Turkish paintings of large scale, bold drawing, and strong coloring, which owes a debt, however, to the mid-16th-century Safavid style at Shiraz, particularly in the figural proportions, facial types and costumes, overall composition, and the device of figures half-emerging from projecting rocks.

Isnik was the center of pottery production during this period. The beautiful underglaze-painted **dish (25)** is typical.

In the 16th century the Mughal Dynasty established its dominion over much of India. Under Akbar and his successors, Islamic traditions developed their own Mughal Indian characteristics. A great school of painting emerged. Initially introduced by two Persian painters from the Safavid court, it later fused with styles of existing Indian cultures and was modified by European influences. The Museum has paintings from one of the largest Mughal manuscripts, the *Dastan-i Amir Hamzeh,* showing the vigorous action characteristic of the early period.

Another painting is a miniature illustrating the *Hasht Behisht*, or *Eight Paradises*. This long narrative poem relates romantic episodes in the life of the idealized king Bahram Gur; on successive nights he visits a different princess, each of whom entertains him with tales. Here **Bahram Gur Visits the Persian Princess (26)** in the purple palace in the sixth paradise. Use of perspective and a more detailed modeling of the figures are characteristic of Mughal painting. Its artist, Manohar, was one of Akbar's most famous court painters.

Lehman Collection

Lehman Collection

Medieval Art

Medieval Art

Objects, Periods, Styles	Numbers in Text
ARCHITECTURAL DECORATION	(27-29)
BARBARIAN ART	(11)
BYZANTINE ART	(12-23)
CAROLINGIAN and OTTONIAN ART	(24), (25)
CERAMICS	(41), (42)
EARLY CHRISTIAN ART	(1-9)
ENAMELS	(18), (19), (58-61)
FURNITURE	(40)
GLASS	(5), (6)
GOTHIC STYLE	(34-39), (43-52), (55)
IVORIES	(7), (8), (20-26), (53-57)
JEWELRY and ORNAMENTS	(16)
LITURGICAL OBJECTS	(8), (26), (30), (64)
METAL OBJECTS: gold, silver, bronze	(8-11), (14-17), (30), (62), (63-65)
RELIQUARIES	(18), (62)
ROMANESQUE STYLE	(27-33), (53), (54)
SCULPTURE	(31-33), (43-52), (63)
STAINED GLASS	(34)
TAPESTRIES	(35-39)
TEXTILES and EMBROIDERIES	(66)

This page helps you to find what you especially want to see and read about.

Medieval Art

The core of the medieval art collection is the extraordinary gift of J. Pierpont Morgan, transmitted by his son, J. P. Morgan, Jr., in 1916 and 1917. Other important gifts by George Blumenthal and by George, Frederic, and Harold Irving Pratt have greatly enriched the Museum's holdings. Forming at first a part of a Decorative Arts Department, the Department of Medieval Art as such was not established until 1933. In 1938, a medieval museum closely connected with the Medieval Department was built at Fort Tryon Park, due to the generosity of John D. Rockefeller, Jr. Known as The Cloisters, because its architectural structure is based upon four cloisters bought earlier by George Barnard, the new building was conceived as an ideal medieval museum, and the collection complements the one at the Metropolitan. The over 4,000 objects in the Medieval Department range, roughly, from the 4th to the 16th century and represent the main aspects of medieval art: Early Christian, Byzantine, the Migrations, Pre-Romanesque, Romanesque, and Gothic; the collection is particularly rich in enamels, ivories, tapestries, and sculpture, and its quality, variety, and comprehensiveness are unsurpassed by any museum outside Europe.

Historically, the beginning of the Middle Ages is generally accepted as A.D. 313, when the Emperor Constantine the Great officially recognized Christianity as one of the religions of the Roman Empire; the end of the Middle Ages is marked by the fall of Constantinople to the Turks (1453) or the discovery of America (1492). In art, however, all limits must be flexible.

The earliest Christians met and worshiped secretly in their homes or in the catacombs, rather than in churches, and left scarcely any art. By the 3rd and 4th centuries, Christians in the western part of the Roman Empire based their artistic productions on Greek and Roman models, thus taking the classical tradition into medieval art. The early Christians were no other than Roman subjects, and the fragment from a sarcophagus, with a beardless Christ giving the Law to the Apostles **(1)**, shows how composition, technique, and costumes depended on Roman sarcophagi. The relationship between Christian and classical art can be seen in other reliefs. A 4th-century representation of Christ as a young Roman shepherd separating the sheep from the goats **(2)** is an allegory of the Last Judgment, when the blessed are to be separated from the damned; in another **(3)**, the common pagan motif of children gathering grapes has a new Christian meaning, the grapes symbolizing the wine of the

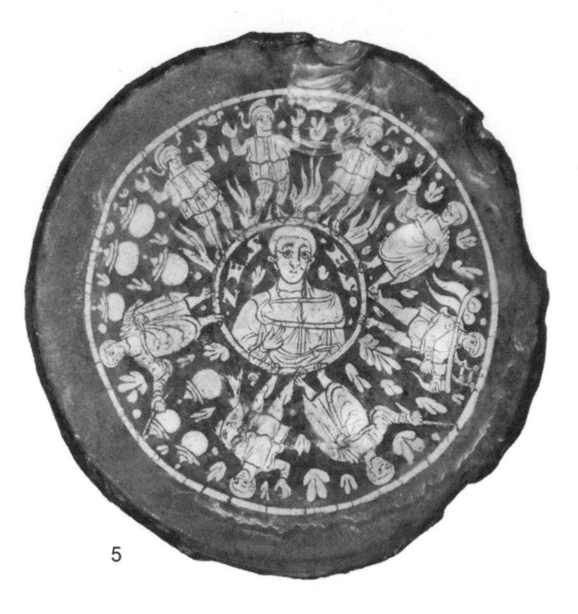

5

10

Eucharist. Old Testament stories were also given Christian interpretation, as in a fragment that shows Jonah swallowed by the whale and reappearing miraculously alive **(4)**, prefiguring the death and Resurrection of Christ.

Gold glass, a technique developed in Hellenistic times, is another indication of the classical roots of Early Christian art. A design cut from gold leaf was applied to a glass surface, the gold was then engraved with a sharp tool and protected with another layer of glass, and finally the two layers were fused together. Some **gold glass roundels (5)** show scenes from the Old and New Testaments; sometimes they have portrait busts, like one with the Greek inscription "Live." The gold glass roundels are bottoms of drinking vessels, but sometimes they were used as identification marks of their owner's burial at the catacombs. The beautiful 3rd-century medallion with the portrait of the musician Gennadios **(6)**, also in gold glass, shows a much better style than the roundels, a more complicated technique, and a realistic approach to portraiture that comes directly from Greek or Roman prototypes.

Although the Early Christian examples of ivories—companion plaques with St. Peter and St. Paul, and another with St. Peter in front view **(7)**—are provincial works, the latter has a barbaric directness that makes it very appealing.

Some of the Museum's Early Christian works come from the eastern part of the Roman Empire, from Syria and Egypt; bronze lamps and pyxes **(8)** (round boxes to hold consecrated wafers) show the influence of Near Eastern models. A marble relief with a seated philosopher is from Asia Minor. Three silver plaques with standing figures of saints—considered to be book covers—were found with other objects, including the famous chalice at The Cloisters, in a buried church treasure **(9)** in Antioch, Syria.

Some of the peoples who lived in present-day Europe preserved their native artistic skills and styles under Roman domination. The 4th-century **spear mounts and a belt buckle (10)**, found in Vermand, northern France, are made of silver with gilding and niello in a geometric pattern that is very unclassical in style.

Rome was the center of the Roman Empire until A.D. 330, when the first Christian emperor, Constantine, founded Constantinople (modern Istanbul) and made it his capital. The new Eastern Empire, known as Byzantium, then became the political and artistic center, and was to endure more than a thousand years. From

13

the 5th to the 7th century the Western Roman Empire was overrun by a series of barbaric nomadic tribes, coming from the north and great distances from the east. The invaders included the Ostrogoths, the Longobards, the Franks, and the Visigoths. Their jewelry and ornaments show a fondness for geometric patterns of an Oriental character, avoiding naturalistic representations. The Museum's collection includes important examples of barbarian art **(11)**: a large gold fibula, or pin, decorated with almandines and hatched wire, possibly from Transylvania; imposing Frankish belt buckles made of iron, inlaid with silver; a Visigothic bit, also of silver-inlaid iron; and a large silver-gilt and niello fibula and a round gold disc decorated with filigree, both Longobardic.

Meanwhile, in Byzantium an art was developing with a style independent of Greco-Roman and Near Eastern influences. Byzantine art is characterized by flat backgrounds and conventionalized figures that in spite of their aloof expressions are strangely alive. Byzantine sculpture attained a high degree of excellence. The 4th-century monumental marble head of the Emperor Constantine **(12)** already shows the large eyes turned upward that give to Byzantine portaits so much spirituality and power. The delicate craftsmanship of the marble bust of a **Lady of Rank (13)**, perhaps her funerary portrait, indicates that she was important enough to afford a first-class sculptor; this is one of the most appealing Byzantine portraits in existence.

A group of bronze steelyard weights **(14)** in the shape of female busts are provincial and barbaric. They vary in size according to the weight desired and were sometimes filled with lead to make them heavier. Some represent an empress, and others, Athena, who as goddess of wisdom also stood for fair measurement and balance.

The most important group of secular Byzantine objects comes from Cyprus. It includes a set of six **silver plates (15)** with scenes from the life of David. Marks on the back indicate that they were made in the 7th century, during the reign of the Emperor Heraclius. Classical influence can be seen in the modeling and freedom of movement of the figures. From the 6th century are a beautiful necklace and two bracelets, made of gold, sapphires, and

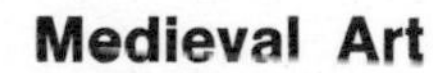

pearls, and a **gold necklace (16)** with a repoussé cross and pendants in the shape of amphorae and leaves with a delicate openwork design.

The so-called Albanian Treasure **(17)** comprises silver and gold vessels, belt buckles, and a 6th- or 7th-century gold drinking cup, the most outstanding piece in the group. It is decorated with busts personifying the cities of Constantinople, Rome, Alexandria, and, instead of Antioch as the fourth city, the island of Cyprus, suggesting that this cup was probably made there. Just as church treasures, like the one from Antioch, were buried to protect them from robbery and destruction, valuable secular objects were also buried for safekeeping, like these from Albania.

Byzantine artists loved to use brilliant colors against gold backgrounds, as in the wall frescoes and the mosaics represented in the Museum by copies only. An equally rich effect was achieved in enamels, which were renowned for their color and the elegance of their execution. The technique used was cloisonné, in which strips, or cloisons, of gold or silver are attached to a gold or silver background. The areas within these partitions are filled with powdered enamel, which when heated becomes a vitreous paste, sometimes translucent, that hardens into a jewel-like surface. The earliest of the Byzantine enamels in the Museum's collection is a small box probably made in Syria about the 8th century. This **Reliquary of the True Cross (18)** is said to have belonged to Pope Innocent IV. In a primitive but beautiful style, the Crucifixion, surrounded by busts of saints, is represented against a green background.

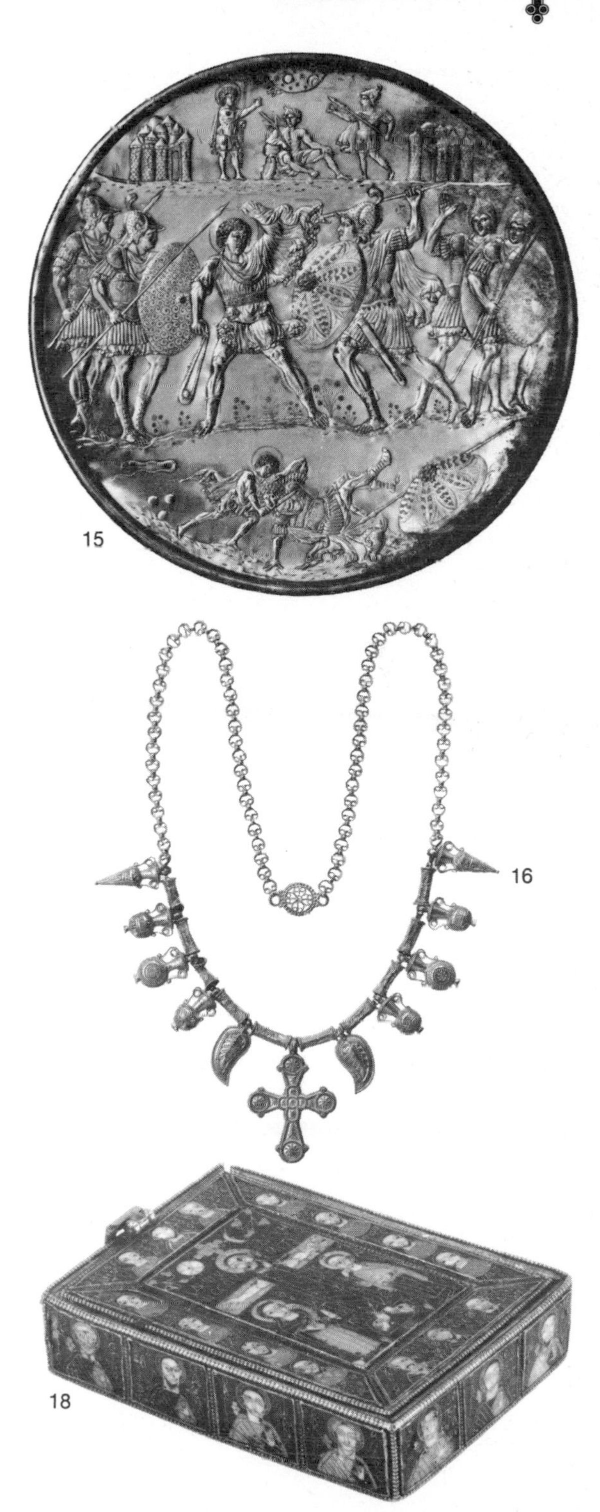

15

16

18

19

Among the later Byzantine enamels are nine **medallions (19)**, which together with three others were attached for centuries to the frame of an icon (now lost) in the monastery of Djumati, Georgia (Caucasus). "Icon" is the Greek word for a devotional image that is still used in Christian Orthodox Churches. The three medallions at the top represent Christ, Mary, and St. John the Baptist, forming the Deësis, a characteristically Byzantine theme; the figures in the other medallions make up a litany of saints to strengthen Mary's and John's intercession with Christ for men's souls. The figures are deliberately stylized, the faces are flesh color, and the attitudes conventional. Thin and intricate cloisons and a glimmering gold background suggest that they were made in the 11th or perhaps the 12th century. Lockets, pendants, earrings, and bracelets, made of gold and decorated with birds in enamel, are examples of secular objects that represent the Byzantine style in Russia.

22

Ivory is another medium in which Byzantine art excelled. Carved ivory plaques **(20)** were used as icons and on boxes, book covers, and furniture. Tablets, called consular diptychs **(21)**, were ceremoni-

23

25

ously presented to senators by newly elected consuls, in this case by Justinian in the 6th century. The fine standing figure of the **Virgin and Child (22)** was cut from a plaque, on which the halos of the two figures presumably remained. Dated around the 10th-11th century, the rigid and conventionalized style of this figure creates an effect of great power and beauty. A **Crucifixion plaque (23)** of about the same time shows the Cross, like the Tree of Life, growing out of the body of Adam; the deeply carved figures are more realistic than the standing Virgin.

In Western Europe during the late 8th and early 9th century, Charlemagne, the emperor of the Franks, in an effort to revive the ideals of the great age of the Emperor Constantine, stimulated a renaissance that lasted more or less to the 10th century. A good example of the art of this period is a Carolingian ivory plaque **(24)**, probably made in the emperor's workshop at Aachen soon after A.D. 800. The imposing and majestic figure of the Virgin Mary is extremely unusual. Her costume includes armor pieces, and she holds a cross-staff in one hand and a pair of spindles, alluding to the Annunciation, in the other. The figure was probably intended to represent the Virgin as Mother of God, leader in battle, and symbol of the Church triumphant over paganism and heresy.

Another great imperial workshop, that of the Emperor Otto I and his sons, is represented by a late 10th-century **ivory plaque (25)** with Christ in Majesty; the background has an open, checkered pattern, probably to let gold show through. It belongs to a series that may have decorated an altarpiece, or frontal, at Mag-

26

deburg. From Cranenburg, near the border of Holland and Germany, came a late 10th or early 11th century **situla (26)**, or holy water bucket. It is made of ivory, with copper-gilt mounts, and represents scenes from the life of Christ, carved in a primitive but appealing style. Very few complete objects of this type have been preserved. Other ivories of about the same time, chiefly from Italy, show a strong Byzantine influence.

After the fall of the Roman Empire, Western Europe was never again united, in spite of the efforts of Charlemagne and his successors. Society and the economy were decentralized; a feudal order began to prevail, and the Church, also feudal in many ways, became strong. Increasingly rich and powerful monastic orders account for the proliferation of ecclesiastical buildings and the creation of a new style that lasted through the 11th and 12th centuries, and, in some regions, into the 13th. This style, which spread rapidly through Western Europe, along the pilgrimage roads leading to the shrine of St. James of Compostela in northwest Spain, was called Romanesque, because its massive stone walls, semicircular arches, and barrel vaults recalled Roman architecture. Byzantine and Near Eastern art, however, were important in the formation of the Romanesque. The single example of Romanesque architecture in the Medieval Department is the doorway **(27)** from the abbey church of San Nicolò at Sangemini, in central Italy. Romanesque architectural decoration, however, is represented by a number of capitals **(28)** that combine reality and fantasy, and illustrate the survival of classic motifs, like volutes and acanthus leaves. Church portals were often adorned with columnar sculptures **(29)**, and the Museum has

30

31

33

three examples—two from Italy and a more formal and linear one from France—that show this aspect of architectural sculpture.

A 12th-century silver **processional cross (30)**, decorated with silver-gilt filigree and gems, is typically Romanesque in its representation of the crowned Christ with open eyes. It comes from an area in northern Spain, never under Moorish influence, where very fine metalwork was made.

Wood was also used during the Romanesque period, and, in spite of its perishability, a number of wooden statues have survived. A favorite theme was the **Virgin and Child Enthroned (31)**, a type known as the Throne of Wisdom, in which Mary holds the Child on her knees, both figures facing front. From the French region of Auvergne, where this type was popular, comes a beautiful 12th-century example made of polychrome oak. These majestic figures have an almost hypnotic force. Another wooden group of the Enthroned Virgin and Child **(32)**, from Oignies in the Meuse Valley, was also once painted and dates from about 1215. The softer posture, the smaller, not-so-frontal child, and the more realistic handling of the drapery folds illustrate the transition from Romanesque rigidity to the amiability of Gothic art.

The differences between the Romanesque and Gothic styles are also illustrated by a group of stone heads from statues on French monuments. A 12th-century **head of King David (33)** from the

34

portal of St. Anne in the Cathedral of Nôtre Dame, Paris, has large, wide-open, deeply carved eyes that give it a frozen expression; whereas a 13th-century head of a bearded king, possibly also from Nôtre Dame, is mild and almost smiling.

In the 13th century feudalism weakened, challenged by powerful kings and by the guilds and fraternities that played an increasingly important role in town life and international trade. Gothic art, which developed from Romanesque around the end of the 12th century, lasted until the Renaissance in the early 16th century.

Stained glass, which decorated the windows of Gothic churches with jewel-like color, was first developed in northern Europe where large openings in the stone were needed to admit light. The 13th-century **window (34)** in the chapel-like alcove in the Medieval Galleries came from the Abbey of St. Germain-des-Près in Paris and represents scenes in the life of St. Vincent of Saragossa, set in a checkered and geometric background typical of French Gothic stained glass.

Stained glass was mainly for churches, but tapestries were made for manors and castles also, as decoration and as protection from the dampness of the walls. They were usually made in sets and represented scenes from the Old and New Testaments and from the lives of saints, as well as allegories, myths, and stories of chivalry. They were woven in vivid colors, usually in wool, but silk and silver- or gold-covered threads were also used. Paris was the chief tapestry-making center until 1400; during the next two centuries Arras, Tournai, and Brussels took the lead. The Museum's earliest tapestry **(35)** is a fragment made perhaps in

36

Constance in the mid-14th century, representing the Crucifixion with Mary and saints, in a flat linear style. A rare **Annunciation Tapestry (36)**, probably woven in Arras in the early 15th century, illustrates the International Style in tapestry, and recalls the paintings of Melchior Broederlam, who worked at the court of Burgundy. The Baptism **(37)** is a scene from an incomplete 15th-century series representing the Seven Sacraments of the Church, with parallel scenes from the Old Testament, and shows the school of Tournai at its best; figures and composition have become more natural and three-dimensional. The three so-called **Rose Tapestries (38)** were perhaps made for Charles VII of France around 1435 or 1440, in Arras or Tournai. They have secular subjects and show courtiers in fancy costumes against a background of stripes and rosebushes. The arming of Hector **(39)** is the subject of a tapestry that probably comes from one of several sets depicting the Trojan War; these were made in Tournai at the end of the 15th century, in the atelier of Pasquier Grenier. Other subjects, like theological allegories favored in the 15th and 16th centuries, and battles, are also present in the Museum's collection.

38

42

Until the 15th century medieval houses were sparsely furnished. The Museum's collection contains a number of pieces of secular furniture, and some choir stalls and lecterns from churches **(40)**, most of them from the 15th and 16th centuries. Chests made of wood, often carved with architectural motifs and other subjects, were used for storage and sitting, since chairs were scarce; others, strengthened by iron strips, were for traveling. Higher backs and canopies identify the chairs intended for ranking dignitaries.

In the 12th and 13th centuries glazed pottery was imported from the Near East; in Spain, Arabs and Christians working together also developed a glaze with a metallic luster. This lusterware, decorated with geometric and vine patterns, was made in profusion for centuries and sent from Spain to the rest of Europe. The Museum has a very distinguished collection—basins, large plates, and pharmacy jars—of this type of so-called Hispano-Moresque ware **(41)**. During the late 14th and 15th centuries the Italians, especially in Orvieto, Siena, and Florence, also developed their special type of pottery, called majolica. It is bright in color and imaginative in decoration, as can be seen in a 14th-century **basin with a crowned lion (42)** and a very large, predominantly green platter with a horseman, both from Tuscany.

46

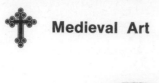

Gothic sculpture, like Romanesque, was at first closely allied to architecture. Soon, however, it acquired a new freedom and the figures began to seem more at ease. A large, polychrome wooden statue of St. Peter **(43)**, from Bellpuig de Balaguer in Catalonia, is still rather rigid in style, but there is some naturalism in the rendering of the head. A monumental 13th-

47

50

century male statue, known as St. James the Less **(44)**, possibly from the Upper Rhine, shows a more relaxed pose and softer garment folds. The Museum has several examples of the Virgin in a new style, developed by the 14th century in France, in which the figure sways to one side in an S-like curve **(45)**. These statues are made of white marble, some adorned with gold leaf in hair and mantle, or of brightly colored stone or wood. It is especially in seated examples, such as the early 14th-century stone Virgin and Child from St. Chéron (Marne), that a new, tender, and human sentiment is expressed in the relationship between Mother and Son. The monumental seated **Virgin and Child (46)** from the church of Poligny, Burgundy, from the 15th century, shows the Virgin represented as an affectionate human mother rather than an awe-inspiring divinity.

One of the rarest pieces of the medieval collection is a small polychrome and gilt group of the **Visitation (47)**, made in the region of Constance in the early 14th century. The youthful figures of Mary and Elizabeth have cavities covered with lids made of crystal cabochons, under which were, perhaps, images of the unborn Christ and John. The simple group is charming and has deep mystical feeling. Three marble sculptures that once decorated Giovanni Pisano's pulpit at the Cathedral of Pisa, as well as an eagle lectern from another of his pulpits **(48)**, are from the same period as the Visitation but are extremely different in concept and style, heralding the Italian Renaissance.

Secular as well as religious art was made for royal and noble patrons. One of the greatest of these, John, duke of Berry, who died in 1419, was buried in a tomb at Bourges from which came the Museum's small marble mourners **(49)** expressing deep grief. The marble head of a smiling princess, also from a tomb, represents the daughter of King Charles IV, **Marie of France (50)**, who died when she was 14.

52

55

During the 15th century saints became more popular than ever, and local, historical, or legendary saints were often colorfully depicted in the costumes of the period. A boxwood statuette shows St. Catherine **(51)** as a very sophisticated and fashionable young lady.

Polychrome and gilded wooden sculpture was favored in Germany, the Netherlands, and Spain. A late 15th-century German wooden relief, representing the **Baptism of Christ (52)**, is now an example of well-preserved polychromy; when it came to the Museum, the perfectly maintained brilliant colors and shining gold were covered with modern paint.

The Medieval Treasury, like the rooms reserved in medieval monasteries and cathedrals to house their most precious objects, contains an outstanding collection of ivories, enamels, metal- and leatherwork, and embroideries from various periods and countries. Ivory carvings were usually made from tusks of African elephants, but in the northern countries—England, Scandinavia, and Germany—walrus tusks were frequently used. Among the Romanesque ivories **(53)** are two walrus panels representing the Doubting Thomas and the Three Marys at the Sepulcher, made in Cologne in the second half of the 12th century for an altarpiece. Also in walrus are the Enthroned Christ and a very small but exquisite Flight into Egypt, both from England. A crucifix, a leaf from a diptych, and a Crucifixion in a jeweled filigree frame are all 12th-century Spanish work **(54)**. Most of the Gothic ivories are French, many from the Parisian workshops of the 14th century. They include religious objects: diptychs, small tabernacles with the Virgin in the middle,

59

and statuettes of all sizes. The **Descent from the Cross (55)** is a particularly beautiful plaque on which the body of Christ is movingly rendered. There are also a number of secular objects **(56)**, such as mirror cases, boxes with scenes of romance and courtly love, and combs, which are often called liturgical but were probably used in everyday life. A Venetian altarpiece **(57)** of the 14th century, made of numerous pieces of bone, has three wings, each with 13 carvings representing the lives of Christ, St. John the Baptist, and St. John the Evangelist.

The Mosan enamels, among the finest ever made, were produced in the 11th and 12th centuries in the valleys of the Meuse and Moselle rivers between France and Belgium, and in the Rhineland, especially at Cologne. They were made in the technique called champlevé, in which hollowed-out areas of a metal base are filled with raw enamel and fired. Their bright, sparkling color is sometimes translucent. The background, and occasionally parts of the figures, were gilded. There are in the medieval collection some extraordinary Mosan enamel plaques, possibly from retables or frontals. One of these is the **Pentecost (58)**.

58

The best-known French center of enameling was Limoges, where champlevé enamels were made to decorate religious and secular objects. The colors are mainly various shades of blue, red, and white. Sometimes the figures were enameled and their heads, in relief, applied to the flat surface, with incised patterns completely covering the gilt background. Other examples have gilt and incised figures and enameled backgrounds. A seated figure of **St. James (59)** was cast in metal and applied to an enameled background. Chasses, or caskets **(60)**, with

63

66

gabled tops have doors at one end and were probably used to keep relics or other valued objects. White enamel is combined with beaten gold and jewels in the beautiful little half-length figure of St. Catherine of Alexandria **(61)**, holding the broken wheel of her martyrdom.

Among the silver objects is a reliquary head of St. Yrieix **(62)**, made to hold part of the saint's skull; the carved wooden head, displayed next to the silver one, was found under the metal casing. Brilliant craftsmanship characterizes a French silver and silver-gilt statuette of **St. Christopher (63)** bearing the Christ Child.

Several objects made of less important metals, such as bronze or copper, are figures of Christ from crosses, and vessels in the shape of lions, horses, and centaurs. These aquamanilia **(64)** were used for washing hands and probably had a liturgical as well as a secular function. Secular table vessels **(65)** are represented by a collection of German jasper, crystal, and silver-gilt cups of different shapes; the double cups were made in Nuremberg in the 16th century.

Some textiles and embroideries, by their very nature perishable, have survived. Among the finest examples are the English embroideries, or *opus Anglicanum*, which were renowned throughout the world in the 13th and 14th centuries. An early 14th-century **chasuble (66)** embroidered in gold thread and seed pearls on a rich, red velvet background, is a fine example of this type of English work.

Musical Instruments

Musical Instruments

Objects, Periods	Numbers in Text
AFRICAN INSTRUMENTS	(17), (18)
AMERICAN INDIAN INSTRUMENTS	(15)
CENTRAL AMERICAN INSTRUMENTS	
CHINESE INSTRUMENTS	(22), (23)
EUROPEAN INSTRUMENTS:	(1-13)
Brass	(1), (2)
Keyboard	(6-10)
Strings	(11-13)
Woodwind	(3-5)
INDIAN INSTRUMENTS	(25), (26)
JAPANESE INSTRUMENTS	(19-21)
NEAR EASTERN INSTRUMENTS	
NORTH AFRICAN INSTRUMENTS	
SOUTH AMERICAN INSTRUMENTS	(14)
SOUTH PACIFIC INSTRUMENTS	(16)
SOUTHEAST ASIAN INSTRUMENTS	
TIBETAN INSTRUMENTS	(24)

☞ **This page helps you to find what you especially want to see and read about.**

Musical Instruments

The collection of musical instruments in the Metropolitan Museum dates from 1889, when Mrs. John Crosby Brown, the wife of a New York banker, made known her intention of donating her private collection to the Museum. In the 1870s Mrs. Brown had become interested in musical instruments when she saw a small lutelike Italian instrument made of ivory, a pandurina. Over the next three decades she gathered together from all over the world specimens of instruments that were representative of their time and their country. With amazing foresight and with the help of her sons, foreign correspondents of her husband's bank, United States consular representatives, missionaries, and the expert advice of scholars, she was successful in bringing together one of the world's richest collections of musical instruments, now appropriately called the Crosby Brown Collection of Musical Instruments of All Nations. In a letter to the Museum's trustees, dated February 16, 1889, she modestly wrote: "The intrinsic value of many of the individual instruments is not very great, but the collection is of value as a whole, as illustrating the musical habits and tastes of different peoples. It will become more valuable every year, as many of the instruments of savage tribes now in the collection are rapidly disappearing, and even now some of them cannot be replaced."

Mrs. Brown's acquisitions were given to the Museum from 1889 to 1904 until the approximately 3,000 objects were finally housed there. Over the years, additional gifts and purchases have extended even more the scope of this collection, which illustrates the development of music and music-making with approximately 4,000 instruments.

In 1942 a curator of musical instruments was appointed to reorganize and rehabilitate the Crosby Brown Collection, and the Department of Musical Instruments came into being. But the acceptance of music into an art museum was for a long time a contested question, and periodic exhibitions showed only a small percentage of these riches. The old instruments were used in concerts organized by the curator from 1941 to 1961, such as the series Music Forgotten and Remembered.

In 1971, however, the first large permanent installation was made possible by the generosity of Mrs. André Mertens, as a memorial to her husband. To a greater extent than ever before, efforts are being made to have the Museum's instruments played in lectures and demonstrations. Audio equipment enables the visitor to hear instruments on display performing music of their time.

Surely no one visiting the galleries devoted to their display will dispute the fact that musical instruments are beautiful. These objects have a two-fold appeal—they are technical tools for producing organized sound, and at the same time most of them are works of visual art in their own right. Aside from the amazing variety of forms and shapes, materials, and even colors, the painted and incised decorations give a virtual history of art styles. And today, when so-called primitive art is finally being recognized, the non-European instruments are also being accorded their share of importance in the world of the visual arts as well as in ethnomusicology.

1

The gallery space is equally divided into display areas for European instruments (west and south sides) and instruments from the Americas, the South Pacific, the Near East, Africa, Japan, China, Tibet, Southeast Asia, and India (north and east sides). Beginning with the European side, a great array of brass instruments meets the visitor's eye. Horns, bugles, trombones, and trumpets are the most important families. They range from primitive instruments—animal horns such as the shofar, and shepherds' and hunters' horns—to magnificent brass instruments of many shapes and technical refinements. Also shown are keyed brass instruments; the experimental mechanisms anticipating the invention of the valve; and, finally, many types of valve horns and valve trumpets. To sound the instruments, the breath and lips of a player on the mouthpiece sets a column of enclosed air into vibration. The illustration shows a **hand horn**, an early 19th-century instrument of a uniquely compact shape; and an **orchestral horn (1)**, which, as a forerunner of the valve instrument, has additional sections of tubing that can be selected by moving a slide, thereby increasing the number of notes that can be played on the instrument. Both horns were made in Belgium.

Straight and curved cornetts (not to be confused with the modern cornet) combine a feature of the brass instruments—the mouth cup—with a characteristic of the woodwind family—finger holes that are covered by the player's fingers to produce the desired pitch. Cornetts were usually made of wood, though one rare example in the collection is made of ivory. Their tone quality is brilliant. The bass

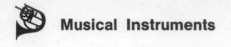

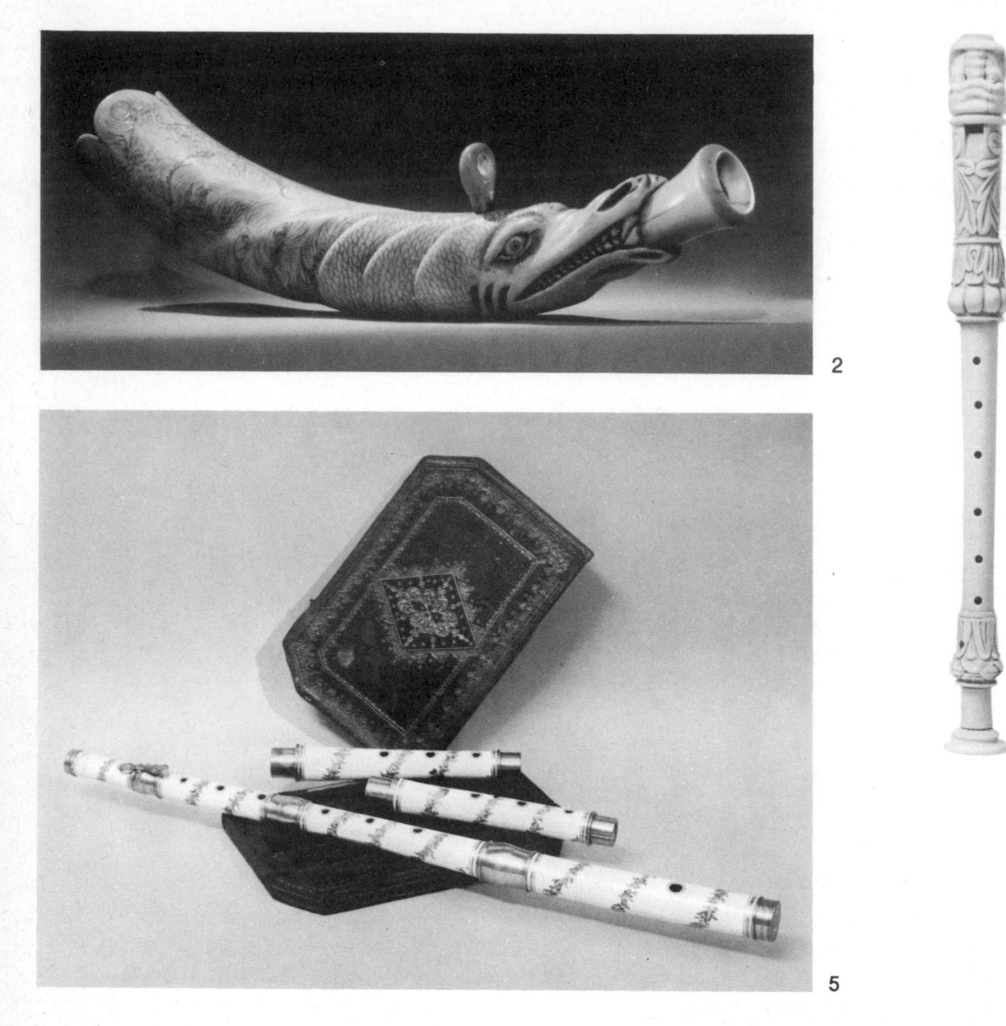

2

4

5

members of the cornett family are the fantastic serpents with their snakelike shapes. A simple French **hunting horn (2)** from about 1700, made of ivory, also imitates an animal form, resembling a monster with gills, scales, and fins. It was hung around the hunter's neck with a cord drawn through the ivory ring at the top.

A totally different group of instruments are those in which a column of air is set into motion by means of a reed, a thin piece of cane; the player, by blowing, causes the reed to vibrate. The instruments of the clarinet family all use a single reed, in contrast to those of the oboe family, which use a double reed. The Crosby Brown Collection includes replicas of the earliest European single-reed instrument—the chalumeau—and other representatives of the entire family of clarinets: contrabass, bass, tenor, alto, and soprano. Illustrated here are a **bass clarinet and basset horns (3)**; the latter are tenor clarinets with a longer tube and narrower bore than the regular clarinets. The basset horn was invented

about 1770, and its somber, velvety tone was employed by Mozart, notably in his Masonic music.

The saxophone is a single-reed metal instrument developed by Adolphe Sax in the 19th century. Four members of this family, from soprano to baritone, are included in the collection. Also represented in the display, by a whole set, is another metal instrument, the sarrusophone, named after Sarrus, a French bandmaster; it uses double reeds, resembling those of an oboe or bassoon. Many oboes and bassoons of different sizes, with their ancestors, are exhibited.

Among the woodwind instruments, recorders and flutes are represented by many specimens. Recorders are held in a vertical position, with the mouthpiece inserted between the player's lips. From the sopranino with its whistlelike sounds the recorder family extends to very large, deep-sounding contrabass recorders that have to be played standing. A French 17th-century **recorder (4)** is made of ivory and is beautifully carved with foliage, its mouthpiece in the shape of a fishlike monster. The soft, gentle tone of the recorder was later superseded by the stronger and more brilliant tone of the flute. The transverse flute was at first made of wood, and only in the 19th century of metal, following the reforms of Theobald Boehm, the great flutist, goldsmith, and expert in musical acoustics. A showpiece from southern Germany is the **porcelain flute (5)** made about 1760, which is shown with its original case.

Magnificent keyboard instruments in the Museum do justice to the motto sometimes painted on Renaissance harpsichords: "Pleasing to ear and eye alike." For indeed the embellishments on some of these instruments—carving, intarsia in wood and mother-of-pearl, painting, and the tracery of a sound hole—are a great visual delight. In addition, the progression of the complicated mechanism of the keyboard action, from that used in a small Italian spinettina to that of an ornate 19th-century English piano, can be seen in the collection. The Venetian

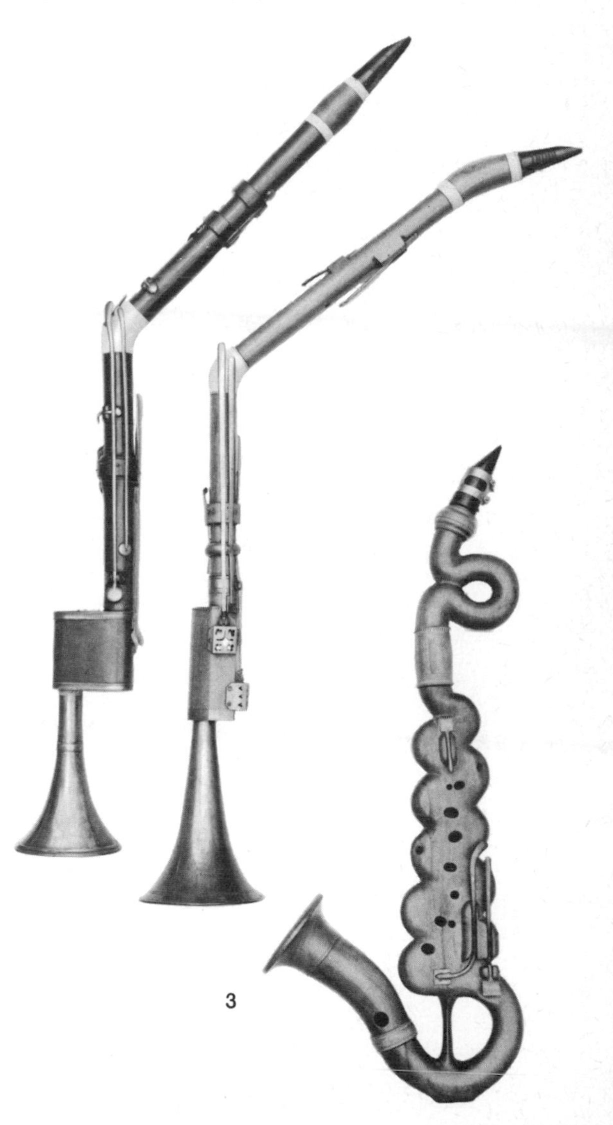

3

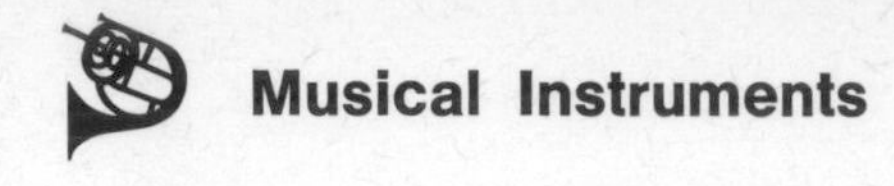

MVSICA · DVLCE · LABORVM · LEVAMEN

7

6

spinettina (6) is beautifully preserved and in perfect playing condition. It was made in 1540 for Eleonora d'Este, the duchess of Urbino, a member of a celebrated music-loving family. The virginal, like the spinet and harpsichord, has strings plucked by quills. This lavishly decorated **double virginal (7)** was made in 1581 by Hans Ruckers the Elder of Antwerp, who was the founder of the most famous Flemish dynasty of keyboard-instrument makers. An elaborate design decorates the side walls of the inside, and the lid, when opened, reveals a painting showing a wide terrace on which elegant people are dining, playing musical instruments, and dancing.

The Museum has many outstanding examples of harpsichords, the most popular keyboard instrument until the invention of the piano. The size of these instruments made them ideal vehicles for decoration. One of the most fantastic is a veritable triumph of Baroque furniture—a **gilded harpsichord (8)** made in Italy in the mid-17th century; its body is supported by three fishtailed Tritons, while two additional sea nymphs

8

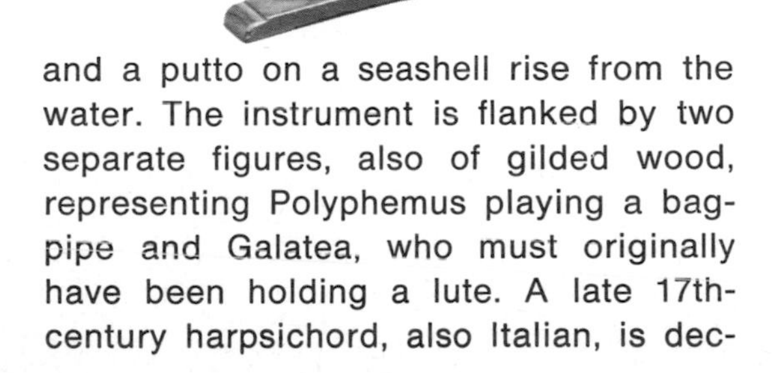

9

and a putto on a seashell rise from the water. The instrument is flanked by two separate figures, also of gilded wood, representing Polyphemus playing a bagpipe and Galatea, who must originally have been holding a lute. A late 17th-century harpsichord, also Italian, is decorated with pastoral scenes; the mermaid between the front columns is the device of the Colonna family. This instrument has a more complex mechanism—three sets of unison strings with three rows of jacks, operated from a single keyboard.

Perhaps the most famous instrument in the Museum stands like a poor cousin among its ornamented relations. Three simple legs support the plain black body of the earliest extant **pianoforte (9)**. It was made by Bartolommeo Cristofori, the inventor of the piano, while he was in

10

Florence as keeper of instruments at the Medici court. Only three of his pianos have survived; the one shown here dates from 1720. Although Cristofori's pianoforte, meaning literally "soft-loud," resembled the harpsichord in shape, soundboard, keyboard, and strings, the ingenious improvement was the hammer mechanism, which replaced the jack-and-quill action of the harpsichord. On this new type of instrument, loudness of sound could be controlled by finger pressure. Cristofori's invention initiated a long line of pianofortes of different makes that competed for a long time with the harpsichord. The Museum possesses many which for reasons of space cannot be shown. One piano on display is the **Erard piano (10)**, built in England in 1840, with a case designed by George Henry Blake. The marquetry is of various woods, ivory, and mother-of-pearl; carved and gilded scrolls, masks, and floral and shell designs add to the profusion of decoration.

With the current revival of interest in Renaissance and Baroque music, many of the instruments that once belonged among the treasured possessions of a cultured household are being played and studied again. One such instrument is the lute, which was widely used in the 15th, 16th, and 17th centuries as a solo or ensemble instrument. Lutes, with their beautiful pear-shaped or almond-shaped bodies, wide fingerboards, and sharply bent necks, were often depicted in contemporary paintings. Toward the end of the Renaissance and in the Baroque period, bass or archlutes were invented, which had two sets of strings, one stopped, the other open, and consequently two peg boxes. Three types of archlutes were the theorbos, the chitarrones, and the theorbo-lutes, all present in the exhibition.

Other types of plucked string instruments are the **guitar and chitarra battente (11)**. The smaller instrument in the illustration is a French guitar from 1770; it has a flat back, gut strings reaching down the sound board to a frontal string holder, and is plucked by the fingers. The larger instrument is a chitarra battente made about 1700; it has a deep body and a vaulted back made of many ribs. Its wire strings are struck with a plectrum. Both instruments were widely used in the 17th and 18th centuries, particularly in Italy, Spain, and France. A curious instrument represented in the Crosby Brown Collection is the lyre guitar. For the sake of appearance, the neck and the stopped strings of a true guitar were combined with the arms and the crossbar of an ancient Greek or Roman lyre. This ladies' instrument was fashionable in the Napoleonic period, and it harmonized well with the flowing dresses of the elegant ladies at court.

Viols and violins belong to the bowed family of stringed instruments. Their sound is produced by drawing a bow across the strings with one hand, while the fingers of the other stop the strings on the fingerboard. Viols were held in a vertical position, between the knees. An ensemble of viols, from the highest treble member to the largest bass instrument, was a common and beautiful combination in the 16th and 17th centuries. The violin, with its capacity for a louder and more resonant tone, was initially considered unpleasantly strident. But as a brilliant solo instrument and in the orchestra the violin eventually replaced its older cousins. The violin makers of northern Italy made the most famous violins, coveted today by the greatest virtuosos. The two in the exhibition by Antonius Stradivarius—the **Francesca violin (12)**, from 1694, and the An-

11

12

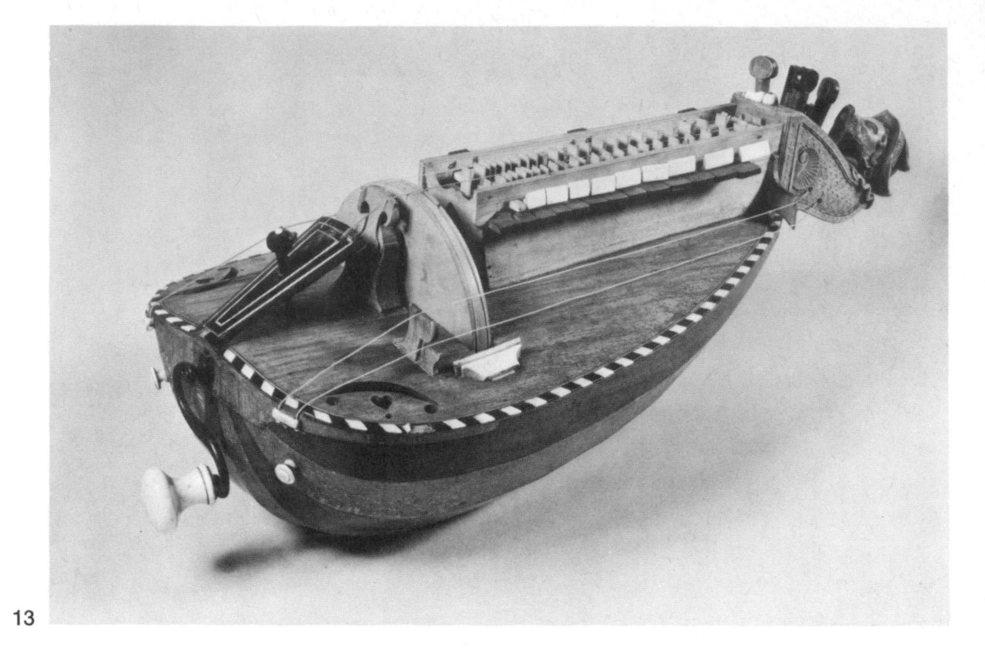

13

tonius, dated 1721—have been played in concerts at the Museum. Tiny kits, or pochettes, were miniature fiddles formerly used by dancing masters, who carried them in their pockets. Tone quality was not so important, hence many were given a playful form or interesting decorations.

The **hurdy-gurdy (13)** was a mechanized fiddle, the strings sounded by means of a rosined wheel. It existed in many shapes, the one shown here having a lute body. In addition to the melody strings in the center, drone strings on the sides sounded a continuous note, much like the drone of a bagpipe.

The wide range of Mrs. Crosby Brown's interest is evident from the instruments she collected from countries around the globe, many of the finest of which are on display. In primitive societies, objects from nature were often used to fashion musical instruments. From Central America comes a group of rattles and scrapers that use dried and hardened gourds some ornamented with feathers; a scraper is rubbed or scraped with a stick to mark time in dance music. Interesting is the Mexican guitar in which the shell of an armadillo forms the back. Also from Mexico are the many charming pottery whistles and rattles made in curious animal and grotesque human shapes, which recall the more sophisticated sculpture of that country. The **whistling jar (14)** from Peru, South America, is one of several in the collection. When the jar is tipped, water flows into the bird-shaped vessel, compressing the air, which then escapes through a whistle hidden in the head of the bird.

Instruments of the Northwest American Indians include unique multiple flutes and many different types of rattles. The **rattle (15)** shown here is in the form of a mythical bird; its breast shows a face and on its back is the figure of a shaman and a bird, probably a kingfisher. These figures are united by their tongues, signifying the conveyance of magical power.

Instruments from the South Pacific use readily available materials, such as bamboo and shells. There are various horns made of pieces of bamboo; also a mouth organ using bamboo pipes. A nose flute of carved wood is played with one nostril of the nose, while the other is blocked. Drums, such as some interesting examples here, are made of hollowed logs; one end frequently is carved to resemble an animal's head, while the opposite end is covered with snakeskin. Both the **bull roarer and time marker (16)** from New Guinea have the same kind of decoration; spiral patterns were incised on the surface and filled with white lime. Whirled through the air by means of a string, the bull roarer makes a whirring sound, said to convey the voice of an ancestor. The time marker, as the name implies, was struck on the palm of a hand to keep time in chants.

From the Near East—Iran, Syria, Turkey, and Asiatic Russia—come different types of Arab musical instruments. Some

15

16

14

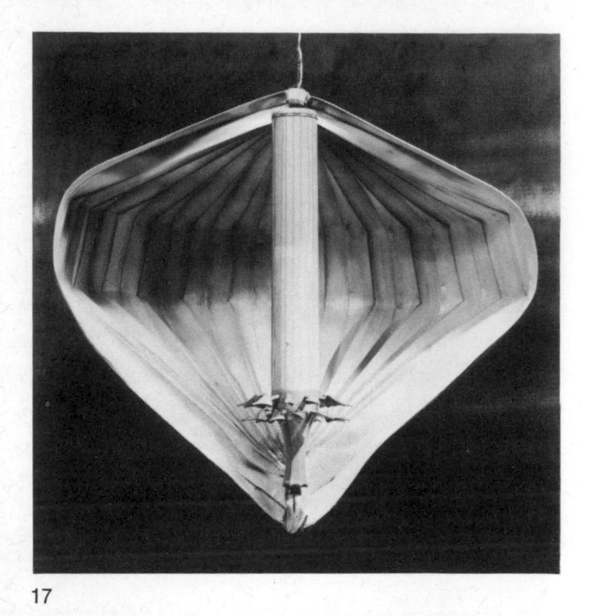

17

were brought to Europe during the expansion of Muslim power, others were introduced during the Crusades. The naqqara, or kettledrum, in use in Islamic countries since the Middle Ages, was the ancestor of the European kettledrum and was called the naker in England. Long-necked lutes and spike fiddles were beautifully inlaid with mother of pearl, wood, or other material.

The African zanza is present in the exhibit in many varieties and from many regions. Basically a wooden box with thin tongues made of metal or split cane, the zanza is played by depressing and releasing the strips with the finger tips. Carved decorations enhance the zanza. A particularly beguiling instrument from Africa, from the island of Madagascar, is the **marovany (17)**; the metal strings are extended along a tube of bamboo, and the sound is projected by means of a dry palm leaf. Many African horns are made of elephant tusks.

Curiously striking are the examples of the **lyre, or kissar (18)**, an instrument which has two arms projecting from

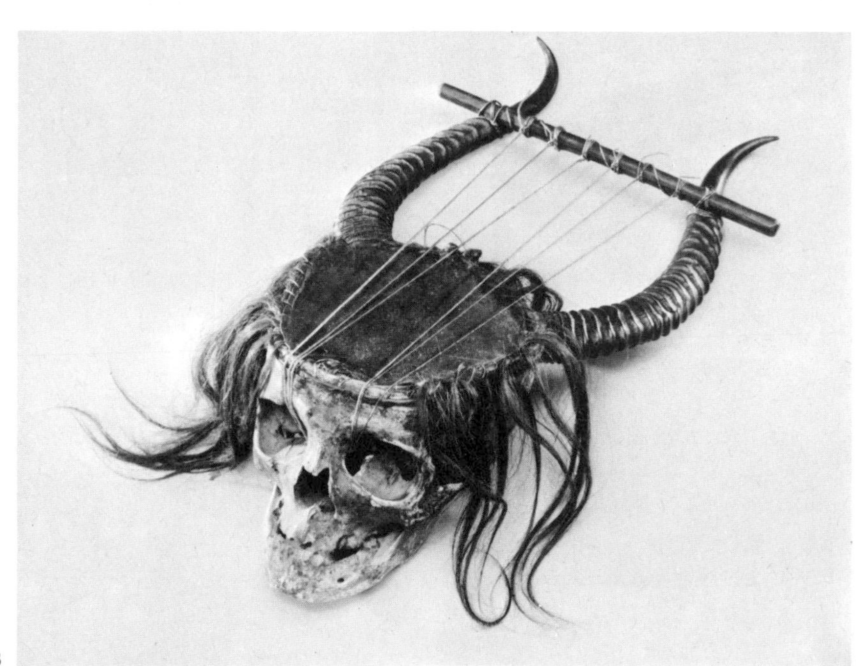

18

19

the body, with strings attached to a crossbar. Some lyres from Central Africa use a human skull with antelope horns. Other African instruments represented are the arched harp, stick and harp zithers, and drums. Of the Benin tribe, famous for sculpture and metalcraft, the exhibit includes a bronze bell decorated with a human mask, and the upper end of a large bronze wind instrument with figural designs.

The musical instruments of the Far East are of very ancient derivation and visually are as sophisticated as any other form of Oriental art. The **gong (19)**, an instrument from Japan, is supported by two grotesque demons. Long-necked fiddles, or kei kin, have bamboo, gourd, or parchment bodies and two to four strings. Represented by many different examples is the classical zither of Japan, the koto, which existed in varying sizes and types, some with only one string, the ichi gen kin, others with as many as 25 strings. The right hand with plectra attached to the fingers plucks the strings, the left controls the pitch.

In many countries instruments with animal shapes had mythological and symbolic meaning and were connected with nature, such as water, rain, the sun and moon, or the rise and fall of tides. The

Japanese slit drum (20), or maku-gyo, used in Buddhist and Taoist services, has a naturalistic fish shape; two other drums vaguely retain portions of the fish form, but recombine the visual elements. Various kinds of bells and gongs, often made of bronze, were also used in religious ceremonies. Other Japanese instruments include a great variety of flutes with their cases, all richly ornamented. A matching set of three-stringed instruments is decorated with a rooster design in lacquer. One is a short-necked lute, biwa, the other a long-necked lute, samisen, and the third a koto. Also shown are two examples of a mouth organ, the sho, similar to the Chinese sheng, which consists of bamboo pipes fitted into a wooden wind chamber, again beautifully decorated with lacquer designs. The bamboo pipes are equipped with small delicate metal reeds. Illustrated here are a **biwa and sho (21)**.

In China and Japan percussion instruments play a very special role in religious belief, and this is true particularly of sonorous stones through whose sound the undiluted voice of nature—using no strings or wind—speaks to the meditative soul. A beautiful example is the large piece of jade suspended in an ornamented teakwood frame. Chinese gongs frequently had luck-bringing animals, such as the bat, incised on their surface. Bells are made of bronze and brass in many visually appealing shapes. The **bronze drum (22)**, with intricate geometric designs and four cast frogs, comes from the Han Dynasty (206 B.C. to A.D. 220). Some bronze bells show geometric ar-

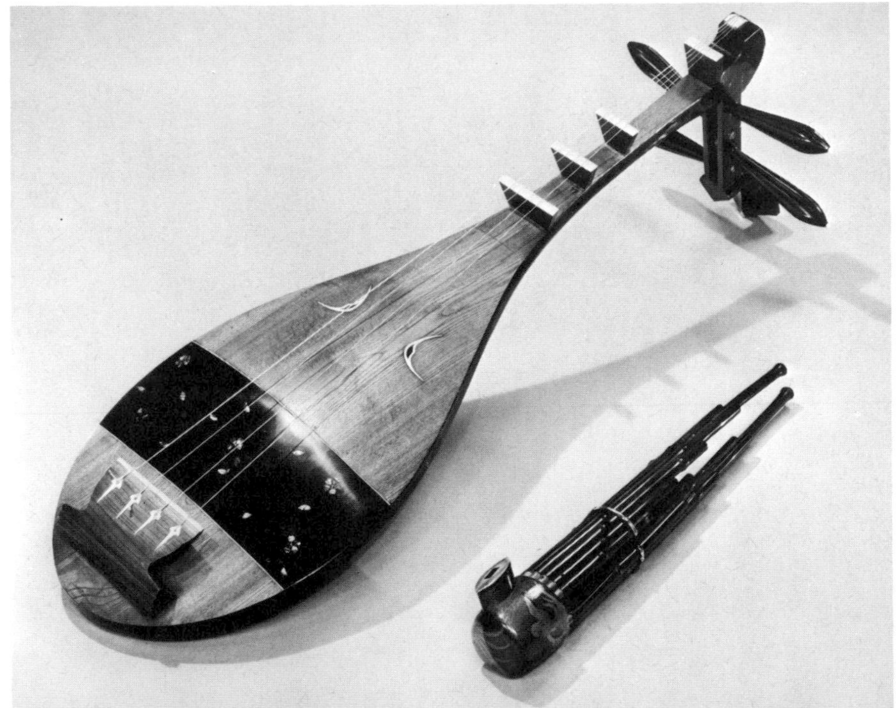

21

22

rangements of projections which originally represented nipples, signs of fertility and eternity.

An instrument of great beauty is the **p'ip'a (23)**, a Chinese lute often used to accompany ballad singing. The Museum's p'ip'a has interlocking ivory plaques, each with a different design.

A copper **temple trumpet (24)** with a bell in the shape of a dragon's head comes from Tibet, as do trumpets made from thigh bones of lama priests. One drum is made of two human skulls.

A number of instruments are from Southeast Asia, including the Burmese arched harp, whose curved neck rises gracefully from the resonating body, which is decorated with delicate painting.

Indian instruments are outstanding for their beauty and variety of shapes. Certain Indian deities closely associated with specific instruments are painted on them in the form of decoration. The peacock, for example, is consecrated to the

24

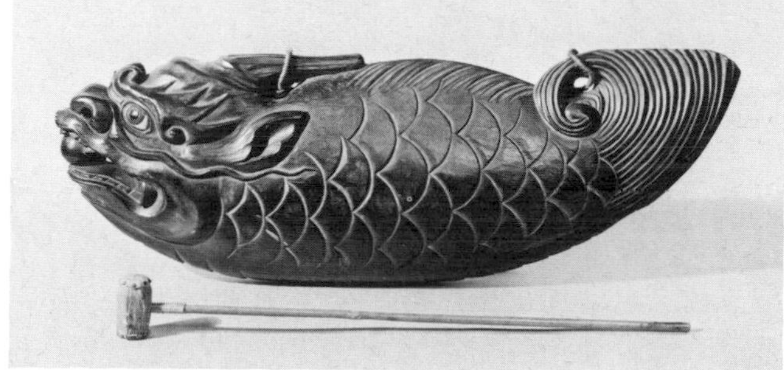

23

20

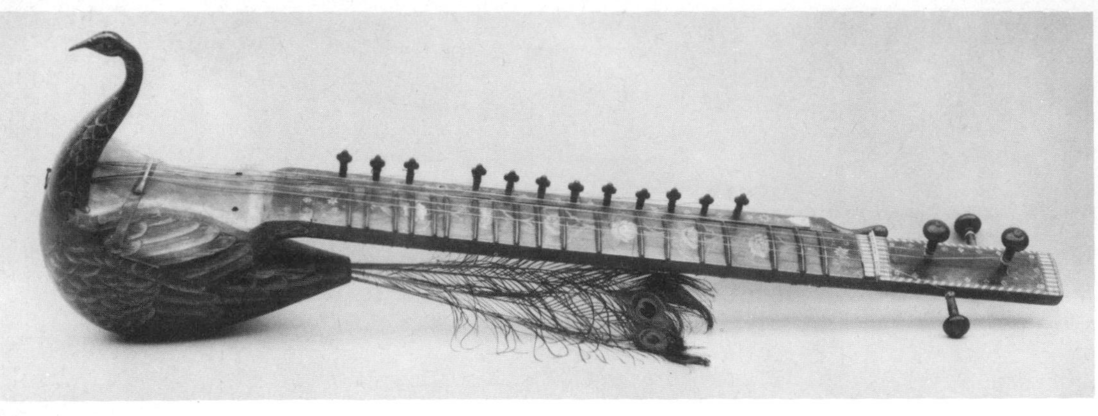

25

goddess Parvati and appears frequently. Sometimes even the instrument is in the shape of a peacock, as the **mayuri (25)**, or peacock lute. The vina is one of the most important instruments in Indian tradition. Technically it is a stick zither with resonators usually made from gourds. At first two large gourds were used; later only one, the other being transformed into an artfully fashioned lute body. The **sitar and vina (26)** are closely related, the sitar being the descendant of the vina and distinguished from it by having movable frets. Many Indian stringed instruments have two sets of strings—one set running over the bridge and stopped by the fingers against the frets, and a larger set underneath, acting as sympathetic strings.

The tambura is the classical Indian drone instrument and is used to sound the same note over and over. The sarod and sursanga are plucked, while the sarangi and the sarinda are played with a bow. The pungi is used by snake charmers; two reed pipes protrude from a spherical wind chamber made from a gourd. The Indian instruments give only a hint of the collection in the Museum and of the variety of Indian music with its intricate rhythmic and melodic patterns.

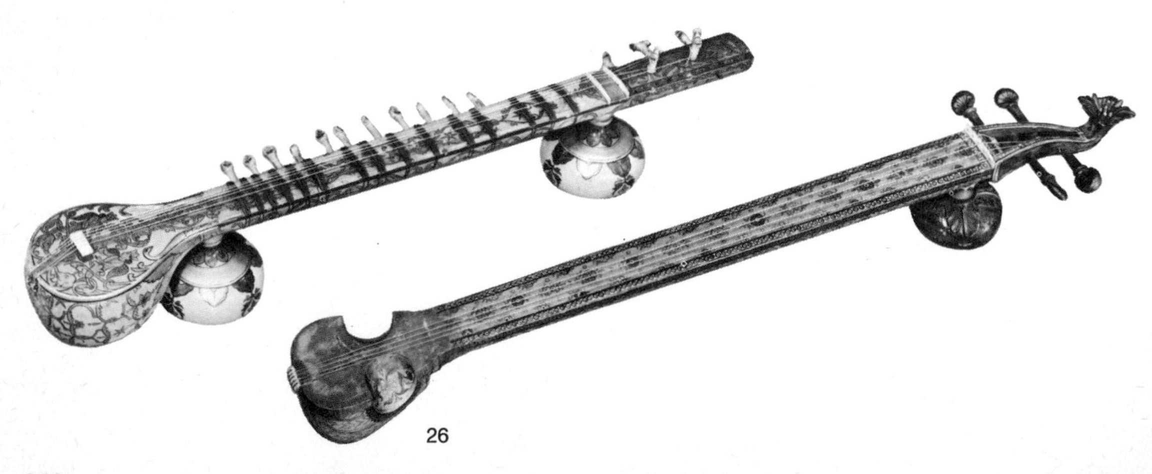

26

Primitive Art

Primitive Art

Prints and Photographs

Prints and Photographs

Objects, Periods, Styles, Artists	Numbers in Text
ARCHITECTURAL DRAWINGS, PRINTS, BOOKS	(10), (19), (21)
CONTEMPORARY PRINTS	(8)
DRAWINGS	(19-23)
DÜRER	
FESTIVAL BOOKS and PRINTS	(11)
FURNITURE DESIGNS	(20)
GOYA	(6)
ILLUSTRATED BOOKS	(9-16)
INTERIOR DESIGNS	(19)
JEWELRY DESIGNS	(22)
LANDSCAPE and GARDEN PRINTS	(15)
ORNAMENT DESIGNS	(14)
PATTERN BOOKS for calligraphy, lace, embroidery	(12-13)
PHOTOGRAPHS	(24-27)
POSTERS	(7)
PRINTS: woodcuts, engravings, etchings, aquatints, mezzotints, monotypes, lithographs	(1-16)
RELIGIOUS PRINTS and BIBLES	(1)
REMBRANDT	(3)
REPRODUCTIVE PRINTS	(4)
SILHOUETTES	(17)
TRADE CARDS and CATALOGUES	(18)

☞ **This page helps you to find what you especially want to see and read about.**

Prints and Photographs

The Department of Prints and Photographs, founded in 1916, is far more extensive than its title suggests. Besides prints and photographs, it includes illustrated books, drawings, posters, silhouettes, and trade cards. The collection has been formed with the intention of showing the high points of the history of printmaking, but this is only one of its many aims. Both the department's first curator, William M. Ivins, Jr., and his successor, A. Hyatt Mayor, collected with fresh insight and an unprejudiced eye in areas whose importance had not been recognized before. The Department of Prints shares exhibition galleries with the Department of Drawings, and prints or drawings are shown separately or together in revolving exhibits. In addition to the loggias of the Blumenthal Patio and the adjoining gallery, the Print Study Room is open to the public by appointment.

The illustrations in this *Guide* were selected not to give a survey of the history of printmaking, book illustration, or photography, but to give some idea of the most remarkable characteristic of the collection—its comprehensiveness. This necessarily limited selection only hints at the range, breadth, and variety of the department's treasures.

1

2

3

PRINTS

Printmaking did not begin in the West until the early 15th century, when paper was made in quantity. One of the most beautiful of the prints from this period is a German woodcut of the **Madonna and Child (1)**. It is surprising how few 15th-century prints have survived in more than one impression, considering the quantity that must have once been made. Sold at religious shrines and pinned on walls, they were not highly valued and therefore few were preserved. This woodcut is in excellent condition; no doubt it was preserved pasted inside a book.

In complete contrast to this religious image is Antonio Pollaiuolo's **Battle of the Ten Naked Men (2)**, dating from the 1460s, about 30 years later than the *Madonna and Child*. It was the first print made by a great artist. Although this was his only engraving, he carefully signed it in the tablet on the left. Ostensibly a battle scene, it is actually a study of anatomy and shows all the men's muscles, almost as if the figures had been flayed. Like Pollaiuolo, several major artists experimented with printmaking only a few times; among them were Pieter Bruegel, Peter Paul Rubens, and Michelangelo da Caravaggio.

Unlike them, Rembrandt devoted a great deal of his time to making prints, and made over 300 etchings. Starting very tentatively in his teens, he became the most skillful printmaker of the 17th century. No artist before or since has taken such full advantage of the unique characteristics of the technique: a plate can produce an image and can then be reworked to print a completely transformed image. The two impressions of the **Three Crosses (3)** reproduced here demonstrate this. The Museum's collection of Rembrandt prints is particularly rich in his later works.

Besides prints made by great painters, there are many so-called reproductive prints, or prints made after paintings. The engraving by Nicolas François Regnault

5

after Jean-Honoré Fragonard's painting **Le Baiser à la Dérobée (4)** is a reproductive print, but it is also a *tour de force* with its visual effects in the rendering of fabrics. Reproductive prints are often of interest in themselves and are indispensable tools in the study of painting. In many cases the paintings from which prints were made have been lost or badly damaged, and reproductive prints are the only visual record. Such prints have often been the basis for the attribution of a painting.

Of all the artists who turned to printmaking in the 19th century, Edgar Degas was the most uninhibited. He experimented with almost every technique, but made more monotypes than any other

4

type of print. Although Giovanni Benedetto Castiglione invented the monotype in the 17th century, it was Degas who successfully exploited this technique. He called monotypes "drawings made with greasy ink and printed." He did not observe the traditional distinctions between printmaking and drawing, and many of his monotypes were finished with color pastels. This monotype of two girls in front of a fireplace, called **The Fireplace (5)**, is one of his most disturbing works.

The outstanding characteristic of prints is that they are originals in multiple, but there are exceptions. The Museum has many unique prints, including Lucas Cranach's woodcut *Agony in the Garden*. Francisco Goya's **Giant (6)**, one of his greatest works, survives in only six impressions, and this is one of the two now in American collections. The brooding figure looks enormous, and it is difficult to believe that such an impressive work is only 11 inches high.

The rare poster by Léon Bakst of the dancer **Caryathis (7)** is one of the few posters that the Russian artist designed. The great period of posters began in the late 19th century, when lithography made it technically possible to print huge sheets in several colors. The Museum owns examples of most of the posters by Toulouse-Lautrec, the best-known of the French 19th-century artists who excelled in this art. There are others by Pierre Bonnard, Jean Edouard Vuillard, Théophile Alexandre Steinlen, and an extensive group by the American Will Bradley.

7

6

Although for many the Metropolitan Museum is associated mainly with the art of the past, it has collected in the contemporary field ever since its founding in 1870. Among the earliest acquisitions in

8

¶ PROEMIO DI SER ALEXANDRO BRACCIO AL
preſtantiſſimo & excellentiſſimo giouane Lorẽzo di Pier frã
ceſco de Medici ſopra la traductione duna hyſtoria di due a/
manti compoſta dalla felice memoria di Papa Pio .ii.

BEnche molti ſieno li exempli Lorẽzo mio excel
lentiſſimo : pequali facilmente in altri ho potu
to comprehendere quanto ſieno ualide & gran
di leforze damore & molte carte habbi riuolte:
doue lincendii ſuoi ſitractano & fannoſi mani/
feſti: nientedimãco alchuna coſa non ha potuto
piu ueramente monſtrarmi laſua potentia: che lo experimento
che ho facto in me ſteſſo: concioſia coſa che nella mia florida eta

a

9

the Print Department were works by Henri Matisse, Jean Edouard Vuillard, Pierre Bonnard, and Pablo Picasso. And the Museum has a large collection of prints by contemporary Americans. In 1971 Robert Rauschenberg was commissioned to make a print to celebrate the Museum's 100th Anniversary, the **Centennial Certificate (8)**.

ILLUSTRATED BOOKS

The Department of Prints and Photographs, unlike many other print collections, has not concentrated solely on the acquisition of single sheet prints but has also acquired books in which prints were used as illustrations. German and Italian 15th-century illustrated books are particularly well represented. One of the most charming is **The Story of Two Lovers (9),** by Aeneas Silvius Piccolomini, who was later Pope Pius II. In it the Botticelli-like lovers gracefully act out their romance. This book was a rarity in 15th-century Florentine publishing, when most books were of a religious nature, like the fiery sermons of Girolamo Savonarola, many of which are now in the Metropolitan Museum.

Books on architecture form an important part of the department's collection. They range from illustrated books on architectural theory to simple how-to-do-it books and elaborate books showing the

works of famous architects. There is an unusually complete group of illustrated editions of Marcus Vitruvius. This plate from Johann David Steingruber's *Architectonisches Alphabet*, from an edition published in 1773, shows a design for a **building in the shape of an A (10)**.

The only visual records of some of the most lavish celebrations of the past are the "fête books" published to commemorate them. Such publications were printed on the occasion of important births, marriages, coronations, royal and state entries, and funerals. One of the 18th century's most extravagant festivities was the **fireworks display (11)** in Paris for the birth of the son of Marie Antoinette and Louis XVI. Here it is shown in an engraving by Moreau le jeune.

Many books, such as herbals, and ana-

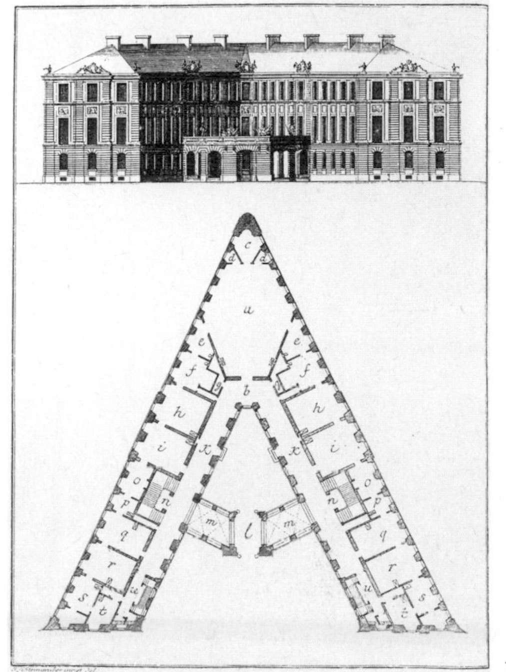

10

11

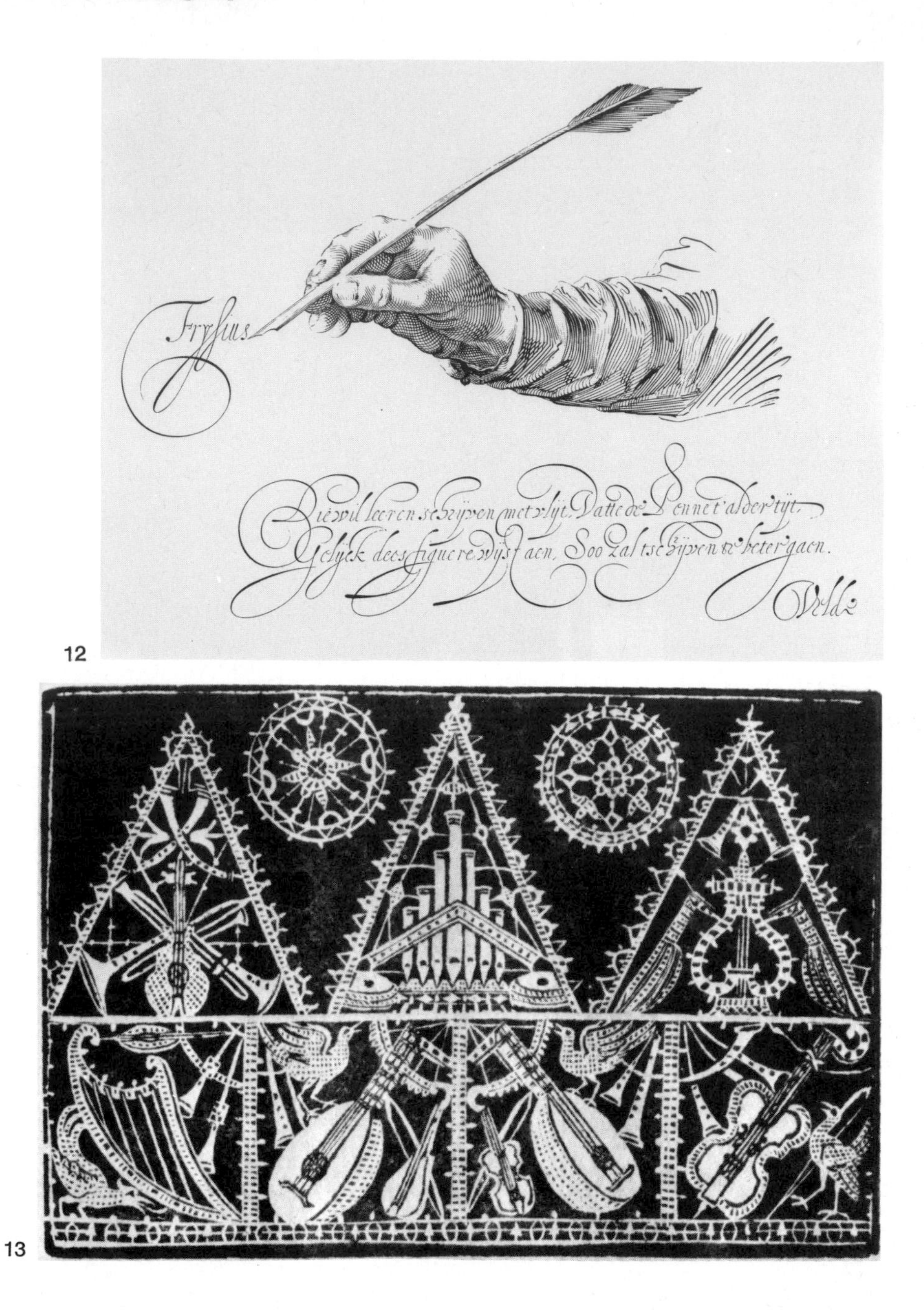

12

13

tomy and drawing books, were instructional. This page from a **writing book (12)** by Jan van de Velde is a good example. Calligraphy, though always more highly esteemed in the East than in the West, was part of every civilized person's education. But it is an art that was always changing, and manuals were continually

14

15

published to teach the newest styles.

Lace books provided designs for lace makers. The Venetians of the 16th and 17th centuries were particularly renowned for their lace, and the **pattern book (13)** by Cesare Vecellio is one of an extensive group of such books in the Museum.

Goldsmiths also relied on books of designs, and this symmetrical **floral bouquet (14)** is one of the plates from *Bouquets d'Orfèvrerie* by Baltasar Le Mercier, published in Paris in 1626. The inventive artist has embellished the design with the amusing setting of a flower-breathing dragon. Such ornament designs are a very important part of the collection, and they are essential for an understanding of the way craftsmen worked.

The history of changes in garden design is well illustrated in many garden books. Where money was no object, the taste in gardens was as changeable as the fashion in clothes. The **labyrinth at Versailles (15)**, shown here in an etching by Sebastien Le Clerc from *Labyrinthe de Versailles* (1677), must have been one of the most delightful ever devised, with its fountain sculptures illustrating the fables of La Fontaine. It, too, yielded to fashion and was replaced by a more naturalistic garden.

Some of the greatest artists have illustrated books, ranging from the *Apocalypse* illustrated by Albrecht Dürer to

Paul Verlaine's **Parallèlement, illustrated by Pierre Bonnard (16).** Bonnard's lithographs, printed in pinkish hues ranging from pale rose to sanguine, frame the text, make charming head and tail pieces, and often spread completely across the page with a sensuous vivacity that makes this one of the most beautiful of illustrated books. It is one of the few "livres de luxe" that looks as if it were meant to be read and not just admired.

Splendides, glorieuses,
Bellement furieuses
Dans leurs jeunes ébats,
Fous mon orgueil en bas
Sous tes fesses joyeuses!

16

SILHOUETTES

The Mary Martin Collection of Silhouettes now in the Museum is one of the finest in the world. The silhouette or profile artist traveled widely making portraits, until the invention of photography in the 19th century superseded his craft. Augustin

17

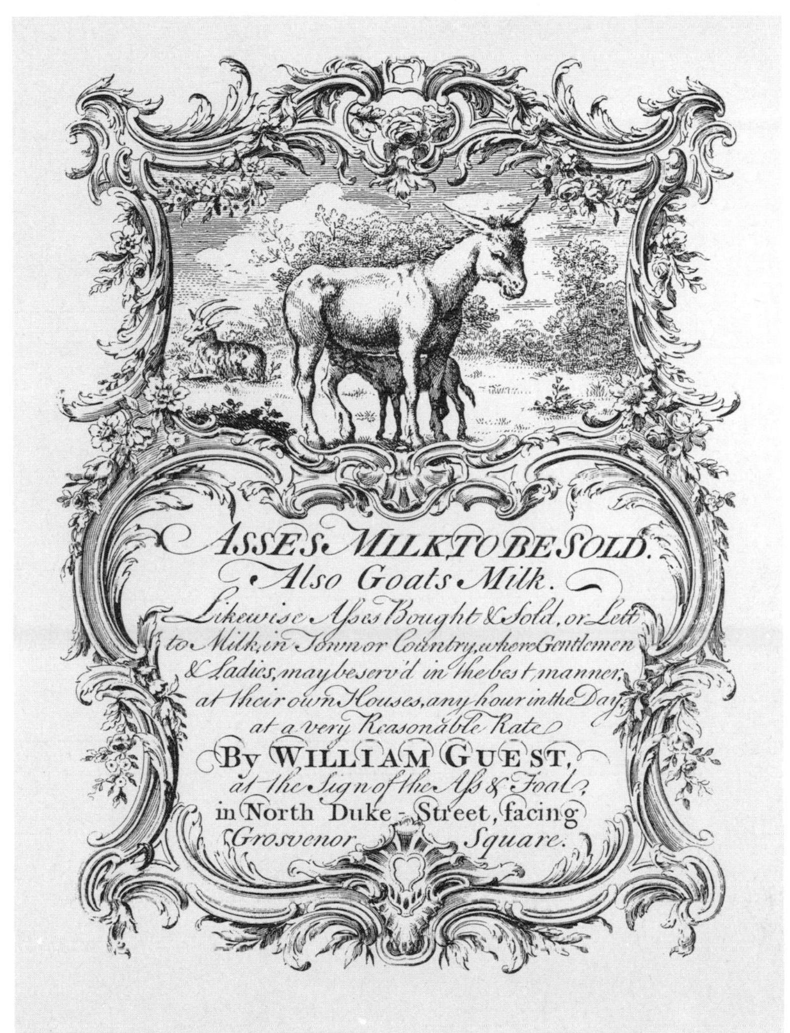

18

Edouart was one of the most talented of the French 18th-century silhouette makers. He was particularly proud of his group portraits rendered in perspective, and the **Magic Lantern (17)** reproduced here was one of his showpieces.

TRADE CARDS

The Museum has two extraordinary collections of trade cards, which show how advertisers presented their wares to the public. This charming advertisement for **asses milk (18)**, from the Bella C. Landauer Collection of European Trade Cards, gives us a glimpse of life in 18th-century England. The Jefferson Burdick Collection consists of American trade cards, tobacco and cigarette insert cards, valentines, and printed ephemera.

DRAWINGS

Although the Museum has a separate

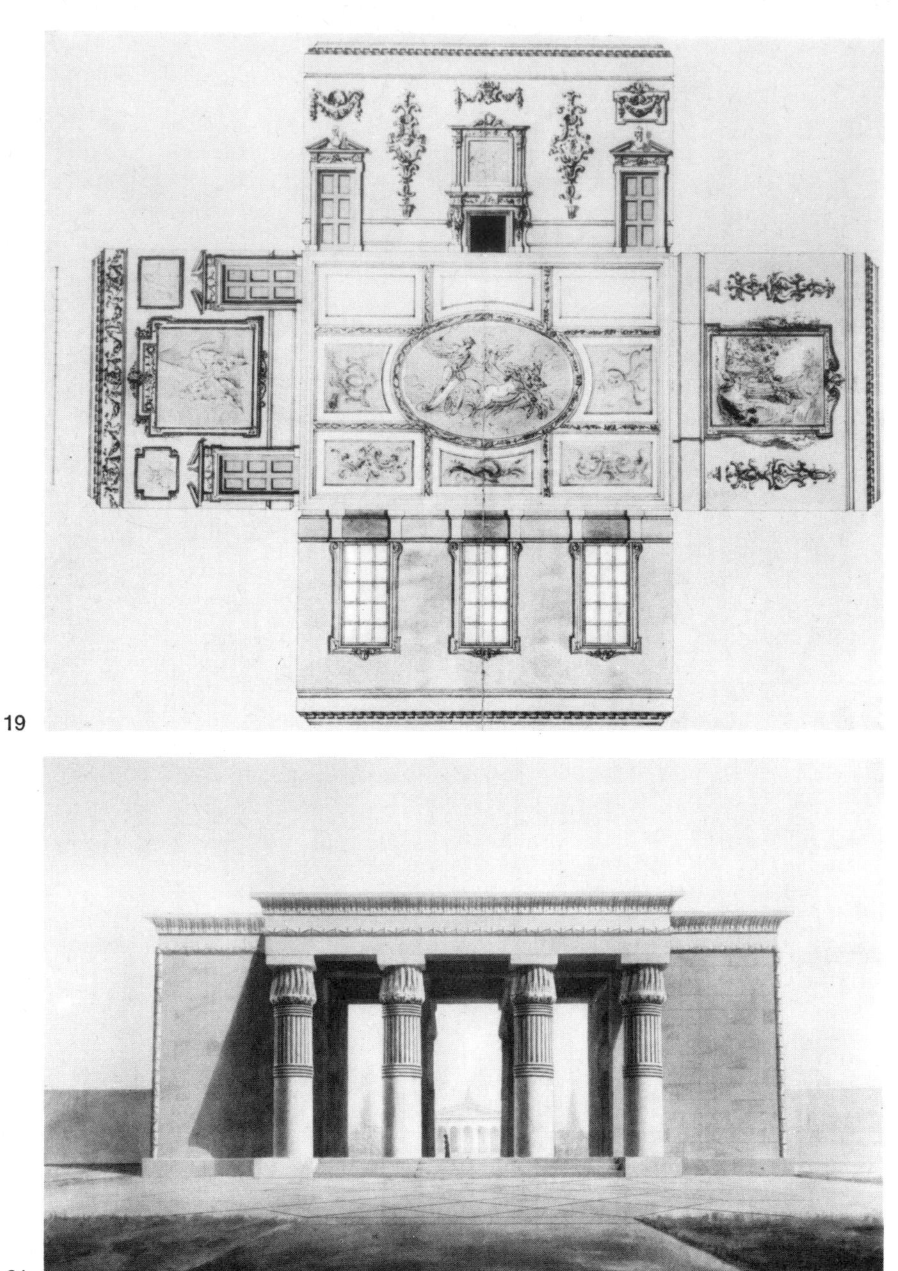

19

21

Department of Drawings, certain types of drawings are kept in the Print Department: designs by jewelers, goldsmiths, cabinetmakers, sculptors, and architects; costume drawings; and preparatory drawings for prints and book illustrations. These provide a history of style in general, as well as a history of architecture,

20

particularly in relation to interiors. Of special interest are the drawings for objects elsewhere in the Museum. The drawing by John Sanderson is for the **Dining Room from Kirtlington Park (19)**, Oxfordshire, which is now installed in the Museum. It was the practice of 18th-century architects to prepare very finished drawings for their clients before the work was executed.

Also dating from this period is the outstanding group of furniture designs by Thomas Chippendale for his *Gentleman and Cabinet-Maker's Director*, one of the most influential furniture books ever published. The Museum is fortunate to have drawings for many of the beautiful pieces in this book; among them is this design for an elaborate **state bed (20)**.

Besides drawings for interiors and furniture, the collection includes many architectural drawings. Among them is a group by the 19th-century American Alexander Jackson Davis, who was one of the most imaginative architects of his day. This design for a **monument in the Egyptian style (21)** is characteristic.

To complement the Museum's costumes, we have an extensive collection of costume and fashion drawings, including an outstanding group by Erté (Romain de Tirtoff) that are the quintessence of the elegance of the 1920s and 30s. Erté, an extraordinarily prolific artist, designed covers for *Harper's Bazaar*, costumes and sets for the theater and movies, and fashion drawings, which were more inspirational than factual, like this **drawing for crystal jewelry (22)**.

Drawings for prints reveal an artist's working method and are included in the

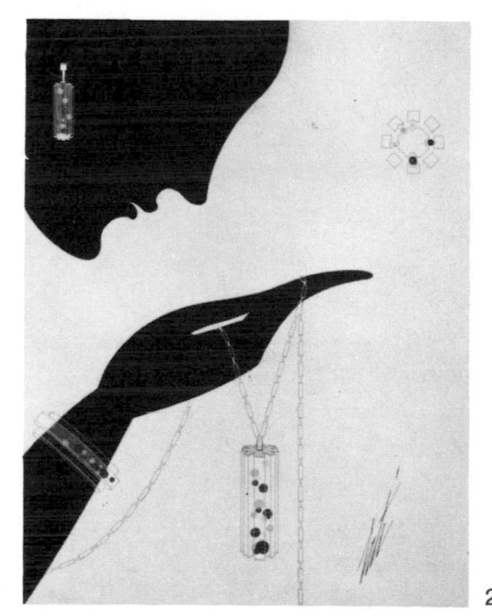

22

23

department. The drawing by Jean Bérain, one of the most prominent artists working at the time of Louis XIV, is for an engraving. It shows the **catafalque of Louis de Bourbon (23)**, Prince de Condé, and Bérain has indicated certain changes that were to be made before printing.

PHOTOGRAPHS

The Museum has one of the outstanding photographic collections in the country. It began in 1928 with the gift of several photographs by Alfred Stieglitz. Five years later he gave the Museum his remarkable collection, a survey of photography from its inception to about 1920. And through the Stieglitz Bequest in 1948 the Museum acquired much of his own work, including his extraordinary series **Equivalents (24)**, dated 1927.

The department's holdings of 19th-century work are particularly strong, and include a group of photographs by Julia Margaret Cameron, who was given a

24

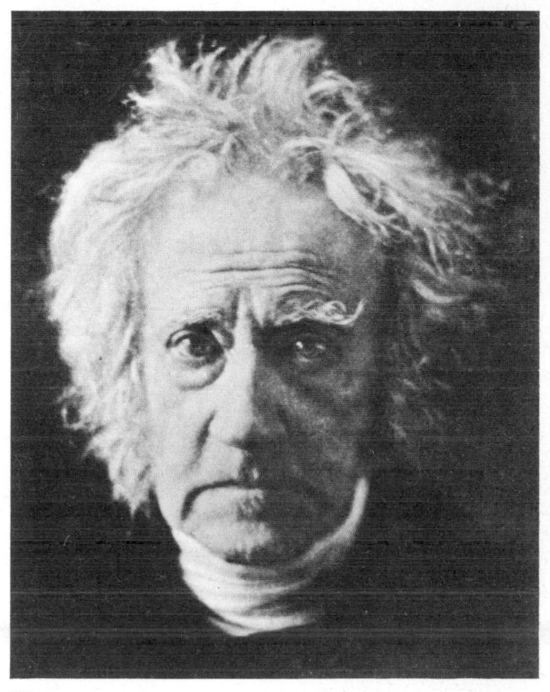

25

26

camera by her son when she was almost 50. In a few years she produced a body of work so impressive as to rank her among the greatest photographers. Her subjects were some of the leading men of the day, including Alfred, Lord Tennyson, Robert Browning, Thomas Carlyle, and **Sir John F. W. Herschel (25)**. Mrs. Cameron also posed her husband and other sitters to illustrate Tennyson's *Idylls of the King*. Although somewhat sentimental, many have a grace equaling the Pre-Raphaelite paintings that inspired them.

Probably no one in the 19th century was more photographed than **Countess Castiglione (26)**, one of the great beauties at the court of Napoleon III, who inspired Adolphe Braun to take numerous photographs of her. This portrait is quite unlike anything done at the time.

Whereas Julia Margaret Cameron was an amateur who experimented briefly with photography, and Adolphe Braun was a professional, Thomas Eakins, the American painter and sculptor, turned first to photography as an aid to his painting. Many of his photographs are of

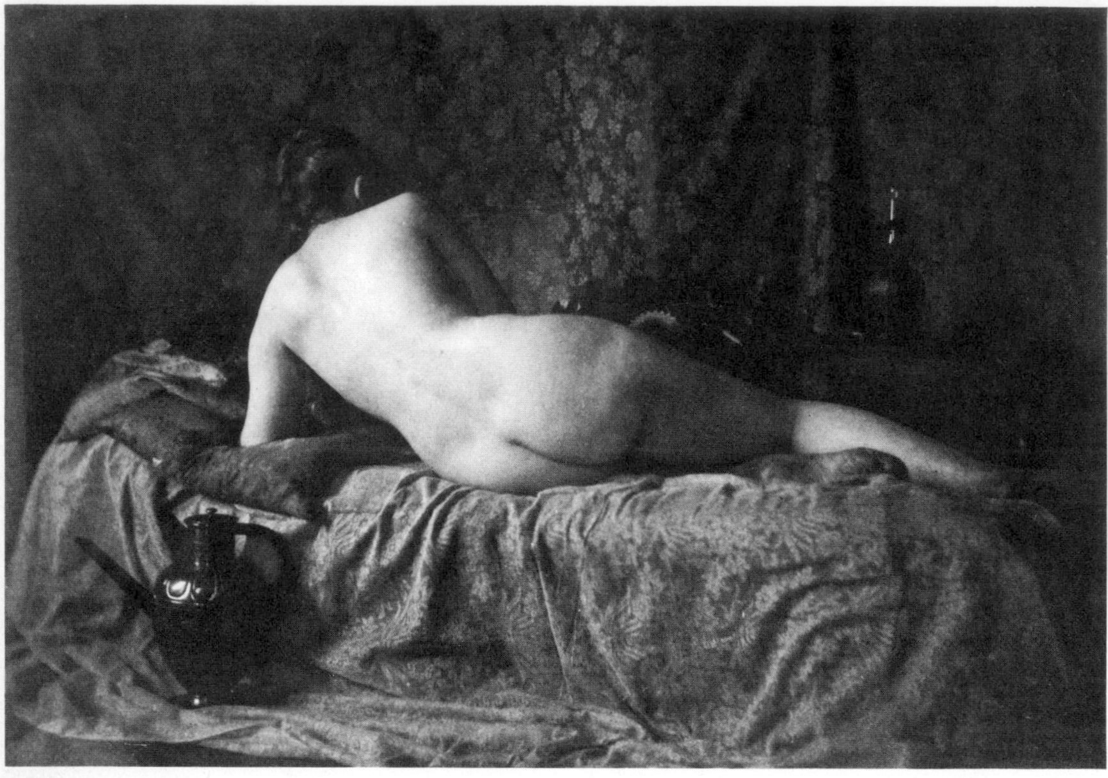

27

nudes, some taken outdoors and others, like this **Nude (27)**, posed in his studio. He also took some fine portraits that are imbued with the same feeling as his paintings. His photographic work was not highly valued, and much was destroyed after his death. We are fortunate in possessing the best group of his photographs, which only recently have begun to be appreciated.

In the years since the first Stieglitz gift, over 5,000 photographs have come to the Museum. It would be virtually impossible to form a comparable collection today, for much of the material is unique, and a great deal is so rare as to be unobtainable. On this firm foundation the collection continues to grow.

Twentieth Century Art

Twentieth Century Art

Objects, Periods, Styles, Artists	Numbers in Text
ABSTRACT EXPRESSIONISM: Pollock, de Kooning, Kline	(17), (18)
ALBERS, JOSEF	(15)
COLOR FIELD PAINTERS: Newman, Louis, Kelly	(19)
DAVIS, STUART	(11)
DECORATIVE ART: Art Nouveau, Art Deco	(20), (21)
DEMUTH, CHARLES	(10)
DOVE, ARTHUR	(7)
GORKY, ARSHILE	(12)
HARTLEY, MARSDEN	(6)
HOFMANN, HANS	(16)
KANDINSKY, WASSILY	(3)
NEW YORK SCHOOL	
O'KEEFFE, GEORGIA	(8)
PACIFIC NORTHWEST PAINTERS: Tobey, Graves	(13)
PICASSO, PABLO	(2)
POST-IMPRESSIONIST PAINTERS: Bonnard, Vuillard	(1)
REALIST PAINTERS: Bellows, Hopper, Wyeth	(14)
REGIONALIST PAINTERS: Benton, Curry, Wood, Burchfield	
SCULPTORS: Maillol, Brancusi, Lachaise	(4), (9)
STELLA, JOSEPH	(5)

☞ **This page helps you to find what you especially want to see and read about.**

Twentieth Century Art

The Department of Twentieth Century Art, created in 1970, has been given the duties of collecting, preserving, and exhibiting painting, drawing, sculpture, and decorative art from 1900 to the present. A primary aim of the department is to keep in touch with art as it is being produced; its responsibility lies in showing the new, giving one-man shows to important 20th-century figures, and in general presenting the best recent art. It is a controversial role, for direction and quality are often problematical without the weight of years behind them.

The Department of Twentieth Century Art has inherited from older departments a collection that is particularly strong in American art. This concentration was made possible by the Arthur H. and George A. Hearn funds, which are restricted to the purchase of American paintings. Another gift that greatly enlarged the scope of the department's holdings was the Alfred Stieglitz Collection, which came to the Museum in 1949, containing many of the remarkable modern works that were first shown in Stieglitz's galleries. Edward Joseph Gallagher III, Chester Dale, and Adelaide Milton de Groot added to the collection in the 1950s and 60s.

The artistic developments in Europe after 1910 are not well represented. This reflects in part the Museum's conservative acquisition policy with regard to European art in the first decades of the century. In addition, it was felt that the founding of the Museum of Modern Art in 1929 relieved the Metropolitan from aggressively pursuing the purchase of works by modern artists.

The most important major exhibit this department has mounted was "New York Painting and Sculpture: 1940-1970," which opened the Museum's Centennial. A show of 408 works, representing 43 artists, it provided an opportunity to evaluate the painting and sculpture that have made New York a world center of contemporary art over the last 30 years. As a result of this exhibition, the Museum received as a gift from the artist Ellsworth Kelly his important painting entitled *13 Panels: Spectrum V*. Three paintings by Robert Motherwell, two by Josef Albers, and one by Helen Frankenthaler had already been donated to the Museum in 1969.

With the completion of the centennial year in 1971, the Department of Twentieth Century Art was allocated its own permanent exhibition galleries, one of which it shares alternately with the Department of European Paintings. There is not, however, sufficient space to install even the majority of the works in the department's collection, and for this reason installations will be changed periodically. It is the purpose of this *Guide* to convey a general idea of the department's strong points, which may or may not be visible to the public at any given moment. Contemporary prints and drawings can be seen, by appointment, in the Department of Prints and Photographs and the Department of Drawings.

In the early 20th century, such developments as Freudian psychology and modern physics represented a major rethinking of the humanist tradition of the Renaissance. In the fine arts it was no longer deemed necessary to convey images in a realistic manner, and linear perspective was bypassed in an attempt to find new aesthetic solutions.

1

Paris in the first two decades of the 20th century was the artistic center of the world. While the Cubists and Surrealists produced the major work in this new history, two men active in Paris, who were friends and near contemporaries, carried on the tradition of the Impressionists: Pierre Bonnard's **Terrace at Vernon (1)** reveals his love of joyous color and gentle intimate scenes; Edouard Vuillard's *Garden at Vaucresson* records a friend's garden near Paris and is suffused with a similar feeling of warmth and privacy. For obvious reasons the two painters were sometimes referred to as "Intimists."

It was the young Spanish painter Pablo Picasso who violently overturned previous conventions. A few years after his move from Spain to France in 1904, he began experimenting with a manner of painting in which the subject was depicted by means of many-faceted planes. Eventually these planes were used to disintegrate the image, expressing the artist's subjective response. They also provided a basis for its reunification according to the principles of Cézanne. Cubism, as the movement came to be called, gained such momentum that most art until about

3

4

2

1940 was influenced by it. Picasso's remarkable **Portrait of Gertrude Stein (2)**, the American writer and a friend of the artist, was done in 1906. It bridges his development from conventional representation to Cubism, for the features of the face, painted in after he had finished the rest of the canvas, have an angularity that anticipates the faceting in his Cubist

works. By 1923, the year of Picasso's *Woman in White*, the original spirit and quality of Cubism had been diluted by its diffusion as an international movement. Responding to a new era, Picasso challenged critical clichés by alternating between two seemingly antagonistic styles. Picasso's Neoclassic style, reminiscent of his blue and rose pictures, is seen in this gentle and refined portrait of the artist's wife, Olga Koklova.

Other artists had gone beyond the bounds of academic Cubism to what seemed at the time to be total abstraction. The Czech painter Frank Kupka, settling in France in the 1890s, used spirals, overlapping planes, and other motifs of cosmological origin to produce abstractions at once decorative and pictorial. Kupka's *Plans Par Verticales* in the Museum dates from 1912-13. His contemporary Wassily Kandinsky was to become perhaps one of the most important and influential abstract painters of the early 20th century. His abstract landscape, **Improvisation No. 27 (3)**, is also from 1912. It is remarkable how close in feeling and form it is to a much later and more Surrealist work, Arshile Gorky's *Water of the Flowery Mill*.

The sculpture of this period reflected traditional styles in art as well as successful experiments. Aristide Maillol's nudes are still classically rounded. In contrast, the figures of the Rumanian sculptor Constantin Brancusi became more and more reduced. In the **Sleeping Muse (4)** the human features are recognizable. Four years later, in a second version of this head, he further simplified the features and polished the head to a finish that mirrored the viewer's own

5

face. His later sculptures continued to suggest observed reality while seeking archetypal form.

A group of American artists called The Eight had in 1908 declared their independence from European art (see American Paintings). Other Americans were caught in the ferment of artistic life in Paris and Berlin. Several were studying in Paris at the inception of the Cubist movement. Among those returning from Europe in the first decades of the 20th century was Max Weber, who in the *Athletic Contest* used Cubist faceting and Futurist methods to express the excitement of New York. Another American, Joseph Stella, also worked with abstract motifs and rhythmic repetitions, as in his well-known **Coney Island (5)**, in which the flashing lights of the amusement park are imaginatively captured.

Marsden Hartley and Lyonel Feininger were two artists drawn to Germany. Hartley became a pioneer and leader of

6

American modernism, though he painted in an abstract idiom for some five years only. The Museum has one of his major works from this period, **Portrait of a German Officer (6)**, dating from 1914; the flags and insignia are used as bold symbols of militarism, without implying either glorification or satire. In his later years Hartley returned to Maine and celebrated its rugged simplicity in *Lobster Fishermen*. His contemporary Feininger lived in Germany for many years and taught at the Bauhaus along with Kandinsky and Paul Klee. His *Church at Gelmeroda* is a fine example of his quiet, architectonic style.

Credited with founding the only American modernist movement in the years between 1910 and 1920, Stanton MacDonald-Wright developed, with Morgan Russell, a style of painting that he called Synchronism; *Aeroplane Synchromy in Yellow-Orange* demonstrates somewhat academically what he theorized: "Color becomes the generating function."

Though Europe provided a fertile field for the semination of new ideas in art, events in New York also had an impact on the future direction of American painting. A key figure in the modernist movement was the great American photographer Alfred Stieglitz, whose galleries and magazines helped to produce an atmosphere in which new art, both European and American, could be exhibited, seen, discussed, and evaluated. Showing for the first time in America the work of Picasso, Matisse, Rodin, Brancusi, and others, Stieglitz introduced to artists and public alike the exciting new art. Also important was the famous Armory Show, held in New York in 1913. A number of what seemed at the time to be shockingly modern canvases, mostly European, created a sensation.

7

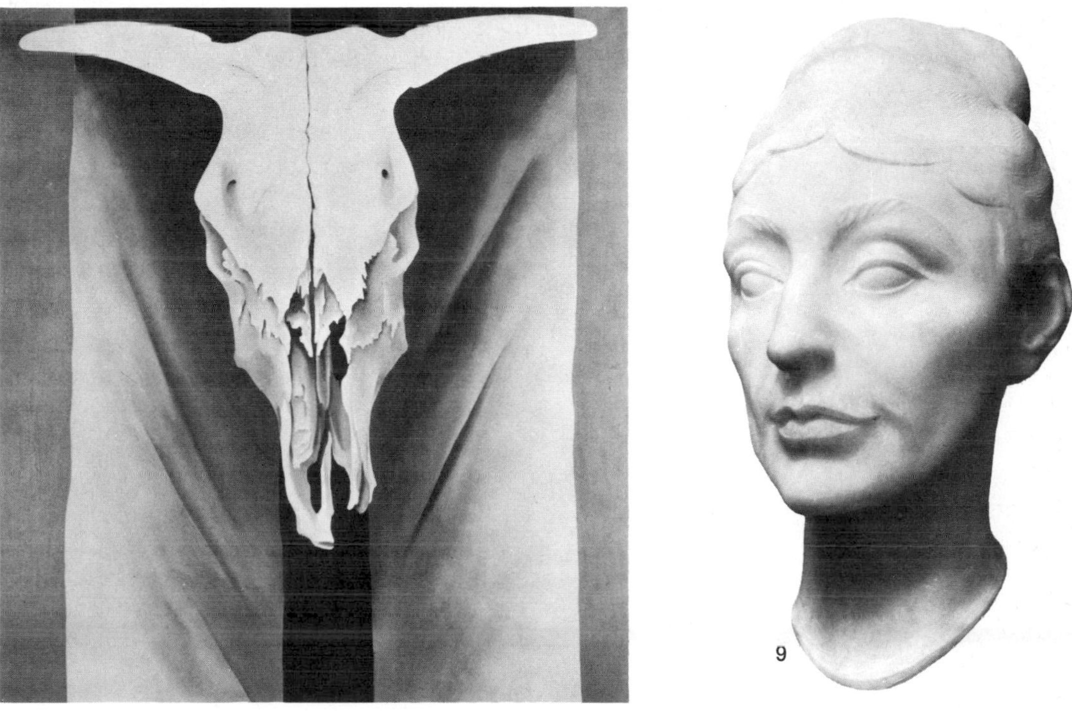

9

8

It was Arthur Dove who painted the first American nonrepresentational pictures in which nature and objects were happily and wittily abstracted. In the Museum's painting *Pagan Philosophy*, we see a provincial artist learning the lesson of Cubism. Pieces of wood shingles and paper are glued in a humorous fashion to the oil painting *Portrait of Ralph Dusenberry*, thus making it one of the earliest modern American collages. His **Hand Sewing Machine (7)** is painted on heavy metal; a piece of blank canvas is used to represent the material being sewn. Here is a subject from the machine age, suggesting that nothing was any longer beyond the scope of an artist.

Dove had been given his first exhibition in 1912 in Stieglitz's Gallery 291. Four years later, Georgia O'Keeffe had her first gallery show there. While O'Keeffe is a keen observer of natural forms, her style is characterized by clean, hard-edged lines and semiabstract forms that are often greatly enlarged. Her *Black Iris* and *Black Flower and Blue Larkspur* have sensuous overtones while remaining essentially close-up views of flowers. In **Cow's Skull: Red, White, and Blue (8)** she presents a symbol of New Mexico, her favorite landscape, where she has lived since 1928. Gaston Lachaise's marble **Portrait Bust of Georgia O'Keeffe (9)**, from 1927, is the work of an important American sculptor.

Of the same generation and also frequenting Gallery 291 was Charles Demuth. Like O'Keeffe he favored the clean, hard line, but his subject matter was often focused on machinery and man-

10

11

12

made objects, though he also did many sensitive water colors of themes from nature. One of his most important paintings is **I Saw the Figure 5 in Gold (10)**; it was dedicated to his friend William Carlos Williams, whose poem "The Great Figure" provided the title and image on which the painting is based. The picture has Futurist and Cubist features in its prismatic breakdown of light, in the use of words and numbers, and in its recurring elements. Charles Sheeler, too, made industrial America his subject and projected it in many precise and sharply focused canvases, such as *Water*, which pictures a Tennessee Valley Authority dam, and *Golden Gate*.

O'Keeffe and Sheeler were both involved in giving contemporary form to a radical sense of the picturesque. They sought new means of isolating and idealizing natural forms, artifacts, and architecture of extraordinary beauty. Other American painters, such as Stuart Davis, devised vocabularies of forms from which they drew in creating complex modernist compositions. By using abstract yet associational forms, Davis builds concrete images that become interesting visual puzzles. Davis explained that the title of his painting **Semé (11)** means "strewn, lots of things"; and the word ANY signifies that "any subject matter is equal in art, from the most insignificant to one of relative importance."

Soon after Arshile Gorky arrived in the United States from Europe in 1920, he became friends with Stuart Davis, who had exhibited in the Armory Show at 19 and was by that time one of the most accomplished abstract artists in America. Gorky's style at first was much influenced

13

by Picasso until in the late 30s it became more fluid and personal. **Water of the Flowery Mill (12)**, done in 1944, four years before his death, is an ambiguous landscape of great beauty, with biomorphic forms suggesting water, clouds, and other natural forms.

A group of painters living in the Pacific Northwest in the 1930s and 40s found quite a different means of self-expression. Mark Tobey's paintings reflect his interest in Japanese calligraphy, which he studied in Japan in 1934. His own private calligraphy came to be called "white writing" and is a distinguishing feature in many of his canvases; sometimes the lines trace large units, at other times they are densely meshed and very compact. In **Broadway (13)** Tobey recalls New York's multitudes, noises, neon signs, and movie theaters. Another well-known Northwest painter is Morris Graves, who was a friend and younger colleague of Mark Tobey. Graves's mystical and magical paintings, such as his *Bird in the Spirit*, reflect his interest in Zen Buddhism.

Of the currents that compose the mainstream of American art in the 20th century, the public found it easier to accept the work of traditional realist painters than the more difficult experimental forms. Now that the situation is often reversed, with modernism having the greatest prestige, there is a danger of undervaluing certain traditional painters. George Bellows in particular was a better painter than most of the provincial modernists of his day. His landscapes are vigorously painted in a rough impasto, while the portraits are conceived in a cool, reserved style, which serves to heighten their emotional impact. Among the paintings by Bellows is the strikingly elegant portrait of *Mrs. Chester Dale*. Historically, Bellows's painting serves as a bridge between the protest of The Eight and later figurative painters.

Edward Hopper was born in the same year as Bellows, in 1882, and studied with the same teacher, Robert Henri. But unlike Bellows, who died in 1925, Hopper won general recognition only after many years of work in solitude. He continued the northern European tradition of lucid painting, which reached its height in the work of Winslow Homer and Thomas Eakins. Typical of his paintings are *From Williamsburg Bridge*, 1928, and **The Lighthouse at Two Lights (14)**, 1929; here, as in many other pictures, Hopper used light to set a mood of isolation and loneliness in rural and urban scenes. Reginald Marsh and Isabel Bishop recreated scenes of Lower Manhattan with a fine technical sureness and social awareness. Protest, both political and social, was angrily voiced by Ben Shahn in *Death of a Miner* and by George Grosz in

14

16

Berlin Street.

Andrew Wyeth is America's best-known realist painter. In *A Crow Flew By*, the dry technique and the spareness of form and color emphasize the quiet dignity of the old man. By rearranging the actual scene, eliminating certain details and emphasizing others, the painter conveys the essence rather than the photographic look of the scene.

Among the regionalist painters of this century represented in the Museum are Thomas Hart Benton, John Steuart Curry, Grant Wood, and Charles Burchfield. They shared an interest in rural America and in the homely aspects of American life.

After World War II, for a variety of reasons, the primary artistic center shifted from Europe to America, in particular to New York. For a period of some 30 years the styles that emerged had their origin in the United States and were of major international influence. Perhaps the most important of these was Abstract Expressionism. This was followed in the 60s by color field painting and such other movements as Pop Art and minimal sculpture. Though the relative quality of these movements is much debated, the discussion itself has added to the richness of the New York School.

Josef Albers came to this country in 1933. Through his painting and teaching he introduced to American artists the philosophy of the Bauhaus. **Pillars (15)**, 1928, reveals Albers's early involvement with the problems of imagery in design. This work came to its highest fruition in the series Homage to the Square.

Hans Hofmann also came from Germany in the 1930s. Enormously inventive, he developed a repertory of skills working concurrently in several dissimilar styles. He then went on to produce his greatest paintings in the 1960s. Hofmann died at the age of 86 in 1966. In **Veluti in Speculum (16)**, 1962, a receding landscape is suggested in painterly terms by

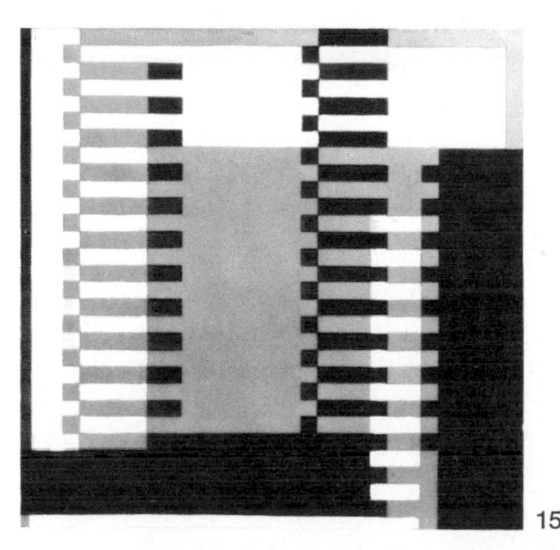

15

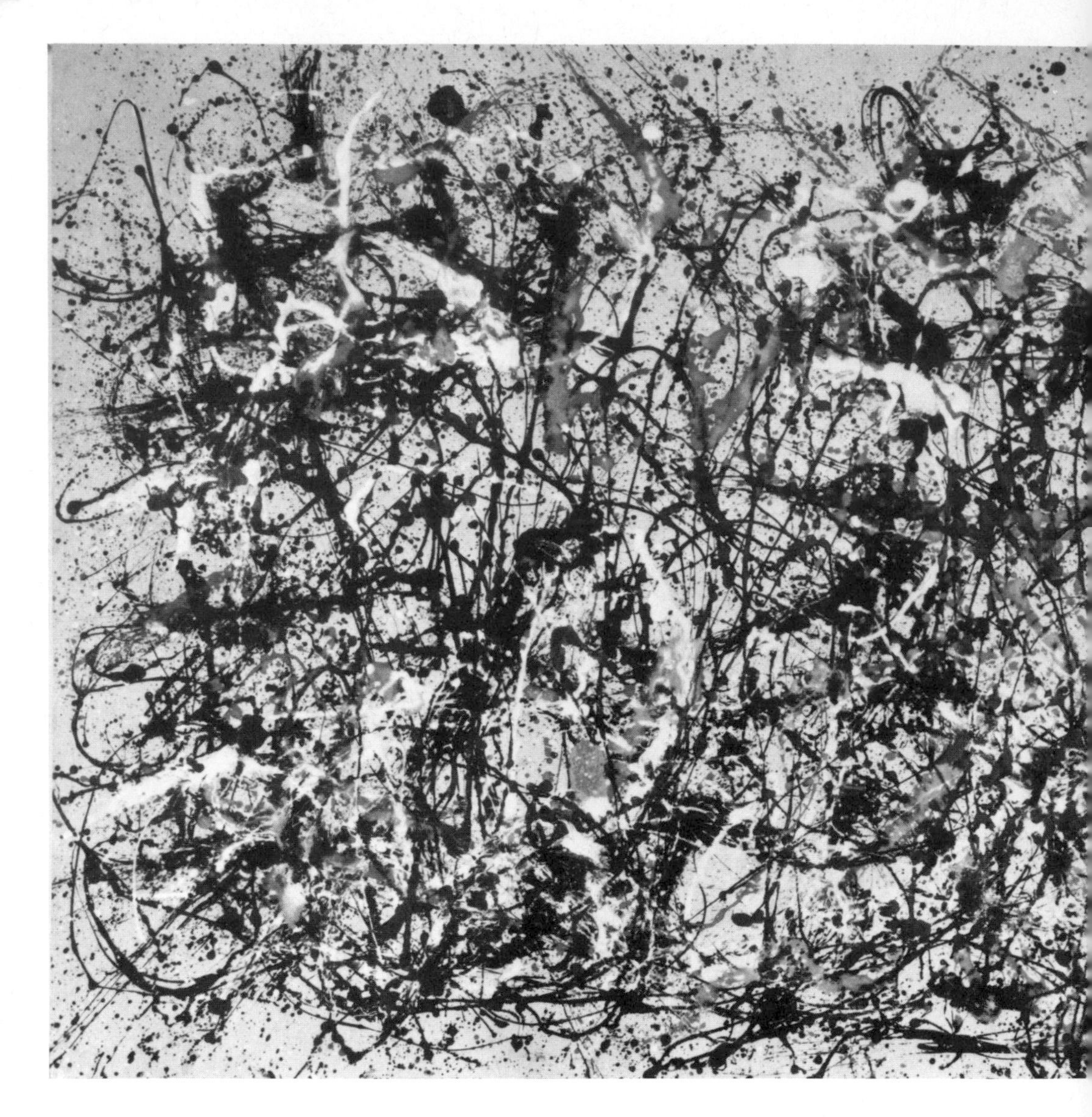

the placing of adjacent and overlapping rectangles of palpable color.

The interest in Abstract Expressionism focused on the work of Jackson Pollock, Willem de Kooning, and Franz Kline, among others. According to early apologists this innovational style made no reference to the perceived world. The work of art was seen rather as a record of the artist's personal feeling as expressed in the act of painting. Pollock's method of "controlled accident," that is, dripping paint onto the canvas, often with the addition of sand, broken glass, and other matter, nevertheless had an object. In his overall pictures, such as the Metropolitan's **Autumn Rhythm (17)**, 1950, Pollock was interested in depicting fields of vision

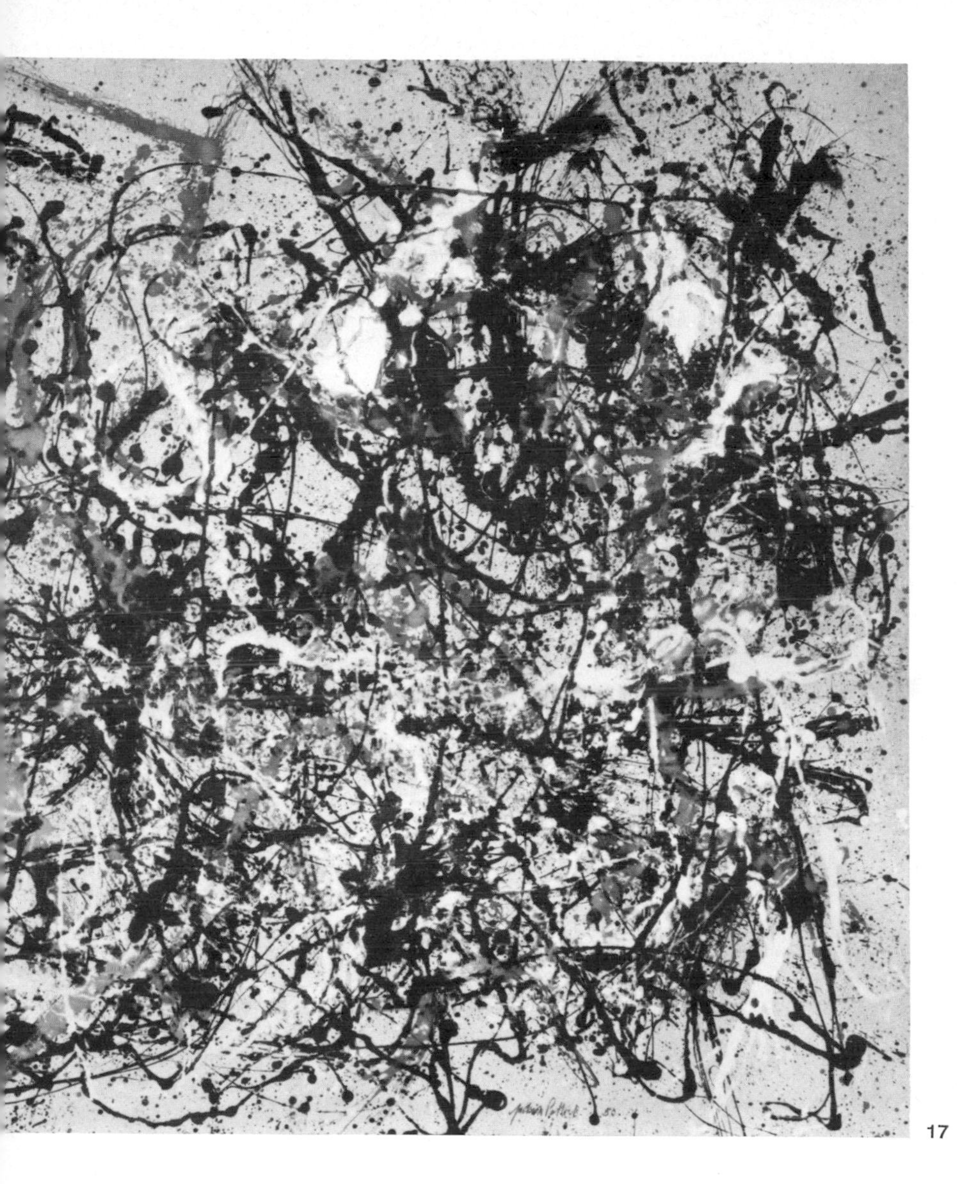

17

rather than objects in space. The atmospheric illusion produced by the skeining lies behind the surface of the picture; the canvas is visionary rather than physical. The ridicule that was heaped on him has since his death turned into praise. His paintings have an international reputation and have served as an inspiration to artists who followed. Franz Kline also allowed his paint to drip, but again the result was never an accident. His more familiar canvases are stark black and white paintings with bold, vigorous strokes; the Museum's *Black, White and Gray* is more muted and softer than his best-known work. Willem de Kooning after his first one-man show in 1948 quickly became a leader of New York

18

painting. **Easter Monday (18)** is characteristic of his energetic style, the opposition in his work of rough brushing and sweet color—light blues, pinks, and yellows.

Other painters used an invented, repeated image in many variations. As Mark Rothko's mature style developed, he painted large rectangles with blurred edges floating against a background with which they subtly blended. *Reds No. 16*, dating from 1960, was purchased by the Museum in 1971. Adolph Gottlieb created his own world of symbols. At first these were reminiscent of primitive pictographs. Later he began his series of "bursts," in which he placed floating spheres above an exploding mass. *Thrust*, 1959, is painted in black and red against a white background. Robert

19

Motherwell's melancholy strength is graphically projected in his expressively painted series Elegies to the Spanish Republic. The Museum has an *Elegy*.

Ellsworth Kelly's fine painting *Blue Red Green* is part of the collection. Alone among successful members of the New York School, Kelly spent his first years as a painter in the Paris of the early 1950s. He thus knew at first hand the excitement of Matisse's late cut-outs. In his work he has intelligently evolved in this tradition. Helen Frankenthaler's contribution to the art of the 50s and 60s is well defined. Not only was she the conveyor of the message—the new freedom adumbrated by Gorky and Pollock—to Morris Louis, Kenneth Noland, and other important young artists, but she has in her own right produced a lovely and important body of work.

In the 1960s there was an inevitable reaction against the excesses of second-generation Abstract Expressionism. The color field painters looked to Barnett Newman and Jackson Pollock as the twin poles of their inspiration. Newman's ability to create the sense of an open expanse without the use of overlapping shapes or lines and his precisely limited use of painterly means provided younger artists with keys to the new medium of acrylics on raw canvas. The monumentality and humanism of Newman's vision are evident in his painting *Concord* in the Museum's collection. Morris Louis's **Alpha-Pi (19)** is a fine example of color field painting. The flow of diagonal bands poured directly onto the raw canvas creates an expanse daringly focused on the periphery.

The Department of Twentieth Century Art has inherited from the Department of Western European Arts and from the

21

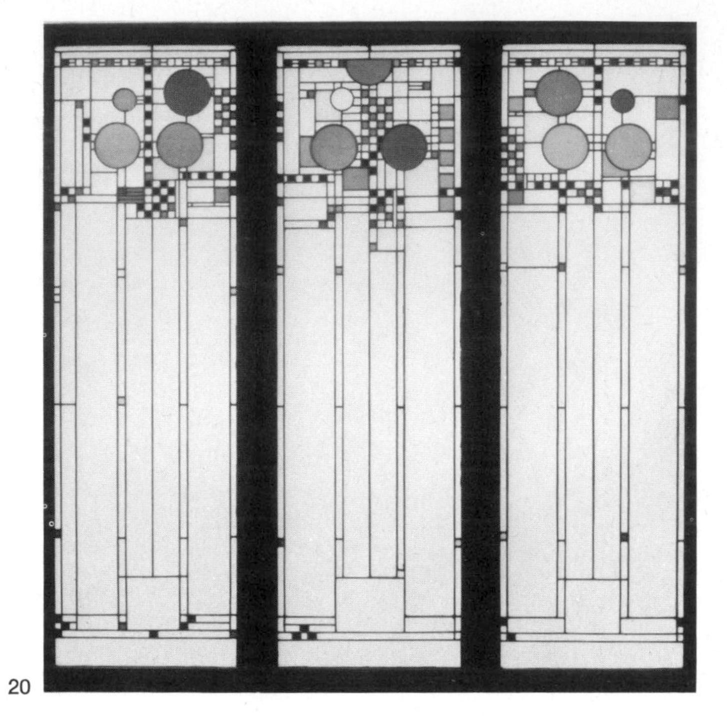
20

American Wing a large number of decorative objects, dating after 1900. Changing exhibitions will do justice to these treasures, from Art Nouveau, Art Deco, and more recent periods. By 1900 the Art Nouveau movement had reached its height, only to exhaust itself some ten years later. The New Style, as it was sometimes called, was indeed the first nonimitative style in years, and it affected all the arts: architecture, interior design, painting and sculpture (to lesser degrees), book illustration and book binding, glass, ceramics, metalware, and textiles. Art Nouveau fostered a close union between art and its technique of production; its floral, sinuously coiling lines can be seen in a great variety of objects by the most famous craftsmen in Europe and America: vases by Emile Gallé, glass and jewelry by René Lalique, and the famous lamps and many other pieces of decorative art by the American master of this style, Louis Comfort Tiffany.

The decorative style that flourished in the 1920s and 30s came to be called Art Deco, after the Paris exhibition of 1925, L'Exposition Internationale des Arts Décoratifs et Industriels Modernes. It was a more rectilinear and symmetrical style than its predecessor, Art Nouveau. In the Metropolitan's new galleries opened in the fall of 1971, exquisite examples from the modern age have been put on display: from America, three windows by Frank Lloyd Wright—this **Triptych (20)**, from 1912, is an example of pioneering abstraction in American decorative arts; and from Europe, a **desk (21)** from around 1900 and other furniture by the Milanese Carlo Bugatti, which convey the designer's fantasy and exoticism.

Western European Arts

Western European Arts

Objects, Periods, Styles	Numbers in Text
BRONZES	(33-35)
CERAMICS: earthenware, lustreware, majolica, porcelain	(45-53)
CLOCKS and WATCHES	(57-58)
ENGLISH ROOMS and FURNITURE:	(8-9), (12-17)
Elizabethan Room	(8)
Lansdowne Dining Room	(15)
Croome Court Tapestry Room	(14)
Kirtlington Park Room	(13)
FRENCH ROOMS and FURNITURE:	(18-25)
Shop Front	(18)
Wrightsman Rooms: Varengeville, Paar, de Tessé	(20-22)
Bordeaux Room	(23)
Crillon Room	(24)
GLASS	(61)
ITALIAN BEDROOM from PALAZZO SAGREDO	(11)
METAL- and GOLDSMITH'S WORK	(58-60)
MINIATURES	
RENAISSANCE INTERIORS and FURNISHINGS	(2-7)
SCULPTURE and RELIEFS (Renaissance to 1900)	(27-44)
SILVER and GOLD	(54-56)
SWISS ROOM	(10)
TAPESTRIES, TEXTILES, and EMBROIDERIES	(7), (26)

☞ **This page helps you to find what you especially want to see and read about.**

Western European Arts

The Department of Western European Arts was created in 1907 when the elder J. P. Morgan gave to the Museum a great collection of French decorative arts; it incorporated the Department of Sculpture and Casts, in existence since 1872. At the outset this condominium included what are now the Medieval, Far Eastern, and Islamic departments, together with the American Wing and the Department of Musical Instruments. Gradually these departments spun off to form separate entities, and in 1932 the Department of Western European Arts was organized along its present lines under the title of the Department of Renaissance and Modern Art. This name was changed to Renaissance and Post-Renaissance Art in 1956 and to the Department of Western European Arts in 1962. However named, it is one of the largest in the Museum and its collections comprise whole rooms from palaces and great houses, furniture, and a wide variety of European decorative arts and sculpture from the Renaissance to 1900.

ROOMS AND FURNITURE

In Florence in the first half of the 15th century a new style in architecture and the visual arts emerged, which differed from the Gothic that had preceded it. The interiors in Renaissance style, as it was called, relied on symmetry, clarity, harmonious proportions, and linear perspective; in part the style was a conscious imitation of classical ideals as used in antiquity by the Greeks and Romans, hence the name renaissance, or rebirth. Without traveling anywhere, a Museum visitor can visit some wonderfully preserved Renaissance interiors now in the

1

Museum. The great Renaissance men were soldiers, merchants, scholars, and art patrons all at once. In the tiny **study (1)**, formerly in the palace of Federigo da Montefeltro at Gubbio, the wood inlay panels were designed to project seemingly three-dimensional half-open cabinets stocked with musical instruments, books, scientific tools, and awards. For lack of space this interior from the 1480s cannot always be shown.

During the Renaissance, Italian craftsmen were in demand throughout Europe, and the **Patio from Velez Blanco (2)**, a castle in southeast Spain, was partially made by them. The noble proportions and the airy loggias of this open court transmit the best of early Renaissance architecture, but not without a distinctive touch of Gothic style still surviving

2

in this remote corner of Spain. The marble decorations around the windows, arcades, and portals were executed by carvers from northern Italy, who borrowed motifs from ancient monuments and combined them with fantastic animal forms. The entire Patio was bequeathed to the Museum by George Blumenthal.

Leaving the Patio, one can see interior furnishings and decorations from the Spanish Renaissance **(3)**. Heavy furniture is set around a carved and partially gilded stone mantelpiece. A great Spanish house would have had on its walls tapestries and embroideries such as those now hanging here; two embroideries made in Spain around 1600 narrate the history of Galcerán de Pinós, a 12th-century Spanish admiral, while a tapestry of the Crucifixion was woven about 1515-25 in Flanders, then under Spanish rule. Little space is at present available for the department's extensive collection of Italian Renaissance art objects. Examples of Italian and northern Renaissance furniture and sculpture can be seen in the European Paintings galleries, including a superb monumental **table (4)** made in the 1560s according to designs by Jacopo Barozzi da Vignola for Cardinal Alessandro Farnese. It was once part of the furnishings of the state apartment in the Farnese Palace, Rome. Its top is a sumptuous inlay of many colored marbles and semiprecious stones forming a border of cartouches in various shapes along two large slabs of Oriental alabaster. A selection of French Renaissance artifacts displayed on the first floor includes stained glass panels and an elaborately carved, painted, and partly gilded walnut cabinet dating before 1600—a Burgundian interpretation of current Italian motifs, probably made for a marriage **(5)**.

An arched doorway leads into a richly paneled chapel **(6)**, its side walls illuminated by a set of splendid 16th-century stained glass from the vicinity of Nancy in northern France. The woodwork elements of this chapel, carved and inlaid in a technique called *intarsia*, were commissioned from the workshop of the great Fra Damiano in Bologna for the Château de la Bastie d'Urfé, near Lyons. The design of the altarpiece of the Last Supper as well as the general organization of the wainscoting were supplied by the architect Vignola.

Renaissance tastes were brought to England via trade and travel. The closeness of artistic rapport is exemplified by a large heraldic table carpet **(7)**, sprinkled with English coats of arms and wildflowers, which was probably woven in Flanders to an English design. This carpet, now hanging on the wall, is dated 1564 and commemorates the Lewknor family of Sussex. One entire room is from the Elizabethan period **(8)**. The carved oak paneling came from a house in Yarmouth that had belonged to a well-to-do merchant, William Crowe. Over the original stone chimneypiece is the coat of arms of the owner's trading company. The elaborate Tudor woodwork is from the end of the 16th century, and the dark oak furniture of the period, carved or with turned legs, harmonizes with the paneling. Furniture was scarce, and the owner must have prized the red-velvet-hung bed with inlaid tester supported on massive bulbous posts, shown in an adjoining gallery **(9)**.

A well-insulated Swiss room **(10)** dates from the last quarter of the 17th century. The carved and veneered paneling, with caryatid figures and wooden reliefs of fantastic animals, comes from a house,

4

13

or little castle, built for a local patriarch of Flims, a village high in the eastern part of Switzerland, near now-fashionable ski resorts. The great earthenware stove was made of tiles painted with scenes from the Old Testament. Carved wooden chairs and a slate-top table for chalking up housekeeping accounts are characteristic of the period.

The opulent interior from the Palazzo Sagredo **(11)** projects a sense of the splendor and zest of living in early 18th-century Venice. A late medieval structure renovated and redecorated about 1718, this palace is situated on the Grand Canal not far from the Rialto. The 32 ebullient cupids who flutter near the stucco ceiling and hold a tasseled canopy over the bed were carried out by the stuccoists Abbondio Stazio and Carpoforo Mazzetti. The custom of receiving formal visits in bed was in vogue at the time, so that the splendors of so ornate a bedroom were not only enjoyed by the occupant but also served to impress the visitor.

The whorled flowers and scrolling acanthus stems of the Cassiobury Park staircase railing **(12)** mark an outburst of English creativity in the decorative arts which coincided with the Restoration and which was to reach its fullest development in the 18th century. These bold Baroque wood sculptures were executed by Grinling Gibbons or his contemporary Edward Pearce between 1677 and 1680 for Arthur Capel, first earl of Essex. Sir Peter Lely's portraits of the earl's sisters and brother, also from Cassiobury Park, a country house now destroyed, hang nearby.

We now span some 70 years to 1748, the year the **Room from Kirtlington Park (13)** in Oxfordshire was finished. The

14

builder of the house, Sir James Dashwood, looks out from a portrait by Enoch Seaman. Although the painting dates from five years prior to the house's construction, Sir James must have known the kind of house he wanted, for in the right background of the portrait appears a representation of a building very similar to the one that was actually built. The fine proportions of this room approach Palladian ideals, and the carved wood doorways also derive from the repertory of Palladian forms. However, the spirited arabesques of the plasterwork decoration are not at all formal, but are more related to the intricate movement of Baroque art.

From the 1760s dates a magnificent interior, the **Tapestry Room from Croome Court (14)**. It was designed by Robert Adam for Croome Court, in Worcestershire, the seat of the earls of Coventry. It receives its name from the Gobelins tapestries that so resplendently cover the walls and the seat furniture. It is one of half a dozen interiors so furnished in French tapestry and superbly represents the contemporary fashion in England for rooms "in the French taste." The tapestries, woven to measure in Paris, include

15

four medallions after François Boucher; Lord Coventry must have been delighted with the splendor of the crimson sea. Almost all the original furniture has been reassembled, although Adam does not seem to have been responsible for its design. The wood and plaster decoration, however, are from designs by this famous 17th-century architect and interior decorator.

An interior of imposing dimensions is the **Dining Room from Lansdowne House (15)**, created by Robert Adam for Lord Shelburne, who became Marquess of Lansdowne in 1784. The room was completed by 1768, when the new owners moved into the house. Joseph Rose carried out the imaginative plasterwork of the room, and the arabesques of griffins and putti, the vases and trophies of arms, leaf garlands, sprays, rosettes, scrolls, and fan-shaped motifs constitute one of the glories of this room. One of Lord Lansdowne's original marble statues is back in its niche; the others are plaster casts of Roman statues that correspond to those admired in the late 18th century. The original furniture had long been dispersed when the Museum acquired the room in 1931, but other pieces of the period were found to complement the architecture. The tables in the room are set with contemporary silver by the famous English silversmith Paul de Lamerie.

Exhibited nearby are English furniture pieces from the 1730s: a pair of chairs and a settee in gilt gesso, with lion-mask carvings on the knees, as well as a side chair and card table of scarlet japanning heightened with gold chinoiserie vignettes, in imitation of costly oriental lacquer. Mahogany came into wide use for furniture-making a few years later, and its reddish veneers form the ground of a cupboard and **coin cabinet (16)** by William Vile that also rely for their effect upon crisp carvings in the heavy, dark wood. The coin cabinet was part of a commission for a larger piece of furniture begun in 1758 for George III while he was still Prince of Wales. Two British lions and the prince's star of the Order of the Garter can be seen in its upper section. An ample mahogany sofa, a ribbon-back side chair, and a pair of fretwork candlestands all derive from designs by Thomas Chippendale, whose reputation was founded on the furniture engravings he published in *The Gentleman and Cabinet-Maker's Director* in 1754. A product of Chippendale's workshop in the 1770s, the beautiful lightwood commode **(17)** from St. Giles's House, Dorset, is ornamented with marquetry motifs in the chaste Neoclassic idiom. Robert Adam drew on firsthand observation of classical forms when designing furniture such as the meticulously carved and painted pier table with matching mirror from 1765, and a bookcase of pine painted to resemble mahogany, made for Lord Frederick Campbell.

16

A **shop front (18)**, dated about 1775, introduces the visitor to 18th-century France. It formerly stood on the Ile Saint-Louis in Paris, and wares which might have been part of the stock of an art dealer and decorator have been reassembled here; these include vases from the Sèvres factory, gilt-bronze candelabra,

18

19

and an ingenious clock fitted into a turbaned female bust. The notable group of furniture with Sèvres porcelain-inlaid plaques was the gift in 1958 of the Samuel H. Kress Foundation and is described in detail in the catalogue of that collection. The **secretary (19)** shown here, set with green-bordered plaques, is signed by the cabinetmaker Martin Carlin, who worked extensively for the great art dealers known as the *marchands-merciers*.

The two interiors given with some of their contents by Charles Wrightsman are

20

earlier in date. The **Room from the Hôtel de Varengeville (20)** has white and gold Rococo paneling that was probably designed by Nicolas Pineau in about 1735. A pair of gilded beechwood armchairs **(21)** dates from about 20 years later. They are covered with Beauvais tapestry depicting animal subjects, after cartoons by the French painter Jean-Baptiste Oudry. These chairs with their finely undercut floral and vegetable motifs were part of a larger set dispatched from Paris to the Bernstorff Palace in Copenhagen, for the use of the former Danish ambassador to Versailles.

In the 30-odd years after the Varengeville room was paneled in Paris, the Rococo style was diffused throughout Europe, and Count Wenzel Joseph von Paar preferred it to the Neoclassical style when he decided to remodel the interiors of the early Baroque Palais Paar on the Wollzeile in Vienna. The dominant blue of the woodwork in the Paar room **(22)** matches traces of the original paint and picks up the blues of the magnificent Savonnerie carpet, which was woven for Louis XIV's Grande Galerie at the Louvre.

Two interiors of smaller dimensions come from France of about 1780. The sage-green walls of the circular room from Bordeaux **(23)** are carved in low relief with decorative motifs and clusters of attributes known as trophies, alluding to abstract concepts such as Architecture (above the door lintel on the left), Farming (the central motif of the panel to the right of the mantelpiece), Music, and the

Arts. On the left, the Crillon room **(24)**, painted in delicate colors on a turquoise ground, was originally a boudoir or bathroom in the Hôtel d'Aumont, now the Hôtel Crillon near the American Embassy in Paris. The fanciful motifs with naturalistic details derive quite closely from Renaissance painted arabesques in the Vatican.

A set of two armchairs and two side chairs made for a cousin of Louis XVI, the duc de Penthièvre, are examples of the finest workmanship of the period. The chairmaker Georges Jacob supervised the incredibly meticulous openwork carving on the gilded frames of this set, which is covered in its original silk-embroidered satin covers. A consummate luxury item of black and gold Japanese lacquer and ebony, trimmed with luxuriant trails of gilt-bronze flowers, this **secretary (25)** and its companion commode were produced in the workshops of Jean-Henri Riesener, the best-known French cabinetmaker of the day, for Queen Marie-Antoinette. Delivered in 1783-84, these pieces were standing in the queen's study of the Château de St.-Cloud at the outbreak of the Revolution, witnesses to the high degree of achievement in French decorative arts before the downfall of the monarchy.

25

TEXTILES AND TAPESTRIES

The Textile Study Room **(26)** is the general repository for textiles belonging to a number of the Museum's departments, including Western European Arts, Far Eastern Art, Islamic Art, the American Wing, Medieval Art, Primitive Art, and Twentieth Century Art. There are some 15,000 textiles in the collections, illustrating the complete development of that art in Europe and the Near East. Also among its resources are the great collections of Chinese and Japanese costumes and textiles built by Alan Priest and Pauline Simmons, and the finest collection of laces in the world outside Brussels.

In the Museum there are tapestries of all centuries from the 16th to the 20th, woven in England, Germany, Italy, and Holland, but from about 1660 to the present day, French manufactories have taken the first place. From the Gobelins in Paris, working primarily for the kings of France, come grandiloquent armorials; mythological scenes, such as the set called Fables; and reworkings of 16th-century designs, such as the so-called Months of Lucas. The manufactory at Beauvais undertook private as well as royal commissions and found an ideal designer in François Boucher; the set of his Italian Entertainments has remained together since the day it was completed in 1762. For tapestries were not meant to be looked at singly, like paintings; they were woven in sets and usually hung border to border. They tell their stories forcefully without neglecting their most important duty—"to be splendid at a distance and full of amusing surprises at near view."

SCULPTURE

European sculpture from the beginning of the Renaissance to the end of the 19th century forms part of the Department of Western European Arts. The first two important sculptures acquired by the Museum, a Jean-Antoine Houdon bust of Benjamin Franklin given in 1872 and an Andrea della Robbia altarpiece given in 1882, forecast the basic orientation toward French and Italian sculpture which was to become characteristic of the collection. With the creation of a larger and more comprehensive Department of Decorative Arts in 1907, sculpture began to be collected in a systematic fashion. In the early years, ten pieces by Auguste Rodin, given by Thomas F. Ryan, and some major Italian and French works included in the Bequest of Benjamin Altman provided a standard of excellence for the years ahead. Exquisite small northern Renaissance sculptures came with the J. Pierpont Morgan Collection. Several Renaissance bronze statuettes presented in the 1920s by Ogden Mills gave an early impetus for collecting in this field. Over the years the department was enormously enriched by purchases and by gifts included in the bequests of

27

Mrs. H. O. Havemeyer, Michael Friedsam, George Blumenthal, and Jules S. Bache. Since 1964 a new era can be said to have opened with the purchase of a number of sculptures made possible by funds donated by the Josephine Bay Paul and C. Michael Paul Foundation, Inc., and by the Charles Ulrick and Josephine Bay Foundation, Inc.; a series of spectacular works, many of them by the greatest masters of French post-Renaissance sculpture, have enlarged the scope of the collection of French sculpture to a level hardly matched outside Paris.

Only a few galleries are devoted entirely to the display of sculpture. A small portion of the rest of the collection is shown in appropriate settings, such as the Renaissance Patio from Velez Blanco, where Italian Mannerist marble figures are shown, the French and English Renaissance galleries, the French 17th- and 18th-century rooms, and the galleries of European Paintings. Antonio Canova's

29

Perseus looms dramatically from the second-floor balcony.

Encouraged by the exceptionally active patronage of Church and nobility, Italy had a brilliant school of sculptors in the Renaissance. Marble, bronze, and terra cotta were the favored materials. The school is especially well represented in the Metropolitan Museum by 15th-century works—some of the finest pieces by Luca and Andrea della Robbia, and marbles by Agostino di Duccio, Antonio Rossellino, Mino da Fiesole, Benedetto da Maiano, and Pietro and Tullio Lombardo. Members of the della Robbia family in Florence carried the glazing of terra cotta figures and reliefs to a high degree of perfection. In this **Madonna and Child (27)** of glazed terra cotta by Luca della Robbia, the white figures were meant to glow from a dark place. Often the figures were made in lower relief in the typical della Robbia blue and white method, as the lunette of *St. Michael* **(28)** by Andrea della Robbia, from the façade of a church in Faenza. Antonio Rossellino, another 15th-century Florentine, used a brownish mottled marble for his relief of the **Madonna and Child with Angels (29)**. The work is unusual in its dense surface decoration, with the halos and the Virgin's hem picked out in gold.

An outstanding sculpture from the Venetian Renaissance is the full-length figure of **Adam (30)**, from about 1490, by Tullio Lombardo. It once formed part of

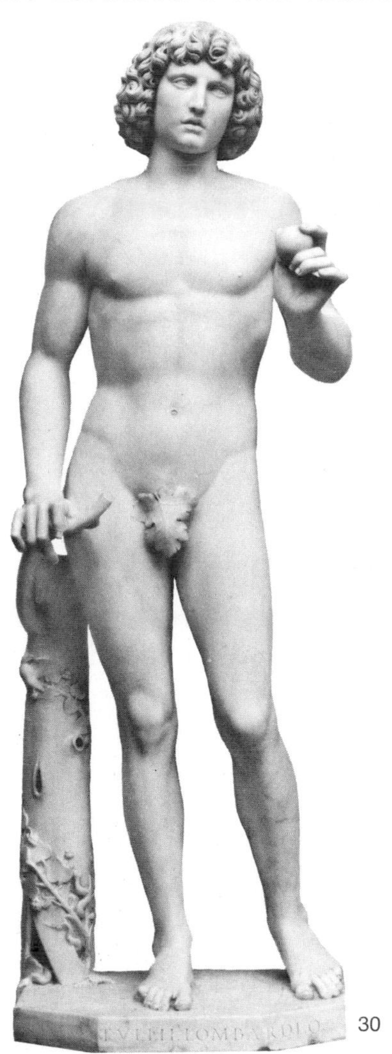

30

the tomb of Doge Andrea Vendramin, now in the church of Sts. Giovanni and Paolo in Venice. Though the figure is certainly based on classical models, the glance, the elegant hands, and the tree trunk with the snake and ivy are Tullio's personal refinements. Outstanding for the purity of its marble and the smoothness of its carving, *Adam* was the first large classical nude to be carved since antiquity!

The Tullio Lombardo *Adam* hints at the 16th-century style called Mannerism, a movement that can be seen very well at the Metropolitan Museum in a small but choice number of marble figures by Domenico Poggini, Battista Lorenzi, Cristoforo Stati da Bracciano, and Giovanni Caccini **(31)**. Equally fine is the group of Spanish 16th- and 17th-century sculptures in polychromed wood. The preaching **St. John the Baptist (32)** by Juan Martinez Montañes, splendidly painted and gilded, speaks with prophetic and natural conviction. Made about 1620-30, the statue comes from a convent in Seville.

33

32

The Baroque, a style that originated in Italy, dominated 17th-century Europe. A late Roman Baroque sculpture, the robust, shrewd characterization of **Pope Alexander VII (33)**, by Melchiore Caffà (1667), is of bronze, a medium that lent itself to the fluid, swagger style.

Bronze was a popular medium for sculpture from the early Renaissance onward. In the 15th century, Italian cities such as Florence, Padua, Venice, and Siena were centers of bronze-casting. The classical nude was a subject reinvestigated by a court artist in Mantua, Pier Jacopo Alari-Bonacolsi, called Anti-

co, in his statuette of the seated **Paris (34)** of about 1500. The finely wrought anatomical details, particularly the gilded hair, are evidence of the artist's training as a goldsmith. Antico is the author of the splendid bust of Antoninus Pius, also in the Museum. This artist is only one of many masters of bronze sculpture represented in the Museum's collection of statuettes, medals, and plaquettes, which includes works of the first importance by Bellano, Riccio, Danese Cattaneo, Tiziano Aspetti, Giovanni Bologna (a number of superb pieces), and the northern sculptors Adriaen de Vries and Hubert Gerhardt.

Venice supported a flourishing bronze industry. Alessandro Vittoria was a leading Venetian marble sculptor; his small **St. Sebastian (35)**, cast by Andrea da Brescia in 1566, and based on Michelangelo, is a masterpiece of Mannerism. (Vittoria was so proud of this model that he is seen holding one in his portrait by Veronese in the European Paintings galleries.)

Collections of medals and plaquettes in bronze and silver, and small sculptures in wood, ivory, and wax have a secondary but treasured place in the Museum. The Renaissance and Baroque styles in Germany are seen in examples of the highest art in boxwood and ivory, such as the vigorous little ivory figure of Neptune **(36)**, signed with the initials of the 17th-century Austrian Adam Lenckhardt; it comes from the Liechtenstein Collection.

Some fine 16th-century French sculptures show the courtly and mannered art of that age to good advantage. The 17th and 18th centuries are yet more brilliantly

35

34

represented by works of the great French sculptors, Michel Anguier, François Girardon, Pierre-Etienne Monnot, Robert Le Lorrain, Guillaume Coustou, Jean-Louis and Jean-Baptiste Lemoyne, Louis-Claude Vassé, Jean-Baptiste Pigalle, Etienne-Maurice Falconet, Augustin Pajou, Clodion, and several major pieces by Jean-Antoine Houdon.

Pierre-Etienne Monnot was a French sculptor in Rome during the last 20 years of the 17th century, undertaking religious and secular commissions for the Roman nobility and foreign patrons. His marble

37

38

Andromeda (37) was made about 1700 for John Cecil, fifth earl of Exeter, who placed it in Burghley House, his country seat in England. Though Andromeda, chained to a rock next to a sea monster and appealing to an invisible Perseus, retells a classical myth, this work is totally Baroque in style. The sculptor has handled the heroine, the monster, the seething water, and the marine plants smoothly and with a fresh sense of naturalism.

The French tradition of sharp, incisive portraiture is epitomized by the bust of **Samuel Bernard (38)**, a powerful financier in the closing years of Louis XIV's reign. The intelligent lined face under its great wig and the flowing jabot are brought to life by the sculptor Guillaume Coustou in the work of about 1720. **Fear of Cupid's Darts (39)** was carved of marble by Jean-Louis Lemoyne between 1735 and 1742 as a royal commission for Louis XV. The young nymph reacts with a self-protective gesture to Cupid, who is about to fire a dart into her breast. It is a sculpture vivaciously alive in its typical Rococo asymmetry and playfulness. Jean-Baptiste Lemoyne, the son of Jean-Louis, was the favorite portrait sculptor of Louis XV during his long reign. He recorded Louis XV **(40)** in all his benign majesty in a bust dated 1757. One of at least six, it was given to Madame de Pompadour for one of her many châteaux. Also now in the Metropolitan is a bust of Madame de Pompadour by Jean-Baptiste Pigalle, another in the magnificent series of French portrait busts.

Reliefs by Clodion were formerly on the courtyard façade of the Hôtel de Bourbon-Condé, Paris. The Museum is fortunate to own the three stucco reliefs

themselves **(41)** and two crisply modeled terra-cotta reductions. The airy, extravagant *Model for a Proposed Monument to Commemorate the Invention of the Balloon*, in terra cotta, is another Clodion treasure in the Metropolitan.

The dominant late 18th-century style, Neoclassicism, reached its highest level in the work of the Italian Antonio Canova. Even after the artist's death in 1822, Neoclassicism remained the most important style of European sculpture for another 30 years or so. A superb work by Canova, **Perseus Carrying the Head of Medusa (42)**, was recently acquired by the Metropolitan. It shows the classical hero after he has slain the hideous monster Medusa. This is one of two versions; the first was made for Pope Pius VII and is still in the Vatican; the Museum's *Perseus* was commissioned by the Polish Countess Valeria Tarnowska and was sent to Poland soon after the statue was completed in 1809. Though Canova's figure was based on the antique *Apollo Belvedere*, his *Perseus* is a fusion of the beauties of the antique with those of "nature," though nature here was refined to a high degree of idealization.

A landmark of Romantic 19th-century French sculpture is a work by Jean-Bap-

39

42

43

44

tiste Carpeaux, **Ugolino and His Sons (43)**. The subject comes from Dante's *Inferno*, where the poet describes the Pisan traitor, Count Ugolino della Gherardesca, imprisoned and starving with his sons and grandsons. The nightmarish intensity of this group and the anatomical realism of his figures were based partly on Michelangelo's frescoes in the Sistine Chapel in Rome. Carpeaux had spent six years in the Eternal City, finishing the plaster model of this group there in 1861.

Among other 19th-century French sculptures in the Museum there are 37 bronzes by Antoine-Louis Barye and 50 quintessential works in marble, bronze, terra cotta, and plaster by the great Auguste Rodin. Three early modern sculptors whose work can also be seen here are Emile-Antoine Bourdelle, Aristide Maillol, and Charles Despiau. Edgar Degas, although primarily known as a painter, is admired for figures cast in bronze after his wax models. Modeled about 1880-81, his **Ballet Dancer (44)** is the most famous of these.

DECORATIVE ARTS

In addition to the objects shown in the period rooms, the Department of Western European Arts has galleries that are devoted exclusively to displays of ceramics, metalwork, and glass. These range from the earthenwares of the French and Italian Renaissance to the porcelains of the 18th century; elegant jewels of the Renaissance; domestic silver; clocks and watches; objects in the base metals—ironwork, pewter, brass, and gilt bronze; glass from 15th-century Venice to the Victorian period; and smaller collections of carved boxwoods and ivory, cameos,

and enameled copper ranging from pieces of the Limoges workshops to those made in Staffordshire in the 18th century. Only a portion of a collection of this scope and size can be exhibited. For this reason the reserves in the storerooms are considered study-storage and are available by appointment to visitors. One gallery is set aside for changing exhibitions, allowing for specialized displays.

It is hardly an exaggeration to claim that together with the ceramic collections of six other departments the Museum houses one of the world's greatest records of man's accomplishment in the use of baked clay. The foundations of the collection were provided by gifts from Henry G. Marquand (in 1894), J. Pierpont Morgan (in 1917), and R. Thornton Wilson (1937 to date). From these sources came collections of Spanish tiles and Delft pottery, important examples of German stoneware and Hafner ware, and a representation of masterpieces in porcelain from Florence, Meissen, Vienna, and Sèvres. Also included in this department is the Helena Woolworth McCann Collection of China Trade Porcelain.

Earthenware is the most versatile of ceramic materials. Made entirely of clay, it remains porous after firing and so requires a protective glaze, which serves a double purpose of usefulness and embellishment. One type of glazed earthenware is Spanish lustreware which, through a complicated process of firing and glazing, simulates the rich patina of metal. This medieval technique is represented here by 16th-century examples from Valencia **(45)**.

Much Valencian ware was imported into Italy, providing inspiration for the

46

tin-glazed earthenwares known as majolica. The opaque white glaze of this ware provided an excellent ground for ceramic painters. The earliest decorative motifs of the 15th century were gradually replaced by pictorial subjects from the Bible or classical mythology, which were frequently borrowed from contemporary prints. The Museum has a splendid representation of the styles of decoration favored in Florence, Siena, Faenza, Urbino, Castel Durante, Deruta, and Venice. The specialty of Deruta was a pale gold lustre, while Gubbio produced a ruby and deeper gold lustre. Among other cities, Urbino was famous for the production of wares called *istoriati*, decorated with polychrome illustrations, scenes from legends, romances, and especially classical mythology. A number of signatures are found on them. A **majolica dish (46)** from a service made about 1486-87 in Faenza for King Matthias Corvinus of Hungary has at its center a female figure combing the mane of a uni-

corn, illustrating a medieval legend. In addition to the king's coat of arms, the decoration of this dish is a compendium of 15th-century majolica ornamentation.

It was the della Robbias in Florence who showed that earthenware could be used as a medium for sculpture. A rare example of ceramic sculpture is the **Lamentation over the Dead Christ (47)**, from Faenza. It is one of the earliest dated works in the history of majolica and was executed by a sculptor in 1487.

From the R. Thornton Wilson Collection of German and Austrian ceramics comes a pair of large stove tiles in glazed earthenware, dating from about 1560. The Adoration of the Shepherds **stove tile (48)**, as well as The Execution of the Five Kings of the Amoriates are attributed to The Master H. R. (Hans Resch), a potter active in Salzburg. Each tile is decorated in relief in shades of colored glaze, with figures placed in the same architectural setting.

Although earthenware was common throughout Europe, the formula for porcelain, treasured in Oriental imports, long remained a mystery. The **ewer (49)** illustrated here, and other objects in the same case, are examples of the earliest attempts at imitating the hard-paste porcelains of China. They were made of artificial soft-paste porcelain and decorated in underglaze blue, as was the Chinese ware known in Europe. These rare pieces were made in Florence between 1575 and 1587, under the patronage of Francesco de' Medici.

The technical secret of porcelain production was not discovered until the early 18th century when a German alchemist, Johann Friedrich Böttger, achieved at Meissen a true, or hard-paste, porcelain similar in composition to the Oriental porcelain. A wide range of Meissen wares can be seen in the Museum, some bearing the monogram of Augustus the Strong, the patron of the Meissen factory. The pair of **porcelain goats (50)** is cast from models by Johann Joachim Kaendler at Meissen. The difficulty in firing pieces of such a large size restricted their pro-

47

48

49

duction to animals and figures made mostly for Augustus's "Japanese Palace." Other objects from Meissen represent a whimsical Rococo adaptation of the Chinese decorative style.

From Meissen the technique of hard-paste spread quickly to other centers. An Austrian beaker with cover **(51)**, dating from about 1720, is an elaborate piece, reminiscent of a goldsmith's work. The arcaded middle section has the portraits of three Hapsburg emperors—Ferdinand II and III and Leopold I—each wearing armor of inlaid gold touched with translucent enamels, a mantle, a crown set with paste jewels, and holding a scepter in the right hand.

In France ceramics as an art form began with Palissy and St.-Porchaire earthenware of the 16th and early 17th century, followed later in the century by the faiences of Rouen, Moustiers, and other provincial centers. In emulation of Augustus the Strong, Louis XV transformed the Vincennes porcelain factory into the royal manufactory at Sèvres. New achievements in design and technique began to change its productions. The

50

covered vase (52) shown here was called after Sieur Boileau, director of the factory from 1753 to 1772. It is particularly admired for its rose ground color, an invention by a flower painter at the factory. The figure decoration is in the style of Dodin, the flowers by Dubois, both important painters at Sèvres. Painted porcelain plaques used as inlays on furniture also come from this period, and many pieces are assembled in a gallery on the first floor.

In contrast to these luxury wares from the Continental porcelain factories were the simpler domestic productions of the Delft and English potters **(53)**. Included in the Museum's collection of English ceramics are examples from Bow and Worcester, a comprehensive group of salt glaze wares, as well as the more refined productions made at Chelsea and, at Etruria, by Josiah Wedgwood.

The silver collections were initiated by the gift in 1897 of the Avery Collection of north European spoons of the 16th to the 19th century. This was followed in 1917 by a gift from J. Pierpont Morgan of Continental tablewares, silver and silver gilt cups in the form of animals, and a German automaton of Diana on a stag **(54)**. English and Irish table silver, including some fine Continental tankards and beakers, was added with the bequest of Alphonso T. Clearwater.

52

The Museum's superb collection of French silver began with a nucleus of pieces by Jacques-Nicolas Roettiers and Martin-Guillaume Biennais. Of great Neoclassic elegance is the circular **stew tureen (55)**, one of eight made for Catherine the Great of Russia by Roettiers, who was among the most famous Parisian silversmiths. The entire service, which may have consisted of 3,000 pieces, was presented in 1773 by the empress to Prince Gregory Orloff. In 1948 the bequest of Mrs. Catherine D. Wentworth enriched the Museum with her magnificent collection of approximately 500 pieces of Parisian and French provincial silver.

The renowned English master Paul de Lamerie is exceptionally well represented by silver from the Jules S. Bache Collection and by other examples presented in 1957 by Mrs. Widener Dixon and George D. Widener. In 1963 some charming silver miniatures came to the Museum with the gift of the Joseph M. and Aimée Loeb Collection. A recent gift of the Honorable Irwin Untermyer brought a distinguished group of English silver and silver gilt objects. An outstanding English piece from the 1760s is the **epergne (56)**, a composite centerpiece of silver, with cast, repoussé, and pierced decorations

56

58

55

in the form of scrolls, flowers, baskets, and circular trays, topped with a finial in the shape of a pineapple. This Rococo fantasy was made by Thomas Heming of London.

The J. Pierpont Morgan gift also provided the nucleus of the watch and clock collection **(57)**. Renaissance clockmaking is admirably represented by the richly decorated astronomical clock of gilded bronze, dated 1568 and signed by the Viennese Caspar Behaim; the silver celestial globe with clockworks supported on the gilded wings of Pegasus by the imperial clockmaker Gerhard Emmoser; and the engraved and gilded brass table clock by Bartholomew Newsam, clockmaker to Queen Elizabeth I.

The development of French and English goldsmithing and enameling, as well as of watchmaking, in the 17th and 18th centuries is illustrated by the works of such masters as Nicholas Vallin, Edward East, Daniel Quare, George Graham, Nicolas Gribelin, Goullons, Julien and Pierre Le Roy, Ferdinand Berthoud, and Robert Robin. In variety, the collection ranges from an exquisitely enameled watch case with Baroque floral decoration, signed by Christophe Morlière, to the handsome silver repeating clock watch by Thomas Tompion, to James Cox's whimsical **Rococo timepiece (58)** incorporated in a

59

miniature secretary cabinet made of gold and agate and decorated with shimmering butterflies.

The technique of enameling on watch cases was closely related to the work of jewelers and goldsmiths. Almost every phase of this art is represented in the Morgan Collection of 1917 with its Renaissance jewels, snuff boxes, and enameled jeweled cups. Perhaps the most famous of these is the **Rospigliosi Cup (59)**, named after the former owners, the Rospigliosi family in Rome. It is attributed to the Netherlandish goldsmith Jacopo Bilivert, who was working in Florence for the Grand Duke Francesco de' Medici in the last quarter of the 16th century.

Among base metals, the three-story *reja*, or screen, made of wrought iron by Master Pedro Juan for the Cathedral of Valladolid, Spain, and now installed in the medieval sculpture court **(60)**, is the most important piece of a large collection of ironwork avquired from Henry G. Marquand, Samuel Yellin, and William Randolph Hearst.

The Department's European glass from 1500 to 1900 **(61)** has been largely formed by the acquisition of entire private collections, such as those of James Jackson Jarves in 1881, Henry G. Marquand in 1883, and Edward C. Moore in 1893. The Museum's Spanish pieces mainly illustrate the traditional aspects of provincial glassmaking; the relatively small collection of French glass comprises not only interesting provincial styles but also products of Nevers and Orléans, where more sophisticated glass was made.

Dutch, Flemish, Austrian, and German glass came to the Metropolitan in 1927 when the great Mühsam Collection was for sale. Included were samples of all styles of glass from these countries and also glass that could be credited to specific artists, such as the enamelers Johann Schaper and Ignaz Preissler, the engravers Herman Schwinger and J. H. B. Sang, the glass experimenter Johann Kunckel, and the Dutch diamond-stipplers Frans Greenwood and David Wolff.

Credits

American Paintings and Sculpture

(4) Bequest of Richard De Wolfe Brixey, 1943; **(6)** Gift of Samuel P. Avery, 1897; **(7)** Rogers Fund, 1907; **(13)** Gift of Edgar William and Bernice Chrysler Garbisch, 1963; **(14)** Maria DeWitt Jesup Fund, 1939; **(15)** Maria DeWitt Jesup Fund, 1959; **(18)** Gift of Edgar William and Bernice Chrysler Garbisch, 1962; **(20)** Bequest of Francis T. S. Darley, 1914; **(23)** Gift of Mrs. Russell Sage, 1908; **(28)** Bequest of Mrs. David Dows, 1909; **(31)** Charles Allen Munn Bequest, 1966; **(32)** Morris K. Jesup Fund, 1933; **(33)** Gift of William B. Astor, 1872; **(38)** Alfred N. Punnett Endowment Fund and Gift of George D. Pratt, 1934; **(39)** Wolfe Fund, 1963; **(41)** Samuel D. Lee Fund, 1934; **(44)** Wolfe Fund, 1913; **(45)** Arthur Hoppock Hearn Fund, 1916; **(46)** Anonymous Gift, 1922; **(47)** Morris K. Jesup Fund, 1968; **(51)** Gift of George A. Hearn, 1910; **(52)** Amelia B. Lazarus Fund, 1910; **(54)** Rogers Fund, 1928; **(56)** Gift of Hugo Reisinger, 1911.

American Wing

(1) Gift of Mrs. J. Insley Blair, 1951; **(2)** Gift of Mrs. Russell Sage, 1909; **(3)** Munsey Fund, 1936; **(4)** Sage Fund, 1926; **(5)** Morris K. Jesup Fund, 1952; **(6)** Purchase, Joseph Pulitzer Bequest, 1940; **(7)** Rogers Fund, 1928; **(8)** Rogers Fund, 1918; **(9)** Rogers Fund, 1925; **(10)** John Stewart Kennedy Fund, 1918; **(11)** Rogers Fund, 1927; **(12)** Rogers Fund, 1925; **(13)** Gift of Mrs. William Bayard Van Rensselaer, in memory of her husband, 1937; **(15)** Gift of the family of Mr. and Mrs. Andrew Varick Stout, in their memory, 1965; **(16)** Funds from various donors, 1966; **(17)** Samuel D. Lee Fund, 1937; **(18)** Rogers Fund, 1912; **(19)** Gift of Mrs. Russell Sage, Bequest of Ethel Yocum, Bequest of Charlotte E. Hoadley and Rogers Fund, by exhange, 1971; **(20)** Gift of Robert Livingston Cammam, 1957; **(21)** Samuel D. Lee Fund, 1938; **(22)** Rogers Fund, 1946; **(23)** Bequest of Alphonso T. Clearwater, 1933; **(24)** Fletcher Fund, 1959; **(25)** Gift of Mrs. Russel Sage and various other donors, 1969.

Ancient Near East

(1) Fletcher Fund, 1940; **(2)** Harris Brisbane Dick Fund, 1955; **(3)** Gift of Walter Hauser, 1955; **(4)** Harris Brisbane Dick Fund, 1959; **(5)** Rogers Fund, 1959; **(6)** Gift of George D. Pratt, 1932; **(7)** Harris Brisbane Dick Fund, 1957; **(8)** Gift of George D. Pratt, 1932; **(9)** Purchase, Joseph Pulitzer Bequest, 1966; **(10)** Rogers Fund, 1947; **(11)** Fletcher Fund, 1963; **(12)** Rogers Fund, 1962; **(13)** Rogers Fund, 1960; **(14)** Rogers Fund, 1953; **(15)** Gift of John D. Rockefeller, Jr., 1932; **(16)** Gift of John D. Rockefeller, Jr., 1931; **(17)** Rogers Fund, 1965; **(18)** Ann and George Blumenthal Fund, 1954; **(19)** Fletcher Fund, 1931; **(20)** Fletcher Fund, 1954; **(21)** Fletcher Fund, 1956; **(22)** Purchase, Joseph Pulitzer Bequest, 1932; **(23)** Rogers Fund, 1951; **(24)** Rogers Fund, 1931; **(25)** Fletcher Fund, 1934; **(26)** Fletcher Fund, 1963; **(27)** Fletcher Fund, 1965; **(28)** Rogers Fund, 1965; **(29)** Rogers Fund, 1947.

Arms and Armor

(1) Harris Brisbane Dick Fund, 1942; **(2)** Rogers Fund, 1955; **(6)** Bashford Dean Memorial Collection, gift of Helen Fahnestock Hubbard, 1929, in memory of her father, Harris C. Fahnestock; **(8)** Harris Brisbane Dick Fund,1923; **(13)** Bashford Dean Memorial Collection, Gift of Edward S. Harkness, 1929; **(14)** Gift of George D. Pratt, 1926; **(15)** Mrs. Stephen V. Harkness Fund, 1926; **(18)** Rogers Fund, 1904; **(22)** Purchase Rogers Fund, 1904, and Pulitzer Bequest, 1922; **(24)** Gift of J. Pierpont Morgan, 1917; **(26)** Rogers Fund, 1932; **(29)** Rogers Fund, 1951; **(31)** Gift of Jean Jacques Reubell, 1926; **(37)** Rogers Fund, 1970; **(40)** Gift of William H. Riggs, 1913; **(43)** Fletcher Fund, 1970; **(48)** Rogers Fund, 1904; **(52)** The Howard Mansfield Collection, Gift of Howard Mansfield, 1936; **(54)** Bequest of George C. Stone, 1936; **(62)** Rogers Fund, 1904; **(64)** Giovanni P. Morosini Collection, presented by his daughter Giulia, 1923.

Costume Institute

(1) Gifts of various donors; **(2)** Gift of Irene Lewisohn, 1937; **(3)** Gifts of Aline Bernstein, Ethel Frankau, Aline Mac Mahon, and Lee Simonson, 1938-39; **(4)** Gift of Mrs. Byron C. Foy, 1956; **(5)** Gift of John Moore, 1968; **(6)** Gift of Lee Simonson, 1961; **(7)** Gift of Newark Public Library; **(8)** Rogers Fund, 1933; **(9)** Irene Lewisohn Bequest, 1962; **(10)** Gift of the heirs of Emily Kearny Rodgers Cowenhoven, 1970; **(11)** Irene Lewisohn Bequest, 1954; **(12)** Gift of Elizabeth R. Hooker, 1962; **(13)** Gift of Mrs. J. Chester Chamberlain, 1952; **(14)** Gift of Mrs. James G. Flockhart, 1968; **(15)** Irene Lewisohn Bequest Fund, 1962; **(16)** Irene Lewisohn Bequest Fund, 1956; **(17)** Gift of Mrs. John C. Cattus, 1952; **(18)** Gift of Alan Wolfe, 1956; **(19)** Gift of the J. L. Hudson Company, 1944.

Drawings

(1) Harris Brisbane Dick Fund, 1949; **(2)** Rogers Fund, 1968; **(3)** Rogers Fund, 1917; **(4)** Purchase, Joseph Pulitzer Bequest, 1924; **(5)** Rogers Fund, 1964; **(6)** Rogers Fund, 1949; **(7)** Gift of Mrs. William H. Osborn, 1961; **(8)** Rogers Fund, 1970; **(9)** Rogers Fund, 1961; **(10)** Rogers Fund, 1965; **(11)** Bequest of Mrs. H. O. Havemeyer, 1929, the H. O. Havemeyer Collection; **(12)** Rogers Fund, 1937; **(13)** Rogers Fund, 1943; **(14)**, **(15)** Rogers Fund, 1937; **(16)** Mr. and Mrs. Henry Ittleson, Jr., Gift, 1970; **(17)** Harris Brisbane Dick Fund, 1941; **(18)** Rogers Fund, 1914; **(19)** Marquand Fund, 1959; **(20)** Harris Brisbane Dick Fund, 1935; **(21)** Bequest of Grace Rainey Rogers, 1943; **(22)** Bequest of Mrs. H. O. Havemeyer, 1929, the H. O. Havemeyer Collection; **(23)** Rogers Fund, 1919; **(24)** Bequest ofStephen C. Clark, 1960; **(25)** Gift of Mrs. Florence Blumenthal, 1910; **(26)** The Alfred Stieglitz Collection, 1949.

Egyptian Art

(1) Rogers Fund, 1920; **(5)** Purchase, 1966; Fletcher Fund, and the Guide Foundation, Inc. Gift; **(14)** Rogers Fund, 1926; **(17)** Rogers Fund, 1952; **(18)** Rogers Fund, 1926; **(21)** Rogers Fund, and Gift of Edward S. Harkness, 1920; **(22)** Rogers Fund, and Gift of Edward S. Harkness, 1919-20; **(24)** Gift of Edward S. Harkness, 1914; **(25)** Gift of Edward S. Harkness, 1912; **(26)** Gift of Edward S. Harkness, 1917; **(27)** Gift of Edward S. Harkness, 1926; **(29)** Rogers Fund, 1926-28; **(37)** Gift of Edward S. Harkness, 1926; **(40)** Gift of Theodore M. Davis, 1907; **(41)** Rogers Fund, 1950; **(42)** Rogers Fund, 1907; **(43)** Gift of Mr. and Mrs. V. Everit Macy, 1923; **(44)** Rogers Fund, 1934; **(45)** Rogers Fund, 1933; **(46)** Rogers Fund, 1934; **(47)**

Credits

Fletcher Fund, 1950; **(48)** Gift of Edward S. Harkness, 1917-18; **(49)** Purchase, Rogers Fund and Henry Walters Gift, 1916; **(50)** Purchase, Henry Walters Gift and Edward S. Harkness Gift, 1926; **(53)** Gift of Edward S. Harkness, 1926; **(55)** Rogers Fund, 1909.

European Paintings

(**1**) John Stewart Kennedy Fund, 1910; **(2)** Munsey Fund, 1936; **(3)** Bequest of Mrs. H. O. Havemeyer, 1929; the H. O. Havemeyer Collection; **(4)** John Stewart Kennedy Fund, 1911; **(5)** The Jules Bache Collection, 1949; **(6)** Bequest of Benjamin Altman, 1913; **(7)** Rogers Fund, 1908; **(8)** Purchase, 1871; **(9)** Funds from various donors, 1956; **(10)** Gift of Henry G. Marquand, 1890; **(11)** Purchase with special funds and gifts of friends of the Museum, 1961; **(12)** Gift of Henry G. Marquand, 1889; **(13)** Fletcher Fund, 1958; **(14)** Harris Brisbane Dick Fund, 1946; **(15)** Munsey Fund, 1934; **(16)** Wolfe Fund, 1931; **(17)** Wolfe Fund, 1918; **(18)** Bequest of Mrs. H. O. Havemeyer, 1929; the H. O. Havemeyer Collection; **(19)** Purchased with special contributions and purchase funds given or bequeathed by friends of the Museum, 1967; **(20)** Bequest of Mrs. H. O. Havemeyer, 1929; the H. O. Havemeyer Collection; **(21)** Bequest of Samuel A. Lewisohn, 1951; **(22)** Fletcher Fund, 1933; **(23)** Bequest of Michael Dreicer, 1921; **(24)** Rogers Fund, 1919; **(25)** Rogers Fund, 1928; **(26)** Bequest of Benjamin Altman, 1913; **(27)** Bequest of Edward S. Harkness, 1940; **(28)** Gift of Harry Payne Bingham, 1937; **(29)** Bequest of Mrs. H. O. Havemeyer, 1929; the H. O. Havemeyer Collection; **(30)** Purchase, 1971; Principally from purchase funds bequeathed by Isaac D. Fletcher and Jacob S. Rogers, supplemented by gifts from friends of the Museum; **(31)** Bequest of Mrs. H. O. Havemeyer, 1929; the H. O. Havemeyer Collection; **(32)** Bequest of William K. Vanderbilt, 1920; **(33)** Bequest of Cornelius Vanderbilt, 1899.

Far Eastern Art

(3) Harris Brisbane Dick Fund, 1949; **(6)** Gift of Miss Florance Waterbury, 1965; **(7)** Harris Brisbane Dick Fund, 1960; **(10)** Rogers Fund, 1917; **(12)** Frederick C. Hewitt Fund, 1921; **(14)** Gift of Robert E. Tod, 1937; **(15)** Bequest of John D. Rockefeller, Jr., 1960; **(16)** Rogers Fund, 1943; **(17)** Munsey Fund, 1931; **(18)** Gift of Heber R. Bishop, 1902; **(21)** Gift of Robert Lehman, 1948; **(23)** Rogers Fund, 1924; **(25)** Kennedy Fund, 1926; **(26)** Rogers Fund, 1938; **(28)** Rogers Fund, 1919; **(29)** Gift of Mrs. John D. Rockefeller, Jr., 1942; **(31)** Fletcher Fund, 1928; **(34)** Rogers Fund, 1941; **(38)** Purchase, Mary Griggs Burke Gift, 1966; **(40)** Fletcher Fund, 1927; **(45)** Purchase, Bequest of Florance Waterbury, 1969; **(46)** Harris Brisbane Dick Fund, 1964; **(49)** Purchase, Bequest of Florance Waterbury, 1970; **(52)** Rogers Fund, 1967.

Greek and Roman

(2) Gift of Christos G. Bastis, 1968; **(3)** Rogers Fund, 1947; **(6)** Purchase, Louisa Eldridge McBurney Gift, 1953; **(7)** Rogers Fund, 1914; **(8)** Rogers Fund, 1921; **(10)** Fletcher Fund, 1932; **(11)** Frederick C. Hewitt, Rogers, and Munsey Funds, 1911, 1921, 1936, and 1938, and anonymous gift, 1951; **(12)** Fletcher Fund, 1938; **(13)** Rogers Fund, 1947; **(14)** Rogers Fund, 1917; **(15)** Purchase, Joseph Pulitzer Bequest, 1963; **(16)** Acquired through exchange, 1972; **(17)** Acquired through exchange, 1972; **(19)** Frederick C. Hewitt Fund, 1925; **(20)** Purchase, John D. Rockefeller Gift, 1932; **(21)** Fletcher Fund, 1927; **(23)** Rogers Fund, 1943; **(24)** Rogers Fund, 1909; **(25)** Fletcher Fund, 1952; **(26)** Rogers Fund, 1962; **(27)** Rogers Fund, 1903; **(29)** Fletcher Fund, 1930; **(30)** Funds from various donors, 1966; **(31)** Purchase, Joseph Pulitzer Bequest, 1955; **(32)**, **(33)** Rogers Fund, 1903.

Islamic Art

(1) Fletcher Fund and funds from various donors, 1931; **(2)** Rogers Fund, 1965; **(3)** Bequest of Cora Timken Burnett, 1957; **(4)** Gift of J. Pierpont Morgan, 1917; **(5)** Rogers Fund, 1944; **(6)** Purchase, Joseph Pulitzer Bequest, 1969; **(7)**, **(8)** Fletcher Fund, 1932; **(9)** Gift of the Schiff Foundation and Rogers Fund, 1957; **(10)** Rogers Fund, 1910; **(11)** Edward C. Moore Collection, Bequest of Edward C. Moore, 1891; **(12)** Harris Brisbane Dick Fund, 1939; **(13)** Purchase, Joseph Pulitzer Bequest, 1933; **(14)** Gift of Alexander Smith Cochran, 1913; **(15)** Rogers Fund, 1918; **(16)** Rogers Fund, 1912; **(17)** Edward C. Moore Collection, Bequest of Edward C. Moore, 1891; **(18)** Rogers Fund, 1941; **(19)** Fletcher Fund, 1970; **(20)** Frederick C. Hewitt Fund, 1910; **(21)** Gift of Arthur A. Houghton, Jr., 1970; **(22)** Rogers Fund, 1912; **(23)** Fletcher Fund, 1963; **(24)** Rogers Fund, 1935; **(25)** Gift of James J. Rorimer in appreciation of Maurice S. Dimand's curatorship, 1933-59, 1959; **(26)** Gift of Alexander Smith Cochran, 1913.

Medieval Art

(5) Rogers Fund, 1916; **(10)** Gift of J. Pierpont Morgan, 1917; **(13)** The Cloisters Collection, 1966; **(15)**, **(16)**, **(18)**, **(19)**, **(22)**, **(23)** Gift of J. Pierpont Morgan, 1917; **(25)** Gift of George Blumenthal, 1941; **(26)**, **(30)** Gift of J. Pierpont Morgan, 1917; **(31)** Gift of J. Pierpont Morgan, 1916; **(33)** Harris Brisbane Dick Fund, 1938; **(34)** Gift of George D. Pratt, 1924; **(36)** Gift of Harriet Barnes Pratt, 1949, in memory of her husband Harold Irving Pratt, 1876-1939; **(38)** Rogers Fund, 1909; **(42)** Fletcher Fund, 1946; **(46)** Rogers Fund, 1933; **(47)** Gift of J. Pierpont Morgan, 1917; **(50)** Gift of George Blumenthal, 1941; **(52)** Rogers Fund, 1912; **(55)** Gift of J. Pierpont Morgan, 1917; **(58)** The Cloisters Collection, 1965; **(59)** Gift of J. Pierpont Morgan, 1917; **(63)** Gift of J. Pierpont Morgan, 1917; **(66)** Fletcher Fund, 1927.

Musical Instruments

(1), **(2)**, **(3)**, **(4)**, **(8)**, **(9)**, **(13)**, **(14)**, **(15)**, **(16)**, **(17)**, **(18)**, **(19)**, **(20)**, **(25)** The Crosby Brown Collection of Musical Instruments, 1889; **(5)** Gift of R. Thornton Wilson, 1943, in memory of Florence Ellsworth Wilson; **(6)** Purchase, Joseph Pulitzer Bequest, 1953; **(7)** Gift of B. H. Homan, 1929; **(10)** Gift of Mrs. Henry McSweeney, 1959; **(11)** Gift of Joseph W. Drexel, 1885; **(12)** Bequest of Annie Bolton Matthews Bryant, 1933; **(21)** Rogers Fund, 1968; **(22)** Gift of Dr. Thongphet Phetsiriseng, 1966; **(23)** Bequest of Mary Stillman Harkness, 1950; **(24)**, **(26)** Gift of Miss Alice Getty, 1946.

Credits

Prints and Photographs

(1) Gift of Felix M. Warburg and his family, 1941; **(2)** Purchase, Joseph Pulitzer Bequest, 1917; **(3)** Gift of Felix M. Warburg and his family, 1941; **(4)** Harris Brisbane Dick Fund, 1935; **(5)** The Elisha Whittelsey Fund and C. Douglas Dillon Gift, 1968; **(6)** Harris Brisbane Dick Fund, 1935; **(7)** The Eisha Whittelsey Fund, 1967; **(8)** Florence and Joseph Singer Collection, 1969; **(9)** Harris Brisbane Dick Fund, 1925; **(10)** The Elisha Whittelsey Fund, 1955; **(11)** Harris Brisbane Dick Fund, 1930; **(12)** Gift of Felix M. Warburg, 1928; **(13)** Rogers Fund, 1918; **(14)** Harris Brisbane Dick Fund, 1930; **(15)** Harris Brisbane Dick Fund, 1931; **(16)** The Elisha Whittelsey Fund, 1970; **(17)** Mary Martin Bequest, 1938; **(18)** Bella C. Landauer Collection; **(19)** The Elisha Whittelsey Fund, 1970; **(20)** Rogers Fund, 1920; **(21)** Harris Brisbane Dick Fund, 1924; **(22)** Purchase, the Martin Foundation, Inc. Gift, 1967; **(23)** Purchase, Harris Brisbane Dick Fund and Joseph Pulitzer Bequest, 1971; **(24)** The Alfred Stieglitz Collection, 1928; **(25)** David Hunter McAlpin Fund, 1943; **(26)** Gift of George Dawes, 1948; **(27)** David Hunter McAlpin Fund, 1943.

Twentieth Century Art

(1) Jointly owned by The Metropolitan Museum of Art and Mrs. Frank Jay Gould; **(2)** Bequest of Gertrude Stein, 1946; **(3)**, **(4)** The Alfred Stieglitz Collection, 1949; **(5)** George A. Hearn Fund, 1963; **(6)**, **(7)**, **(8)**, **(9)**, **(10)** The Alfred Stieglitz Collection, 1949; **(11)** George A. Hearn Fund, 1953; **(12)** George A. Hearn Fund, 1956; **(13)** Arthur Hoppock Hearn Fund, 1942; **(14)** Hugo Kastor Fund, 1962; **(15)** George A. Hearn Fund, 1970; **(16)** Gift of Mr. and Mrs. Richard Rodgers and the Francis Lathrop Fund, 1963; **(17)** George A. Hearn Fund, 1957; **(18)** Rogers Fund, 1956; **(19)** Arthur Hoppock Hearn Fund, 1967; **(20)** Purchase, 1967. Edward C. Moore, Jr., Gift and Edgar J. Kaufmann Charitable Foundation Gift; **(21)** Purchase, 1963, Edward C. Moore Gift, 1963.

Western European Arts

(1) Rogers Fund, 1939; **(2)** Ann and George Blumenthal Fund, 1941; **(4)** Harris Brisbane Dick Fund, 1957; **(13)** Fletcher Fund, 1931; **(14)** Gift of Samuel H. Kress Foundation, 1958-59; **(15)** Rogers Fund, 1930; **(16)** Fletcher Fund, 1964; **(18)** Gift of J. P. Morgan, 1920; **(19)** Gift of the Samuel H. Kress Foundation, 1958; **(20)** Gift of Mr. and Mrs. Charles Wrightsman, 1963; **(25)** Bequest of William K. Vanderbilt, 1920; **(27)** Bequest of Benjamin Altman, 1913; **(29)** Bequest of Benjamin Altman, 1913; **(30)** Fletcher Fund, 1936; **(32)** Purchase, Joseph Pulitzer Bequest, 1963; **(33)** Edith Perry Chapman Fund, 1957; **(34)** Edith Perry Chapman Fund, 1955; **(35)** Samuel D. Lee Fund, 1940; **(37)**, **(38)**, **(39)** Purchase, 1966 and 1967. Funds given by the Joseprine Bay Paul and C. Michael Paul Foundation, Inc., and Charles Ulrick and Josephine Bay Foundation, Inc.; **(42)** Fletcher Fund, 1967; **(43)** Purchase, 1967. Funds given by the Josephine Bay Paul and C. Michael Paul Foundation, and Charles Ulrick and Josephine Bay Foundation, Inc.; **(44)** Bequest of Mrs. H. O. Havemeyer, 1929; The H. O. Havemeyer Collection; **(46)** Fletcher Fund, 1946; **(47)** Rogers Fund, 1904; **(48)** Gift of J. Pierpont Morgan, 1917; **(49)** Gift of R. Thornton Wilson in memory of Robert Francis Kennedy, 1925-68, Senator from New York, 1968; **(50)** Rogers Fund, 1969, and Gift of Mrs. Jean Mauzé, 1962; **(52)** Gift of R. Thornton Wilson, 1950, in memory of Florence Ellsworth Wilson; **(55)** Rogers Fund, 1933; **(56)** Gift of Lewis Einstein, 1952; **(58)** Gift of Admiral F. R. Harris, 1946, in memory of his wife, Dena Sperry Harris; **(59)** Bequest of Benjamin Altman, 1913.

Index

Page numbers in bold face indicate illustrations.

Abstract Expressionism, 283-284, 287
Accessories, clothing, 79, 84, 86
Adam, Robert, 36, 37, 40, 294, 295, 296
Albers, Josef, 274, **283**
Allston, Washington, 15
Amelung, John Frederick, 31
Andokides Painter, 168
Antico, 302-**303**
Architecture
  American, 26, 27, 29, 32, 33, 34, 38
  books on, 262
  drawings, 10, 91, **268**, 269
  Greek, 162-163, 165
  Renaissance, 290, **291**
  Romanesque, 216
Art Deco, 288
Art Nouveau, 40, 288
Ash Can School, 24
Avignon School, 131

Badger, Joseph, 11
Bakst, Léon, **261**
Baroque style, 126, 140, 302, 303, 304
Barye, Antoine-Louis, 306
Beds, 38, 292, 293
Bellegambe, Jean, 131
Bellini, Giovanni, **126**
Bellows, George, **24**, 282
Benton, Thomas Hart, 283
Bérain, Jean, **270**
Berlinghiero, 123
Biennais, Martin-Guillaume, 310
Bierstadt, Albert, 17
Bihzad, **186**, 187
Bingham, George Caleb, **18**
Bishop, Isabel, 282
Blackburn, Joseph, 11
Blake, William, **100**, 101
Blakelock, Ralph, 20
Bodhisattvas
  paintings, 155, 160
  sculpture, 152, **153**, 154, **155**, 159
Bologna, Giovanni, 303
Bonheur, Rosa, 134
Bonnard, Pierre, 261, 262, **266**, **275**
Bookcases, **38**, 40, 296
Books, illustrated, 258, 262-266, 268
Botticelli, Sandro, **125**
Boucher, François, 100, 132, 300
Bouts, Dieric, 137
Bows and crossbows, **65**, 70
Bradley, Will, 261
Brancusi, Constantin, **276**, 277, 278
Bronzes
  ancient Near Eastern, 42, 45, **48**, 52, **53**
  Chinese, **150**-151
  Egyptian, 120
  Etruscan, **173**
  Greek, 163, **165**, **167**, 169, 173
  medieval, 211, 212, 224
  Western European, 306
Bronzino, **123**
Bruegel, Pieter, the Elder, **138**, 259
Buddhas, 152, **153**, **154**, 155, **158**-159, 160
Bugatti, Carlo, **288**
Burchfield, Charles, 283

Cabinets, 292, **296**
Caffà, Melchiore, **302**
Calligraphy, 180, 181, **264**, 281
Campin, Robert, 137
Canaletto, Antonio, **98**, 99, 127
Candlesticks, 31, **39**
Canova, Antonio, 300, **305**
Caravaggio, Michelangelo da, 127, 259
Carpaccio, Vittore, 92, 126
Carpeaux, Jean-Baptiste, 306-**307**
Carpets, *see* Rugs and carpets
Carracci, Annibale, **94**, 95, 126
Cassatt, Mary, **22**
Ceramics, 307
  American, 26
  Chinese, 146-150
  European, 306, 307-310
  Greek, ancient, 167
  Islamic, 179, **181**, **182**
  Japanese, 146, 158
  Korean, 160
  see also, Earthenware; Porcelain; Pottery
Cézanne, Paul, 135, 275
Chairs, 27, 29, 30, 31, 32, **33**, 34, **36**, **37**, 200, 293, 296, 298, 299
Chandeliers, 31, 37
Chardin, Jean-Siméon, 132
Chests, **27**, 30, 31, **32**, 220
Ch'i style, 154
China, *see* Ceramics
Chippendale, Thomas, 269, 296
  style, 31-32, 34
Christus, Petrus, 137
Church, Frederic Edwin, 10, **16**, 17
Claude Lorrain, 131
Clocks and watches, 31, 34, 37, 297, 306, 311-312
Clodion, 303, 304-305
Clothing, 74-88
  children's, 86
  men's, 85
  regional, 87, 88
  sports, 84-85
  women's, *see* Dresses and gowns
Clouet, Jean, 131
Cole, Thomas, **16**, 17
Collages, 279
Colt, Samuel, 69
Commodes, 296, 299
Constable, John, 144
Copley, John Singleton, 10, **11**, 31, 34
Copper, 43, **45**, 46, **47**, 224, 307
Corot, Camille, 134
Correggio, Antonio, 122
Cortona, Pietro da, **95**
Costumes, 74-88
  Chinese and Japanese, 299
  drawings, 79, 269
Courbet, Gustave, 134
Coustou, Guillaume, 303, 304
Cox, James, 312
Cozens, John Robert, 100
Cranach, Lucas, the Elder, 138, **139**, 261
Crewel work, 29
Cristofori piano, 231
Crivelli, Carlo, **124**, 125
Cropsey, Jasper Francis, 17
Cubism, 104, 135, 275, 276-277, 279, 281
Cupboards, 29, 30, 33, 34, 296
Curry, John Steuart, 283
Curtains and draperies, 26, 29, 37
Cypriot art, 162, 163-164

Daggers, 60, 65, **66**, 71, 72
Daubigny, Charles-François, 134
Daumier, Honoré, 102, **103**
David, Gerard, 138
David, Jacques-Louis, **133**
Davies, Arthur B., 10, 24
Davis, Alexander Jackson, **268**, 269
Davis, Stuart, **280**, 281
Decorative arts

American, 26-40, 274, 288
European, 290, 293-296, 298-299, 306-312
Islamic, 180, **182**, 183, **184**
Degas, Hilaire-Germain-Edgar, 102-**103**, 134, **135**, **260**, **306**
De Kooning, Willem, 284, 285, **286**
Delaune, Etienne, 64
Demuth, Charles, 104, 279, **280**, 281
Desks, 30, 32, **40**, **288**, **297**, 299
Dior, Christian, 77
Doors, 30, **178**, 179, **187**
Doughty, Thomas, 17
Dove, Arthur, 279
Draperies, *see* Curtains and draperies
Drawings, 10, 90-104, 258, 267-270, 274
architectural, 10, 91, **268**, 269
fashion, 79, 269
jewelry designs, 268, **269**
landscapes, 91, 96, **101**
portrait, 90, 95, **102**, **103**
Dresses and gowns, **75**, 76-**77**, **78**, **79**, **80**, **81**, **82**, **83**, **84**, **86**, 87
Duccio di Buoninsegna, 124
Duplessis, Joseph Siffred, 132
Durand, Asher Brown, 17
Dürer, Albrecht, 64, **94**, 95, **139**, 265
Dyck, Anthony van, 140

Eakins, Thomas, 10, **19**, 104, 271, **272**, 282
Earl, Ralph, 13
Earthenware
American, 31
Chinese, 146, **147**
European, 306, 307-309
Islamic, **179**
Japanese, 158
Eight, The, 24, 277, 282
Embroideries, 222, 224, 291
Empire style, 36, 40
Enamels and enameling, **182**, 210, **213**, **214**, 222, 223, 312
Engravings, **258**, 259, **263**, **265**
Etruscan art, 162, 172-173
Exekias, 168
Eyck, Jan van, **136**, 137

Fashions, *see* Clothing
Federal style, 34, 36, 37, 39
Feininger, Lyonel, 277, 278
Feke, Robert, 11
Firearms, 58, 65, 67 68, **69**
Fireplaces, 29, 32
Florentine School, 124, 125
Fouquet, Jean, **94**, 95
Fragonard, Jean-Honoré, 100, 132, 260
Frankenthaler, Helen, 274, 287
Furniture
American, 26-40
drawings of, **269**
European, 288, 290-299
Islamic, **181**
medieval, 220
Futurism, 277, 281

Gaddi, Taddeo, 124
Gainsborough, Thomas, 100, **143**
Gallé, Emile, 288
Gauguin, Paul, **135**
Gems, Greek, 162
Ghirlandaio, Domenico, 126
Giambono, Michele, 125
Gibbons, Grinling, 293
Giotto di Bondone, **124**
Giovanni di Paolo, 125
Glackens, William, 24
Glass
American, 26, 29, **30**, 31, 39, 40
Egyptian, 120
European, 34, 37, 306, 312
gold, 211
Islamic, 178, 179, **186**, 187
Roman, 162, 173, 176
stained, **218**, 292
twentieth century, 288
Goddard, John, 33
Goes, Hugo van der, 137
Gogh, Vincent van, 135
Gold, 44, **45**, **47**, **51**, 53, **172**, 212, **213**, **265**
jewelry, 163, 172
Gorky, Arshile, 277, **280**, 281, 287
Gothic style, 27, 210, 217, 218, 220, 222, 290
Gottlieb, Adolph, 286
Goya, Francisco, 90, 101-**102**, **142**, **261**
Goyen, Jan van, 130
Granacci, Francesco, 122
Graves, Morris, 282
Greco, El, **141**
Greek art, 162-173
Greuze, Jean-Baptiste, 100, 132
Grosz, George, 282
Guardi, Francesco, 90, **98**, 99, **127**
Guns, *see* Firearms

Habib Allah, 190, **191**
Halberds and partisans, 59, 66, 68
Hals, Frans, **128**, 129
Harnett, William Michael, **20**
Hartley, Marsden, 277, **278**
Hassam, Childe, 22
Hathaway, Rufus, **13**
Helmets, **47**, **59**, 60, **64**, 65, 70, 71, **72**
Henri, Robert, 24, 282
Hepplewhite, George, 36
Hesselius, John, 11
Hicks, Edward, **14**, 15
Highboys, **29**, **32**
Hofmann, Hans, **283**
Hogarth, William, 100, 143
Holbein, Hans, the Younger, 66, 139, **140**, 190
Homer, Winslow, 10, 22, **23**, 104, 282
Hooch, Pieter de, 130
Hopper, Edward, **282**
Houdon, Jean-Antoine, 300, 303
Hudson River School, 17
Hurd, Jacob, 29

Impressionists, 22, 134, 135, 275
Ingres, Jean-Auguste-Dominique, **102**, **133**
Inness, George, 17
Interior decoration, *see* Decorative arts
Ivories
ancient Near Eastern, 42, **46**, **48**, **51**
Byzantine, 214
Chinese, 34
Egyptian, 108, 119, **120**
European, 303, 306
Islamic, **180**, 187
medieval, 210, 211, 214, **215**, **216**, 222
musical instruments, 227, 228, 229, 239
whale and walrus, 31, 222

Jacob, Georges, 299
Jade, Chinese, **151**
Japanning, 29, 34, 296
Jewelry
American, 39
ancient Near Eastern, 44
barbarian, 212

Index

Byzantine, 212-213, 214
drawings of, 268, **269**
Egyptian, 106, 114, 119
Etruscan, 173
European, 306, 312
Far Eastern, 160
Greek, 163, 164, 172
twentieth century, 288
Johnson, Eastman, 19
Jordaens, Jacob, 140

Kaendler, Johann Joachim, 308
Kandinsky, Wassily, **276**, 277, 278
Kelly, Ellsworth, 274, 287
Kensett, John F., 10, 17
Kierstede, Cornelius, 39
Klee, Paul, 278
Kline, Franz, 284, 285
Knights, 58-63
Korin, Ogata, **157**
Kouros, 165, **166**
Kresilas, 170
Kuan Yin, 154, **155**
Kupka, Frank, 277

Lace, **265**, 299
Lachaise, Gaston, **279**
Lacquer ware, 146, 151
La Farge, John, 10
Lalique, René, 288
Lamerie, Paul de, 296, 310
Lamps, 26, 39, 211
candelabra, 296
Tiffany, 40, 288
see also Chandeliers
Landscapes
American, 15, 17, 22, 23, 33, 34
drawings, 91, 96, **101**
Dutch, 130
English, 144
Flemish, 138
French, 131, 134
Spanish, 141
twentieth century, 279, 282, **283**
water color, 100
Lannuier, Charles-Honoré, 36
La Tour, Georges de, 131
Lawrence, Sir Thomas, 144
Lawson, Ernest, 24
Lehman Pavilion, 193
Lely, Sir Peter, 293
Lemoyne, Jean-Baptiste, 303
Lemoyne, Jean-Louis, 303, 304, **305**
Lenckhardt, Adam, 303

Leonardo da Vinci, **92**, 93
Leutze, Emanuel G., 17
Lighting, *see* Candlesticks; Chandeliers; Lamps
Lippi, Filippino, 92
Lippi, Fra Filippo, 126
Lombardo, Tullio, **301**
Longhi, Pietro, 127
Lorenzetti, Pietro, 125
Louis, Morris, **287**
Luks, George, 24
Lustreware, 179, 180, **181**, 182, 220, 307

MacDonald-Wright, Stanton, 278
Maitreyas, **152**, 154
Majolica, 220, **307**, **308**
Manet, Edouard, **134**
Mannerism, 302, 303
Manohar, **192**
Mantegna, Andrea, 126
Mantelpieces, 33, 36, 37, 291
overmantels, 32
Manuscripts, illustrated Islamic, 178, **180**, **185**, **186**, 187, **189**, **190**, 191-**192**
Marble, *see* Sculpture
Marin, John, 104
Marsh, Reginald, 282
Masks, 70, 107, **120**
Master of the Barberini Panels, 126
Matisse, Henri, **104**, 262, 278, 287
McIntire, Samuel, 36, 37
Medallions, **214**, 295
Memling, Hans, 137
Memmi, Lippo, 125
Metalwork
ancient Near Eastern, **46**
brass, 306
European, 306
iron, 212, 306, 312
Islamic, 178, **181**, 182, **183**, **186**, 187
medieval, 222
see also Bronzes; Copper; Gold; Pewter; Silver
Michelangelo Buonarroti, **93**
Millet, Jean François, 134
Miniatures, 10, 13, 39
Minoan art, 164
Mirrors, 34, 37, 167, 296
Molyn, Pieter de, 130
Monaco, Lorenzo, 124
Monet, Claude, 134, **135**
Monnot, Pierre-Etienne, 303-**304**

Montañes, Juan Martinez, **302**
Moore, John, 78
Moreau, Gustave, 133
Moreau le jeune, **263**
Moretto da Brescia, 122
Morse, Samuel F. B., 15, 17
Motherwell, Robert, 274, 286-287
Mount, William Sidney, 17, **18**
Mummies, 107-108
Murillo, Bartolomé, 141
Mycenaean art, 164-165

Nattier, Jean-Marc, 132
Naturalism, 19, 114, 220
Needlework, 31
see also Crewel work; Embroideries
Negroli, Philippo de, 64
Neoclassicism, 12, 34, 37, 102, 277, 305
Neroccio di Landi, 125
Newman, Barnett, 287
Niccolò di Pietro, 125
Niello, **211**, 212
Noland, Kenneth, 287

O'Keeffe, Georgia, **279**, 281
Oudry, Jean-Baptiste, **99**, 298

Paintings
American, 10-24, 26, 34, 36, 274-288
Chinese, 155-**156**
Dutch, 128-130
English, 143-144
European, 122-144
Flemish, 136-141
French, 131-136
German, 136-141
Italian, 122-128
Japanese, 156-157
Roman wall, 162, 173, **175-176**
Spanish, 141-143
Tibetan, 160
twentieth century, 274-288
Palmer, Erastus Dow, 19
Paneling, wood, 27, 29, 30, 31, 32, 33, 290, 292
Pannini, Giovanni, 127
Paolo Veneziano, 125-126
Patio from Velez Blanco, 290-**291**
Peale, Charles Willson, 10, 13
Peale, James, 10, **14**
Peale, Raphaelle, **14**, 15
Peale, Rembrandt, 15
Pearce, Edward, 293

Pennsylvania Germans, 30
Peto, John Frederick, 20
Pewter, 26, 31, 306
Photographs, 258, 270-272
Phyfe, Duncan, **35**, 36
Picasso, Pablo, **104**, 262, 275, **276**, 278, 281
Pigalle, Jean-Baptiste, 303, 304
Pistols, *see* Firearms
Plaques
  ancient Near Eastern, 48, **51**
  Egyptian, **118**
  ivory, 48, 214, **215**
  medieval, 211, 214, **215, 222,** 223
Pointillism, 104
Pollaiuolo, Antonio, **258**, 259
Pollock, Jackson, **284**, 287
Porcelain
  American, 26
  China trade, 31, 33, 34, 37, 307
  Chinese, 149-150
  European, 37, 307-310
  Japanese, 158
Portraits
  American, 10-15, 19, 31, 33, 34
  Byzantine, 212
  drawings, 90, 95, **102, 103**
  Dutch, 129
  Egyptian, 109-116
  English, 143, 293, 294
  Flemish, 137, 141
  Florentine, **123**, 125
  French, 132, 134
  German, 139
  medieval, 211
  Roman sculpture, 173-**174**
  Spanish, 141, 142
  twentieth century, 276, 277, 278, 282
Posters, 258, **261**
Pottery
  American, 26
  ancient Near Eastern, 42, 43
  Chinese, **146**
  Delft, 307
  Egyptian, **107**
  English, 37
  Etruscan, 173
  European, 307
  Greek, 162, 163, **164**, 165
  Islamic, 178, 179, **181, 182,** 187, **192**
  Japanese, 158
  medieval, 220
Poussin, Nicolas, **131**
Powers, Hiram, **18**, 19
Pratt, Matthew, **12**
Praxiteles, 172
Prendergast, Maurice, 10, 24
Pre-Raphaelite movement, 144
Prints, 258-262
  American, 10, 26
  costume, 79
  Far Eastern, 146
  twentieth century, 274
  see also Engravings; Posters

Queen Anne style, 33
Quercia, Jacopo della, **91**, 92

Raeburn, Sir Henry, 144
Raffaellino del Garbo, **92**
Raphael, **93**, 122
Rauschenberg, Robert, **262**
Realism, 20, 24, 282, 283
Regnault, Nicolas François, 259, 260
Reliefs
  Assyrian, 42, 49
  Egyptian, 109, 111, 118
  French, 304-305
  funerary, 53
  Greek, **170**-171
  medieval, 211, 222
  Near Eastern, **54**
  Roman, **174**, 175
Rembrandt, 90, 96, **97, 129, 259**
Remington, Frederic, 23
Renaissance style, 290, 303
Reni, Guido, 126
Renoir, Pierre-Auguste, 134
Revere, Paul, Jr., 40
Revolvers, *see* Firearms
Reynolds, Sir Joshua, 143, 144
Ribera, Jusepe de, 141
Riesener, Jean-Henri, 299
Rifles, *see* Firearms
Rimmer, William, 19
Rimpa School (Japan), 157
Robbia, Andrea della, 300, 301, 308
Robbia, Luca della, **300**, 301, 308
Robinson, Theodore, 22
Rockefeller, Michael C., Collection of Primitive Art, 241
Rococo style, 11, 31, 32, 34, 39, 132, 298
Rodin, Auguste, 278, 300, 306
Roettiers, Jacques-Nicolas, 310
Rogier van der Weyden, **137**
Roman art, 162-163, 173-176
Romanesque style, 210, 216, 217, 222
Rosa, Salvator, 127
Rossellino, Antonio, 301
Rossetti, Dante Gabriel, 144
Rothko, Mark, 286
Roundels, **210,** 211
Rousseau, Théodore, 134
Rowlandson, Thomas, **100,** 101
Rubens, **96, 140,** 259
Ruckers, Hans, the Elder, 230
Rugs and carpets, 178, 187-**188,** 190-191, 298
Ruisdael, Jacob van, 130
Russell, Morgan, 278
Ruysdael, Salomon van, 130
Ryder, Albert Pinkham, **20**

Saddles, 61, 70
Saint-Gaudens, Augustus, 23, **24**
Sanderson, John, **268**, 269
Sarcophagi
  Egyptian, 108
  Roman, 162, 173, **174**, 175, 210
Sargent, John Singer, 10, **21,** 104
Sarto, Andrea del, 122
Sassetta, 125
Schuech, Israel, 66
Screens, Japanese, 157
Scrolls, Japanese, 156-157
Sculpture
  American, 10, 18-19, 23
  architectural, 216-217
  Attic, 162
  bronze, 174-175, 300, 301, 302-303, 306
  Byzantine, 212
  Central Asian, 160
  ceramic, 308
  Chinese, 151-155
  copper, **47**
  Cypriot, 164
  Egyptian, 106, 108-118
  European, 300-306
  Gothic, 220
  Greek, **163**-164, 165, **166, 167, 169-170, 171, 172**
  Indian, 146, 158-159
  Ivory, **48**, 303
  Japanese, 158
  Khmer, 160
  marble, **18**, 19, 163, 165, **212**, 221, 300, 301, 302, 303-304
  medieval, 210, **217**, 220
  minimal, 283

Index

plaster, 306
Roman, 162, 173, **174**
Southeast Asian, 146
stone, **43, 44, 53,** 162, 163-164, 165
stucco, 160
Tibetan, 160
twentieth century, 274, 277, **279**
wax, 303
wood, **217**, 220, 221, 222, 303
Seals and sealstones
ancient Near Eastern, 42, **44,** 46, 51
Greek, 164, 165, **169**
Secretaries, *see* Desks
Segna di Buonaventura, 124
Seurat, Georges, **103**
Scrimshaw, 31, 222
Shahn, Ben, 282
Shaker furniture, 30
Shaw, Joshua, 15
Sheeler, Charles, 281
Sheraton, Thomas, 36
style, 34
Shields, 60, 65, 71
Shinn, Everett, 24
Shop front, 296, **297**
Sienese School, 124-125
Silhouettes, 258, 266-**267**
Silver, 26, **28**, 29, 32, **39**, 40, 46, 53, 54, **55, 56**, 120, 163, 172, **211**, 212, **213**, 310, **311**
tableware, 296, 306, 310
Sloan, John, 24
Smibert, John, 11
Snuffboxes and bottles, 39, 84, 151, 312
Sofas and settees, 33, 34, 36, 296
Spinelli, Parri, 92
Sphinxes, 113, 114
Staircases, 27, 29
railings, 293
Steen, Jan, 130
Stelae (Egyptian), 108, 112, **113,** 114, **118**
Steles (Chinese), **152**, 153, 154
Stella, Joseph, **277**
Stieglitz, Alfred, 270, **271,** 278
Steinlen, Théophile Alexandre, 261
Stirrups and spurs, 61, 70
Stuart, Gilbert, 12, **13**, 31
Sue ware, 158
Sully, Thomas, **15**
Sung ware, 148
Surrealism, 275, 277
Swords, 56, 58, 65, **66**-67, 68
Oriental, 69, 70-71
Turkish, **72**
Viking, **59**

Tables, **27**, 30, **31**, 32, 33, 34, **36, 292**, 293, 296
Tapestries, 210, 218, **219**, 291, 298, 299-300
Gobelins, 294-295, 299
Ten, The, 22
Ter Borch, Gerard, **130**
Terra cottas, 163, 165, 167, 171, 301, 306
Terbrugghen, Hendrick, **128**
Textiles, 26, 37, 74-88, 146, 218, 224, 299-300
Theüs, Jeremiah, 11
Tiepolo, Domenico, 90, 99
Tiepolo, Giovanni Battista (Giambattista), 90, 96, **97**, 127
Tiffany, Louis Comfort, 288
Tiles, 29, 108, 293, 307, **308**
Tintoretto, 123
Titian, **123**, 125
Tobey, Mark, **281,** 282
Tombs, Egyptian, 106, 109
Toulouse-Lautrec, Henri de, 261
Townsend, John, 32
Trade cards, 258, **267**
Trumbull, John, 12, 13
Turner, Joseph Mallord William, **101, 144**
Twachtman, John Henry, **22**

Valentines, 267
Vases
French, 296, **310**
Greek, 162, 163, **164**, 165, 167-168, 172
Vedder, Elihu, 21
Velazquez, Diego Rodríguez, 141, **142**
Vermeer, Jan, 129-**130**
Veronese, Paolo, **122**, 123, 303
Vignola, Jacopo Barozzi da, 292
Vile, William, 296
Vitruvius, Marcus, 263
Vittoria, Alessandro, **303**
Vuillard, Jean Edouard, 261, 262, 275

Wallpaper, 31, 32, 34, 37, 38
Watches, *see* Clocks and watches
Water colors, 10, 23, **100**, 101, 104, 281
Watteau, Jean Antoine, **99, 132**
Weapons, 58-72
Weber, Max, 277
Wedgwood, Josiah, 310
Wei style, **153**-154
Weir, Julian Alden, 22
West, Benjamin, 11, 12
Whistler, James Abbott McNeill, **21**
Windows, 29, 37, **218, 288**
Wollaston, John, 11
Wood
carvings, 180, 187
paneling, 27, 29, 30, 31, 32, 290, 292
sculpture, **217**, 220, 221, 222, 303
Wood, Grant, 283
Worth, Charles Frederick, 79, 84
Wright, Frank Lloyd, **288**
Wyeth, Andrew, 283

Yüeh ware, 147, 148

Zurbarán, Francisco de, 141

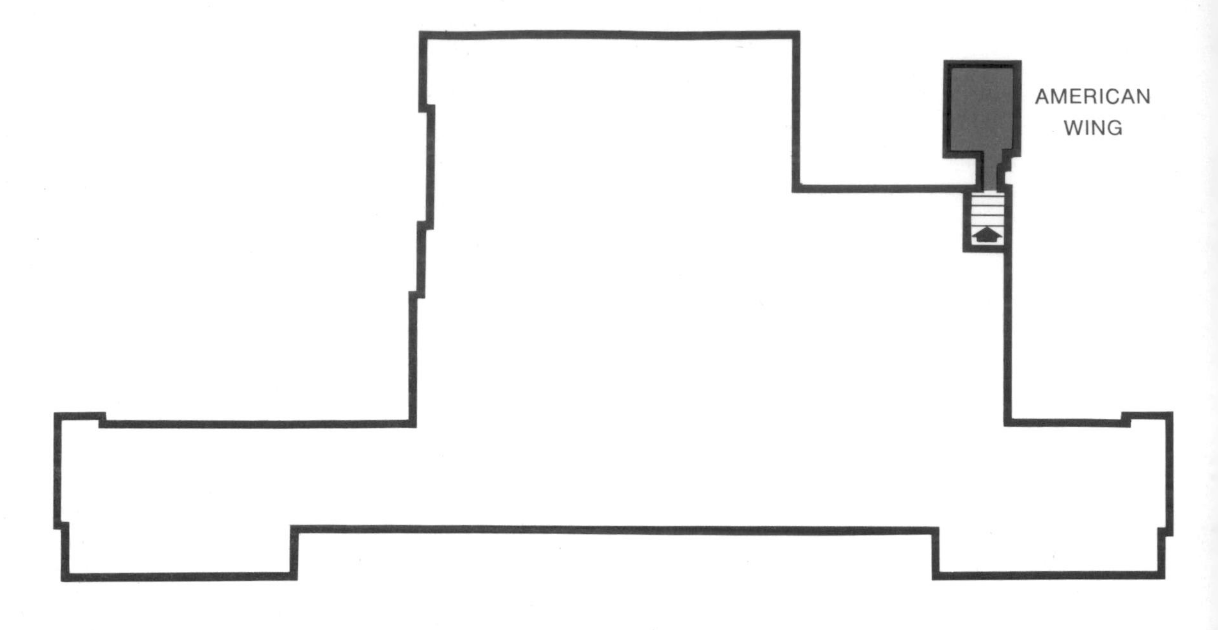

Changir
Exhibit

DRAWIN
PRINT
PHOTOGR

Drawin
Print
Photogr
Stud
Room

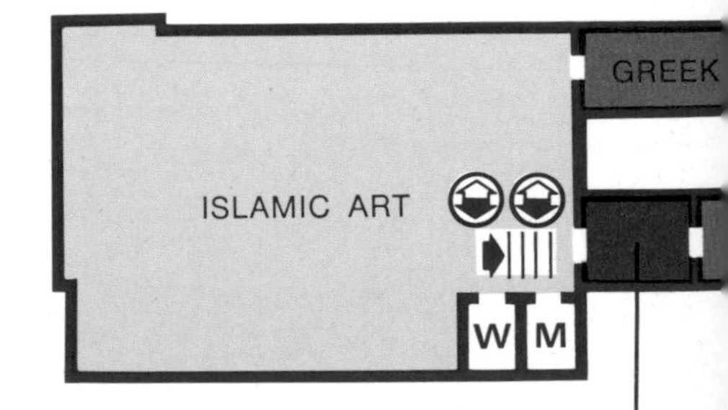

ANCIENT
NEAR EASTE
ART

STAIRS

ELEVATOR

ESCALATOR

W WOMEN'S ROOM

M MEN'S ROOM

COAT CHECK

TELEPHONE

S SMOKING